CW00570671

RETURN TO CHINA

ALSO BY LIANG HENG AND JUDITH SHAPIRO

Son of the Revolution

RETURN TO CHINA

LIANG HENG and JUDITH SHAPIRO

A SURVIVOR OF THE CULTURAL REVOLUTION

REPORTS ON CHINA TODAY

CHATTO & WINDUS
LONDON

Published in 1987 by
Chatto & Windus Ltd
40 William IV Street
London WC2N 4DF

All rights reserved. No part of this publication may be reproduced, stored in a retrieval system, or transmitted in any form, or by any means, electronic, mechanical, photocopying, recording or otherwise, without the prior permission of the publisher.

British Library Cataloguing in Publication Data

Liang, Heng
    Return to China: a survivor of the
    cultural revolution reports on China today.
    1. China—Social conditions—1976–
    I. Title   II. Shapiro, Judith
    951.05'8   HN733.5
    ISBN 0–7011–3125–X

Copyright © 1982, 1983, 1984, 1985, 1986 by Liang Heng and Judith Shapiro. Map copyright © 1986 by Rafael Palacios.

Portions of this work were originally published in *The New York Review of Books* and *Life* magazine.

Printed in Great Britain by
Redwood Burn Limited, Trowbridge, Wiltshire

TO OUR FATHERS

CONTENTS

RETURN TO CHINA

CHANGSHA

More than anything, I feared seeing my beloved father again. I liked to remember him as he had been when I was a child, handsome and active, a brilliant journalist, a man who loved in his spare time to write poetry, play the accordion, and conduct waltzes for the *Hunan Daily*'s dance band. The Cultural Revolution had transformed him into a quavering invalid who lived in his memories but wept at any mention of the past. I understood more than anyone how much he had lost—but my love for him was most bearable at a distance. At the thought that I would soon stand before him, after a separation of four years and half the earth, my whole nervous system tightened as if to explode.

It was a cold, gray, drizzling Changsha afternoon, typical of the long Central South China winters I knew so well, where you never feel warm, never feel dry, and your hands are so stiff you can hardly hold a pen. I dressed myself in a nice Western tweed jacket and tie from a shop near Columbia University (appearances mean a lot in China), and Judy and I set out on foot, for Father had a new address not far from our hotel. Through a compromise worked out between the Hunan Province Foreign Affairs Office (which was concerned about China's international image) and the newspaper where he had once worked (which wasn't), Father had only a few months earlier been moved back to Changsha, the provincial capital, from a tiny, broken, dirt-floored room in the county primary school where my stepmother had taught until her retirement. The *Hunan Daily* had agreed to restore its formal relationship with him, once again issuing his salary, but not to provide housing in the newspaper compound, which, leaders claimed, was too limited to be given to a stroke victim unable to work.

The Xiang River Hotel, where my American wife Judith Shapiro and I had been married amid controversy nearly five years before, lay in the tight knot of streets that was the true heart of Changsha. Even this old quarter was changing. Directly across the street from the hotel, a glass-faced eleven-story building shot up incongruously from among the old trapezoid-roofed houses of black tile and wood: it was the new dormitory for the hotel staff, doubtless (I had been told cynically) far better kept up than the hotel itself.

Always a city with its pulse exposed, Changsha seemed even dirtier and more chaotic than I remembered it. It looked as if it were under reconstruction after a war—bamboo scaffolding and piles of bricks and sand blocked the sidewalks, so that we were driven willy-nilly into the muddy streets. Guardrails had been erected between the sidewalks and the pavement, apparently to fence pedestrians in, but they only added to the congestion, for cyclists loaded with marketing barreled along the sidewalks in utter disregard of safety, unable to find an opening out again. On the streets, the maelstrom of cyclists rang their bells continuously, cursing each other in the vulgar local dialect that made my heart jump with painful familiarity, fighting with overcrowded buses, Russian Volgas, and new Toyota minibuses for space. Now there seemed to be more bicycles than ever, and bright orange imported motorcycles, whose drivers, wearing only sunglasses for protection, drove as if to flatten all in their path. The only motorcycles in Changsha when I left in 1981 had been pea-green military ones, with sidecars.

I could scarcely believe I was here. I had departed for the United States as a dissident, believing I would never see China again. Like so many of my generation, I had once worshiped Chairman Mao as a god, and at twelve, I had joined the Cultural Revolution. I wore a red armband and denounced my primary-school teachers; I traveled to mountains and cities all over China "making revolution." I wept with ecstasy when, with tens of thousands of others, I caught a glimpse of Chairman Mao in Beijing's Tiananmen Square.

But by the end of the Cultural Revolution, my family had been so twisted and torn apart by political movements that it hurt to remember that we had once lived together. My mother was labeled a rightist and sent to labor camp when I was only four; my idealistic father divorced her to try to rid the family of the stigma and save himself for a bright political future serving the party in which he so deeply believed. Then, when the Cultural Revolution began, Father was denounced, beaten, and humiliated for "taking the capitalist road in news reporting" and sent to Mao Zedong Thought Study School. Later I followed him to the countryside to be "reeducated" by the peasants. My older sisters were sent away too, with the slogan "The farther from Father and Mother, the nearer to Chairman Mao's heart." Then at the age of fifteen, when I was a student at a rural middle school, I was accused of being a counterrevolutionary traitor. A politics cadre locked me in a classroom for days, beat me, and tried to force me to confess to a crime I knew nothing about.

Together with thousands of ex–Red Guards like myself, I gradually learned that I had been exploited for political purposes. I began to ask questions about the fit between feudal Chinese culture and Mao's terrifying version of communism, about why there was such a discrepancy between the beautiful worlds described in our books and the harsh reality around us. Many called us China's "lost generation," for we had lived our childhoods uprooted by the winds of politics. But we were also China's thoughtful generation, for we had awakened to the folly of our traditions, with their passion for hierarchy and obedience to authority.

After the Cultural Revolution, I became a student in the Chinese literature department of the Hunan Teachers College. In this more liberal era, there was an election for representatives to the local People's Congress. I nominated myself as a candidate, giving public speeches saying that I did not believe Marxism-Leninism should be taken as a revolutionary religion. To the displeasure of college leaders, I earned large numbers of votes in the primary. But ultimately, the party triumphed over the students—I was saved from labor camp only because by then I had married Judy, one of the first Americans to live and teach in China following the normalization of U.S.-China relations. Deng Xiaoping, the most powerful man in China, had granted our appeal for permission the previous year.

The failure of the "election movement" was a final source of disillusionment for me, and I set my eyes on the future and a new life in the West. I took to freedom as if I had been born to it. In New York I attended graduate school, and discovered to my surprise and pleasure that my disagreements with my professors were rewarded as signs of intellectual independence, not criticized as symptoms of "bad thought." Together with my wife, who rendered my thoughts into English, I recounted my memoirs of growing up under socialism, *Son of the Revolution,* opening my heart freely without having to consider political repercussions or fear that I would be unable to publish if I said too much. Later, I experienced what seemed to me an unimaginable privilege, after living so long in a land where jobs were assigned by the state: I chose my own occupation, securing a foundation grant to start a magazine for visiting scholars and students from China.

Many Western readers of *Son of the Revolution* assumed that the Chinese government must regard me as a traitor for telling my story. While I too had my doubts about how the book would be received by the authorities, I knew the matter was not a simple one. Many of the architects of the post–Cultural Revolution reforms had been victims of the tragedies I described—Deng Xiaoping himself, like the top staff members of the *Hunan Daily,* had been paraded in a dunce cap; Red Guards had turned his eldest son into a cripple. Still, many Democracy Wall activists who had put up posters during the liberal "Beijing Spring" of 1978–79 remained in prisons and labor camps. Although there had been no official reaction to the book, I had little hope that China would view me kindly.

In 1984 an official in the Chinese embassy in Washington at last gave me a sense of the government's attitude. The reformers took a more generous view of it than "the more orthodox comrades," he told me. What I had written was the truth. The trouble was, "your negation of the Cultural Revolution came earlier than ours did."

I understood what he meant—in a patriarchal society, the son should wait for the father to speak first.

Another problem, the official said, was that the book stopped too soon after the Cultural Revolution. Great changes for the better were under way in China. In fact, he suggested to my surprise, it was high time I go back and have a look for myself.

I was indeed curious to see for myself what Deng's much-discussed economic reforms had accomplished. Judy had already returned to China several times, and could attest that the general mood of the country was good. Still, we feared that I could have difficulties if I traveled as a Chinese national, and for the spouse of an American the waiting period to change citizenship was three years. Now, with my U.S. passport secure in my tweed pocket, I walked once again through the streets of the beloved and hated hometown where I had spent almost every year of my life. Once again I had become part of a blur of Hunanese humanity. At any moment, it seemed to me, the crowd must reveal the familiar face of a friend or an enemy. Then, as Judy and I turned onto a side street, I realized I was just footsteps away from fulfilling the most dreaded and longed-for purpose of my trip.

Father's place at Number 144 Yinpan lay among Changsha's residential back alleys. The wooden door stood open, and we passed through a series of dark, damp stone hallways off which many other families lived, coming at last to a courtyard. The surrounding balconies were hung with bright laundry, lending a festive air to the otherwise drab scene. In the middle there stood yet another bleak stone structure. An inquisitive-looking old woman who had been washing cabbage at a noisy outdoor spigot told us that Old Liang lived in there.

I knocked quietly. My stepmother, Zhu Zhidao, opened it, as red-faced and thick-built as ever. She called my name with a little shriek and just stood there, staring and speechless, a pair of iron tongs dangling forgotten in her pudgy hand. Father was sitting in the semidarkness inside, wearing a heavy wool hat and his old blue padded jacket. Our long-awaited appearance was too much for him, and he burst into tears.

He struggled to stand, but I urged his trembling body back into the old cane chair, afraid for a moment of what the shock might do to him. He stared up at us through the familiar thick glasses, his smooth skin peculiarly ageless for a sick man. I looked back at him until I could bear it no longer.

"So how is America?" he finally whispered, his voice so weak that I could hardly hear him.

As my stepmother busied herself getting tea and oranges, I sat on the wooden bed near him and fumbled in my wallet for one of my editor-in-chief business cards, printed in English on one side and Chinese on the other. Father took the white rectangle gingerly, for he had never seen such a thing before, and examined it carefully, bringing it up close to his glasses and turning it over several times. Suddenly he burst into a huge smile, beaming with joy and pride, and I felt my tension disappear. He wanted to know everything about the magazine, from my dreams and ambitions for it to matters of production and distribution. I spoke carefully, for my stories brought on frequent fits of weeping. In editorial work Father had once been a professional, and although he had not sat at his desk since he had been forced to leave it nearly twenty years before, through me he was reminded, if only for a few moments, that he had once been a man of expertise and competence.

I knew how he longed to return to the staff of the paper he had helped to found in 1949. Most of his similarly persecuted colleagues had done so long before, for Deng Xiaoping's policies emphasizing the contribution intellectuals could make to the modernization drive had gone far to reverse Maoist prejudices toward people with professional abilities. Father had been one of the unfortunates because of his illness. Still, his old dream of being among the editors again, of smelling the printer's ink and hearing the clack of the press as the papers came off fresh and warm, had remained as strong as ever. He lived in a dream world, only partly understood by my stepmother, who had been little more than a live-in nurse to him for most of their lives together. Over the years, Judy and I had written many letters to the authorities requesting that he be brought back from the countryside—not so much, I knew, for the better living standards the city offered, but so he could be near the newspaper again.

Now I worried not only about Father's psychological state but also about how his health would fare in his new home. Although far better than the old one, it was so damp from the runoff of a tree that the walls and even the quilts felt moist; the outhouse, which served the compound of hundreds, was much too far away for Father, who could barely walk even with the aid of a crutch. Judy and I resolved to appeal to the newspaper once again. Perhaps we would have more success if we spoke on humanitarian rather than political grounds. We left Father reading the first two issues of my magazine, *Zhishifenzi* ("The Chinese Intellectual"), happier than he had been in many years.

It turned out that I knew most of the new leaders of the newspaper from my childhood. Many were ex-rightists like my mother, returned from labor camps, prisons, and the countryside with the downfall of the Gang of Four and now promoted to important positions. They welcomed us warmly, unlocking a musty Honored Guests' Room full of heavy leather chairs, and fetching us tea. When we told them why we had come, they expressed sympathy for Father. His trials sounded all too familiar to them.

However, they told us sadly but firmly that many others were in similar situations. The vast majority of the editors and journalists had suffered, and restoring their political reputations had been far easier than taking care of their daily needs. The paper had been able to provide proper housing for earlier victims, those persecuted during the 1957 Anti-Rightist movement. But there were far too many maltreated during the Cultural Revolution to help them all. The legacy of historical problems was, one official confided, simply overwhelming.

I knew from long experience that confrontation gets you nowhere in China. Perhaps it was our conciliatory attitude, perhaps it was my Western jacket, perhaps it was Judy's foreign "face," beautiful Chinese, and expression of understanding of China's problems that made it difficult for them to refuse us. Two days later we were told that out of the eleven households to be permitted to move into a newly erected cement-block building in the newspaper compound, Father's was one. They had assigned him a first-floor apartment so he wouldn't have to be carried up and down stairs, and there was a small veranda where he could sit until his dying days, smelling the printer's ink and watching the world go by.

Father wept when we told him and nervously counted the days until the building was finished and we had the key in hand. I shared his nervousness—with so many families lobbying for so few spaces, there was always a chance that something could go wrong. Moving day was memorable for all of us. As I pushed

Father in his wheelchair through the gates of the compound, old colleagues stared, puzzled, finally recognized him, and stopped and spoke to him with tears in their eyes, shaking his hand and asking where he had been all these years. They had all been victims together; now they had come home.

After he was settled, Father had one urgent request: to visit the leaders responsible for taking him back so he could thank them. One of them, Old Chen, was an old colleague; when I was a child, he had been a particularly lively and talkative "uncle." He had been attacked, like so many activists, during the Anti-Rightist campaign, and had spent many years in the countryside. Now once again he was a leader at the newspaper.

One evening, then, we brought Father to visit his modest apartment in his wife's work-unit compound, a nearby hospital. The building was typical of millions of new constructions, made entirely of huge concrete slabs, like Father's own. The floors, walls, and ceilings were all scratchy gray, and the wooden window trim and doors had been painted the sickly yellow so mysteriously common throughout China. However, even in the weak light of the bulb hanging overhead, the Chen family's meticulous attempts to make something clean and livable were apparent. A small television stood in a prominent position on a table, the English letters "T.V." lovingly embroidered on its green velvet dust cover; under the glass on the desk lay the family photographs, one, hand tinted with archaic-looking reds and greens, of a daughter in a white Western-style wedding gown that I knew belonged to the photo shop. In such small things could recent happinesses be seen.

Old Chen had grown soft-spoken through nearly twenty years as professional victim, and he had a nervous, high-strung manner. Like many sufferers, he seemed of an indeterminate age, but I knew him to be in his late fifties, like Father. His current situation and prominent position might have been Father's, I thought, had Father only kept his health.

His hands trembling, Father placed the bag containing our

gifts, a solar-powered pocket calculator and two pairs of nylon knee-high stockings, on the table. Against the obligatory flood of protests from the old journalist, Judy spoke firmly. It was a familiar ritual. "A small token of our friendship. Worthless mementos for your family."

Settled before steaming cups of bitter green tea, Chen and Father soon reestablished their relationship. We were able to turn the conversation to our own interest: the current situation for journalists. Chen sighed when we broached the question, and told us a story to illustrate how difficult things still were.

When a purge of party leaders who had risen to power through violence during the Cultural Revolution was announced in early 1984, he said, a number of local party secretaries in Shaoyang (a middle-sized city where my two sisters were living) realized that their close association with the Gang of Four had marked them as inevitable targets. Joining together with like-minded leftist officials from the Municipal Party Committee, they claimed that they themselves were being persecuted by local reformers. They hoped thus to strike first, ousting those who would oust them. It was a well-worn tactic: they would deflect the threat to their power by relying on their unbreakable "relationship net." Unfortunately, power in China is still based primarily on personal connections.

A *Hunan Daily* journalist, himself a onetime victim of such people, got wind of the situation and went to Shaoyang to investigate. He wrote an article about the damage these leaders had done but immediately ran into trouble. The leftists' relationship net extended from the city to the provincial capital, as in many of China's bureaucratic administrations. The Provincial Propaganda Department, which had direct jurisdiction over the *Hunan Daily* (the paper was the official "voice" of the Hunan Provincial Party Committee), killed the piece before publication and reprimanded the reporter.

The man was frightened, but he did not give up. He sent his

article to the *People's Daily* in Beijing, telling them what had happened. It was still true, said Chen, as it had been for years, that higher-level papers had more freedom than regional ones to publish articles critical of local leaders: those under attack had no way to exercise control. However, publication in a national paper still depended on whether the local issue had a bearing on policies being promoted countrywide.

Fortunately, the situation in Shaoyang was seen as an example of the urgent need to rid the party of some of its members. The *People's Daily* sent a writer from Beijing to Changsha on special assignment. The two journalists went to Shaoyang together, where they interviewed both ordinary citizens and the reform-minded officials struggling against the entrenched leftists in the region. The resulting article, written under a pen name, was an even stronger indictment than the first, for it included statistics on how many intellectuals, artists, and officials had been tortured and murdered during the Cultural Revolution as a direct result of the leftists' orders.

I stole a glance at Father, who was listening to Old Chen's tale with rapt attention. He had always said that living by the pen was the most dangerous of occupations, yet had urged me to take the same path. In China, the obstacles to journalistic integrity were "layer upon layer," yet under similar circumstances, I believed, he would have done the same.

Under pressure from Beijing, Chen continued, the Hunan Provincial Party Committee was forced to approve the piece for publication in the *Hunan Daily;* it appeared in the *People's Daily* as well. The National Party Rectification Committee then ordered the Provincial Party Committee to conduct an investigation into the leftist officials' pasts, and to make a public self-criticism for its role in obstructing the original inquiry. Eventually, many Shaoyang leaders were transferred, and some got prison and labor camp sentences.

I had lived most of my life in close connection with China's newspaper world, and Old Chen didn't need to tell me that the Shaoyang case was a rare exception. It was extremely unusual for a journalist's appeals to be given such attention at the top, or even for Beijing's efforts to yield such visible results. Far more often, the journalist himself was criticized or transferred, or guilty local officials would make token self-criticisms and the situation continue unchanged. Journalists were instructed that they were "tools to express the voice of the party," or, as it was also put, "conveyors of the party spirit to the masses, and collectors of the opinions of the masses for the party." It was little wonder that most reporters chose to remain silent about the abuses they uncovered. I was impressed that this reporter had dared take on the very bureaucracy he was supposed to represent, despite the obvious danger to himself.

I asked Old Chen who had dared to bite the rear of the tiger. Only when I insisted that I wished to meet the man did our host admit that he himself was the determined investigator.

"You!" Father cried out in nervous amazement. I hastened to calm him down.

"Old Chen is a brave man," I said. "But you see, the risk was worth it." I could only admire the journalist of the story more now that I knew he was the seemingly timid ex-rightist sitting across the table from us. Someone who has suffered so long for airing his criticisms does not lightly speak out again.

Such resilience was not unusual, however. At times it seemed a miracle to me that so many Chinese had retained their courage and the faith that through their efforts China might yet be made a better place. Although fate had denied Father his own reprieve, I was sure that that evening it meant a great deal to him to be reunited with those whose second chance had come.

MOTHER WAS NOW too old to have a second chance, but seeing her was far less painful to me than seeing Father. Before Judy and I had left China, she and my stepfather, Uncle Lei, had been installed in a new apartment complex for people with "foreign connections" (it had been easier to help her, as she had never lost her Changsha residence card). Like Old Chen, she had been a target of the Anti-Rightist movement nearly twenty years earlier, but she had long ago come to terms with her role as someone on the fringes of society. The extraverted personality that had brought her so much sorrow had grown careful and shy, and Uncle Lei, a graduate of Beijing University who had relatives in Taiwan, was similarly inclined to avoid trouble. They knew how to protect themselves and lived out their retirements quietly and at peace.

When my sisters and I were children and Mother was driven away from us, we didn't know enough to pity her and dared not go to see her. Now we tried to use the time remaining to make up the love and attention we should have given her over the years. Whenever there was a vacation, my sisters came from Shaoyang to stay with her. They sat in her apartment endlessly, knitting sweaters and long underwear and showing off their two lovely little girls, who could sing, dance, and recite Tang dynasty poetry in piercing oratorical style. Now because it was already February and time for Spring Festival, the Chinese New Year, they had brought their husbands as well, and we were able to spend many days visiting Mother together.

When at last they had managed to come back from the countryside, my sisters had been given teaching jobs. They had married, through introduction, likable and hardworking engineers. Neither of my sisters seemed to have any interest in matters of politics and state, not even Liang Fang, the elder of the two, who had once been the most politically sophisticated and active Red Guard of the three of us. Now she devoted her energies to her family and placed her hopes for the future on her daughter, the only child she was allowed to have because of population control policies.

Where once it would have been my sisters' happiness to go anywhere the state required, they now said they avoided responsibilities that would take them away from home. They had grown up believing that life's purpose was to serve the revolution, but today they had found a different answer. "Political struggle consumed my entire youth," Liang Fang commented suddenly to me one evening. We were sitting in Father's new apartment, and he was dozing on a straw couch. "First there was the business with Mother, which you were much too young to understand. Then, from the time I was sixteen till I was twenty-six, the revolution made it impossible to live a normal life. I'll never be able to make up what I've missed."

Of the three of us, only I had still been young enough to qualify when Deng Xiaoping reinstated university entrance examinations in 1977, and Liang Fang told me that now, with the new emphasis on job qualifications, she was often passed over in favor of less competent, younger people who were college graduates. The whole country had gone diploma crazy, she complained. Even athletes, artists, and policemen were desperately studying written Chinese, math, and politics so they might keep the jobs they had held for years, or qualify for raises and leadership positions. Going to extremes was China's great failing, but I thought I knew why things were being done this way. If the least flexibility were allowed, the uneducated bureaucrats would squirm back through the loopholes and remain in power. It was people like my sisters, with real ability but no degrees, who lost out.

Liang Fang looked thoughtfully at her seven-year-old daughter, who was sitting on the bed trying to master a hand-held electronic game we had brought. "It's different for her," she said fondly. "She's got her whole life ahead of her." She told me that she spent every spare minute helping the child with her schoolwork. But, she confessed, speaking softly so her daughter would not overhear, she often felt conflict even about that. Should she teach her to think for herself, or teach her to live safely and happily? What should she say when the child returned from school and told her that Teacher had instructed everyone to love the party? Did Mama love the party? Liang Fang sighed. "How can I tell her what I really think?" she asked. "We can love our parents and children, but support, not love, is all we owe to the party."

My sisters seemed to want the same family happiness for Judy and me that they had found for themselves. They urged us to have a child, and a boy at that. In America, they pointed out, we were not bound by the one-child family policy, and it was up to us to see that the family name of our branch of Liangs did not die out. They knew how busy we were, they said, but if we would only produce it, we could bring it to China. We could trust them to raise it well for us, and then we could come pick it up when it was grown.

This was an unusual proposal to Western ears, although a common enough arrangement in China. My second sister had journeyed all the way to Shanghai to give birth, just so she could leave the baby with her mother-in-law for a few years. Judy diplomatically refrained from commenting on their desire for a male child in the family, and promised that we would consider the idea. Truly, for all its faults, China was a wonderful place for small children. I had often thought of returning for a few years if we ever did decide to have a family. Nearly everyone seemed to regard children as an absolute pleasure.

GLAD AS I WAS to see my relatives, I sometimes found it difficult to juggle the needs of the two families.

One unseasonably warm morning, I pushed my father in his wheelchair to the hotel where Judy and I were staying so he could take a bath. (The older buildings in China rarely have running water, and even the new ones, with rare exceptions, have no hot water—since our arrival in Changsha, we had averaged about three guest bathers a day.) Father took much longer in the tub than I had expected, and I began to become nervous. At noon, my mother was scheduled to make a visit for the same purpose.

I had sensed from rare hints that Father regretted his harsh treatment of Mother after she had been labeled a rightist, and now recognized how unfairly she had been accused. Perhaps he even regretted the divorce. As for Mother, she had heard about Father's poor health and occasionally asked after him. It seemed to me she understood his motives and had forgiven him. Despite her good second marriage, she might even have missed him sometimes.

Still, in China, divorce is a great humiliation, especially one that occurs under political circumstances. According to custom, my two sisters and I never mentioned one parent to the other, pretending that that early period of our lives had never taken place. We did everything we could to avoid potentially embarrassing situations. At times, this required great mental agility, the skills of a social secretary, and a duplicitousness that, for whatever good purpose, often made me unhappy and uncomfortable.

Father finally finished his bath, but not quickly enough. As I was helping him into a hired automobile, I spotted Mother coming through the gate. With an impulse I could not have explained, I suddenly found I very much wanted them to see each other. "Father, Mother is there!" I said excitedly, pointing to the plump woman in the dark green padded jacket. As if lost in a dream, Father stared at me, uncomprehending. "My mother," I repeated impatiently. "Don't you want to talk to her?"

Obediently, automatically, without time for further thought, he nodded. I ran to Mother and spoke quickly to her. She too seemed stupefied and embarrassed. Had she imagined such a meeting to herself? With flushed cheeks, she patted her short gray hair and thick clothing, saying, "How can I see anybody, dressed in this dirty old jacket?"

At my urging, she walked slowly to the waiting car and bent

her head to look in the open window. "Old Liang," she said tentatively. "Hello."

Father's mouth fell open. He looked at her without words, clutching his well-worn crutch. To me, it seemed an eternity.

Although she knew about his stroke, Father's invalid appearance must have been a great shock to her. "Old Liang," she said, her voice breaking. "Take care of yourself." Tears streamed down her face and she turned away, unable to continue. She walked quickly up the ramp into the hotel, and I did not pursue her. I climbed into the car next to Father and took his hand.

As we pulled away into the street, he seemed more dazed than anything else. "Her eyes," he finally said. "They don't seem so bright as before."

"Father!" I exclaimed, the tears breaking in my own throat. "It's been twenty-five years!"

"I feel sorry," Father whispered. He was silent for the remainder of the short distance to his home.

My parents would probably never see each other again. But for me, this brief meeting was one of the most important results of my visit, perhaps even more important than arranging for Father to return to the newspaper. Ideological absolutes had led us Chinese to treat one another in ways that ran counter to any human feeling. Now the political movements had passed and were officially pronounced disasters. If we were to heal our wounds, surely a first step would be to recognize they existed. Despite their great separateness, my parents were deeply linked. I had allowed them one moment in which to know how very much this was so.

A GHOST
MADE
FLESH

THERE WERE FEW PEOPLE I was more anxious to see than Peng Ming. At one time, as a young Red Guard, I had worshiped the ground on which he stood. Now, my sisters told me, he had been released from prison and was back in Changsha, working as a composer at the Hunan Television Station.

Peng Ming's father was a journalist like mine, and when I was growing up in the *Hunan Daily* compound, his family lived across the hall and shared a kitchen with ours. Peng Ming was about ten years my elder, and when he went away to study composition at the prestigious Central Institute of Music in Beijing, we saw him less often. Then came the Cultural Revolution, and he came home to organize local young people to go on a "New Long March" to Chairman Mao's revolutionary base in the Jinggang Mountains. Father at last permitted me to go along, and at the age of twelve I became one of the youngest of millions of Red Guards.

Peng Ming treated me as an adopted brother during those years, enabling me to see and understand far more than would otherwise have been possible at my age. Uninvited, I went all by myself to Beijing to join him, where he allowed me to help out by carrying musical instruments for one of the Central Institute of Music's propaganda teams and by selling newspapers attacking the "bourgeois" arts establishment. I was like a mascot to Peng Ming's Red Guards; I was their leader's little sidekick. They called me "Little Hunan," after the home region I shared with Chairman Mao.

Peng Ming was a man of astonishing articulateness and dedication, intense critical sensibility and vision. He had always been a Marxist, but a Marxist who believed that hierarchical and corrupt China bore little resemblance to any society about which Marx had ever written.

He gradually rose to great heights as a leader close to the ultraleftist "Cultural Revolution Directorate" itself. The Directorate, led by the Gang of Four, was a group of extremists who came close to destroying the country; but one had only to remember the Peng Ming of that time to despair of understanding the complexities of the Cultural Revolution or of making simple judgments about who was right and who was wrong.

To Peng Ming, the Cultural Revolution was an antifeudal exercise in radical democracy. He fervently believed that it was necessary to rid China of the entrenched elites that incapacitated the administrative bureaucracy, the academic establishment, and literature and art circles. China, he used to tell me, was a backward peasant nation. Only if the ranks of power were open to all the people could China develop into a truly democratic and egalitarian socialist society. Peng Ming, like many other more mature and theoretically inclined Red Guards, had motivations similar to those of the Democracy Wall movement rebels who were briefly active later, in 1978–79, until a crackdown left many of them in prisons and labor camps. The democrats called for free speech and the end of feudalism and the privileged bureaucratic class—indeed, many participants in that doomed movement could have been found among yesterday's Red Guards.

After I left Beijing to rejoin Father in Changsha, we were sent to the countryside and I lost touch with Peng Ming. I wrote him a letter once, which was intercepted by Beijing security forces; it was then that I was locked in a classroom and beaten, and told to confess my role in a criminal political conspiracy about which I knew nothing. As for Peng Ming, he seemed to have vanished without a trace.

Only later did I learn that he had been labeled a counterrevolutionary. Members of the Gang of Four had sacrificed his group in order to consolidate their own positions; he was a victim of factional struggle at the very top. Because he would not confess to something of which he was not guilty, he spent five years in solitary confinement in a secret jail for important prisoners of state. From prison, he was sent to labor camp. His rehabilitation came only in 1979, when he was at last assigned work composing music. Although we were both in Changsha at the time, I didn't know if he was alive or dead. In those days most of us felt as if we were just stirring from the battlefield, patting ourselves all over to find the wounds, stumbling about in the ruins to see who else had survived. There had been so much dislocation that it was reappearances, not absences, that surprised us.

Judy and I were invited to visit Peng Ming on a weekend, and we rode on borrowed bicycles to the Hunan Television Station. It was in a northern suburb, densely surrounded by trees. The sounds of musical instruments floated from the cement-block apartments, and handsome men and women, television actors no doubt, walked about with net bags bursting with Sunday meat and vegetables. We located his building at last, among some twenty identical to it: like so many in Changsha, the hallways were dark and smelly, filthy with chicken droppings, straw baskets of coal briquettes, and crumbling red bricks.

Peng Ming's wife, a middle-aged woman with glasses, clearly an intellectual, greeted us warmly. Inside, in sharp contrast to the exterior, the apartment was immaculate: two narrow rooms crowded with new furniture, a brightly shellacked upright piano wedged into a corner by the window. This cramped home must seem a small paradise to one who had been so long in prison, I thought. Peanuts were being sand-roasted in a wok on the coal stove in the center of the room; plates of tangerines and hard candy lay waiting for us on a table before the new, homemade sofa of honor. Peng Ming himself came rushing in five minutes later, a bag of yellow cakes in his hand.

He was a tall man, razor thin as ever, with startling sharp cheekbones and round wire glasses in the old style of an intellectual from the thirties. He had lost none of his fire and brilliance, seeming, if anything, even more talkative than before, as if making up for all those years in which he had been deprived of conversation. Energy sparked from him like electricity, his charisma as powerful as it had been in radical days. His long musician's fingers seemed to vibrate with expression, and his ready smile transformed his face into a thousand lines, giving him a charm that was irresistible.

For me, the most urgent task was to catch up on the parts of his life that I had missed, particularly those years in solitary confinement. It was hard to believe that they had really occurred as Peng Ming leaped to the piano to play us a newly written tune, as if life had always been normal.

I was not afraid to broach this subject, nor was Peng Ming afraid to answer it. We knew each other too well for that, and Peng Ming was not one to drop five years out of his life. He himself had written extensively on his experiences, he told us, believing that someday such a record might be important for future generations. The prison was perhaps the most important one in China: it had housed top political prisoners from the Dalai Lama's brother to National Chairman Liu Shaoqi; the Gang of Four was there now. When we said we wanted to hear a full account, my friend urged us to tape record what he said. Then he drew out some of his manuscripts and, consulting them occasionally, spoke for nearly an hour without interruption.

"I had no idea where I was being taken," he said, "only that it wasn't too far from Beijing. They held my head down when they drove me there, a public security bureau officer on each side. I couldn't see a thing. When we stopped, I was led to a questioning room, where I was ordered to sign an acknowledgment of arrest. This was absurd: my arrest was a fait accompli when I was seized weeks earlier.

"I demanded to know what I was accused of and who was prosecuting me, but no one would answer. I was tempted not to sign, so that it would be an arrest under protest, but then I thought, why should I be afraid, wasn't China supposed to be a Marxist state? Someday my innocence would be clear. They confiscated my clothing and gave me a black monkey suit. There were no pockets and the drawstring was short, so I couldn't hang myself with it, I suppose. Then they shaved my head.

"We went out into a long, gray-walled corridor open to the sun. It was about five yards across and very long, seemingly ending at the foot of the distant mountains. Over the walls, I could see U-shaped buildings about four stories high, each one behind a gate. There must have been about twenty different prisons. Finally, a gate was opened to me. They ushered me inside, unlocking many doors and locking them again behind us.

"They put me into a small cell. After a while, they brought some bedding and a newspaper. It was dated the week before, so I asked for a new one. The sentry said sharply, 'Whatever day we give you, that's the day you read.' Later, someone came into my cell to tell me the rules: 'This is an organ of the dictatorship of the proletariat under the leadership of Chairman Mao. There is to be no shouting. There is to be no speaking to anyone, including the sentries. It is especially forbidden to tell anyone your name.'

"The door didn't open again for over a year. I didn't know where I was, why, or how long I was supposed to be there. Sometimes, on a windy day, I heard a faint loudspeaker and I could catch the words 'China-Vietnam Friendship People's Commune'; I guessed it must be nearby. . . .

"My cell was about fifteen feet long and nine wide, with only a small wooden bed and two damp cotton quilts, one to lie on and one to cover myself with. There was a window of nontransparent green glass that opened at the top, and in front were a mosquito screen and iron bars. All I could see was a little sky. The ceiling was fitted with two light bulbs, a strong one for daytime, a weak one for night; they wanted to be able to keep an eye on me at all times. The bulbs were covered with steel wire to keep me from trying to electrocute myself. There were double doors, one of steel and one of wood, and at the bottom was a small hole for food and newspapers. At eye level was the little window, steel-encased from the outside; a sentry shot it back several times an hour to check on me. There was a similar window in the little washroom, so I was under observation even when I was going to the toilet.

"One day I asked for something else to read. The warden refused. I insisted that I be given the works of Marx, Lenin, and Chairman Mao. He still said no. I said, 'You think I'm a bad man, don't you?' He said, 'Of course you're a bad man. Why else would you be here?' I said, 'If I'm a bad man, I should have the chance to reform myself.' A few days later, I got my books. On each of them was stamped, 'Qincheng Prison Library.' . . .

"At first, I ran in place six hours a day. I didn't want to wear out my shoes, so I ran barefoot. Eventually, I wore quite a deep impression in the dirt floor. After they gave me books, I ran only four hours a day. I had to stand at attention as soon as the wake-up bell sounded, and I wasn't allowed to sit for too long because they were afraid I'd get sick. At night, I had to sleep facing the door so they could watch me. I began to have a painful stiffness all down that side of my body. It bothers me even today.

"I got a bar of soap every two months and as much tooth powder as I wanted, but no toothpaste because they were afraid I would eat the tube and kill myself. I made something from the cardboard boxes. I managed to hide it and bring it out with me. In fact, I have it here."

Peng Ming turned to his desk, riffling impatiently through

the papers in a drawer. From a faded envelope, he drew out something a bit bigger than a postcard: it was a scene, of sorts, composed of revolutionary symbols. Each one had been painstakingly torn into shape from colored paper by hand. There were the hills of Dazhai, the model farm brigade; the oil fields of Daqing, the model in industry. Tiananmen Square, the heart of Beijing, was there, as was the five-starred national flag; there were also three human figures, a worker, a peasant, and a soldier, representing the revolutionary masses. In the middle of the sky, in crudely torn red characters, hung the slogan, "Long Live the Revolution!"

It was awesome to see and touch this "artwork," so expressive of Peng Ming's faith, such a testament to the thousands of hours of life that this talented and dedicated man had been forced to waste. The pitiful symbols captured the noble socialism in which he believed, not the distorted one that had led to his imprisonment. I felt as if his whole courageous, idealistic spirit lay there in my hands.

"I worked on this when there were no books," Peng Ming said, "always keeping my secret. I could always avoid the sentry by working for only a few minutes just after he had checked on me. Then I hid it away again. I felt it was a great victory when it was finally completed." Peng Ming paused for a moment, taking the tattered collage back from me and looking at it with a mixture of sadness and pride.

"If there were books, of course, that was much better." Peng Ming returned his treasure to the desk and resumed his story. "They would pass me a slip of paper with my number on it, and I would write down a request. Of course, Marx, Lenin, and Chairman Mao were the only authors available. If they had what I wanted, they'd slip it through the food hole—what happiness that was! During those five years, I read almost every work of Marx, Lenin, and Mao published in China, including Marx's and Lenin's memoirs. I learned my lessons well, too. Sometimes someone would come to the window and demand, 'What have you been thinking?' I would always give the same answer, 'I'm ready to serve the party at any time.' Whenever I was given paper and pencil, I wrote letters to Chairman Mao about my innocence. But I'm sure they were never sent.

"Once they put a paper slogan up on my cell wall, 'Leniency to those who admit their crimes; severity to those who refuse.' Since I felt that this slogan was not applicable to my case, I took it down and put it under my pillow. A soldier came in immediately and demanded that I hand it over. When I refused, more came in. Four of them beat and kicked me. When I protested, they said, 'Who claims we can't beat a counterrevolutionary?' Later, I called for a warden and said, 'I'm not a counterrevolutionary.' He said, 'If you're not, then who is?' I said, 'If you can wait, I can wait. Someday I'll walk out of here smiling.'

"At first, I longed to be interrogated, because I thought that way I would be cleared. Later, I learned to dread it. It was always three days at a stretch, with thirty or forty examiners shooting questions at me. They could rest, I couldn't. They always told me all I had to do was confess my guilt and I could return to the ranks of the revolution; otherwise I would be a counterrevolutionary forever. They sat me on a hard ceramic stool and asked their questions. I always answered, 'I'm ready to serve the party at any time,' no matter what they asked. They thought I was crazy.

"Sometimes, late at night, I'd hear another prisoner cry, 'Chairman Mao, I'm a man, not a ghost!' Then there would be a huge kicking at a metal door. Sometimes I heard a woman weep. . . .

"I was afraid of losing the ability to speak, so I often talked softly to myself. Once I thought I would go crazy if I couldn't talk to somebody, so I shouted, 'Report!'—the signal for a warden. Instead, four security bureau officers came in with shackles and handcuffs, and locked them on me. They didn't take them off for ten days. It wasn't until I got sick and the doctor came to look at me that I was released.

"They didn't want me to die, you see, because my existence was the sole evidence of the conspiracy they claimed I had organized.

"In 1973, they took me to the interrogation room to listen to a document. It was the first and only time. They read, 'From now on, fascist-style interrogations are to be eliminated in Qincheng Prison. If they occur, prisoners are permitted to appeal.' The relatives of some of the old Central Committee members who were incarcerated there must have found out what was going on and protested. And in fact, after that things did get somewhat better. . . .

"I remember the first time I was allowed to go outside. There was a small building, divided into twenty or thirty rooms, all of them open to the sky. Inside, it was like looking at clouds from inside a well, except there was a kind of long road on top, so two armed sentries could pace back and forth and look down at you.

"I couldn't figure out why I seemed to be the only one being taken out; it was only much later that I realized the guards had it timed exactly. As each prisoner rounded a corner, another one was taken from his cell. That way we never set eyes on one another. Perhaps that was the virtue of the U-shaped prison. Of course, you could always shout, 'I am so-and-so, I am innocent,' but that just brought you trouble.

"I saw another prisoner only once, by pure chance. I was being led out for my airing, and the sentry took me around a corner before the man in front had disappeared around his. I saw black clothes and a shaved head just like my own. He looked back and saw me, too. I thought about that human contact for days. Another time, there was some kind of mixup, and I was shoved into someone else's cell to let somebody pass. It was exactly like mine, but the walls were padded with rubber.

"The time for being 'put in the wind' was limited to an hour.

At first, it came once a month, then three times a month, and finally every day. Once I caught a little sparrow. I was mad with happiness! The sentry yelled and stamped his foot, but I just cradled my little sparrow against my chest.

"In 1975, I began to notice that fewer doors seemed to be opening when it was time to go outside. My position in the outdoor rooms seemed to have moved closer to the front. I guessed that some prisoners had been released. My newspaper began to be more up-to-date, too; there must have been fewer people to share it with. Then one day the door opened, and I was led to the interrogation room. 'Please sit down,' I heard. 'Today we have an important announcement.'

" 'Please!' I could hardly believe my ears. 'I'm ready to serve the party at any time,' I said.

"A waiting security official picked up a document from his desk and read, 'Our great leader Chairman Mao personally releases you.' He put it down and stared at me, as if wondering what I was still doing there. 'That will be all.'

" 'I want to see the document,' I demanded. 'I want to know what crime I've been accused of.'

" 'There's no need for that,' he said. 'We've communicated the spirit of the document. There's no crime involved. You're a comrade. You'll be released.'

" 'Then what have I been doing here the last five years?' I cried.

" 'The Central Committee needed to investigate you.'

"The meeting was over. Then they took me back to my cell and locked me up again. First they called me 'Comrade'—then they locked me up.

"The next morning, they brought me a new pair of pants and a jacket. They said I wasn't allowed to take anything from the jail. Still, I smuggled out my cloth shoes, as a souvenir of five years of absurdity.

"I was released with a large group. The wardens, sentries, and security bureau officials stood on both sides of the road to see us off, as if we had been guests all those years. I turned to look again at the place that took away my best years and strength, then climbed into the bus waiting to take me back to human life. I was a ghost made flesh; I wondered if everyone would be afraid of me."

Peng Ming had finished his story, and he sat back and took a long drink of tea. We were all silent for a long time before speaking. Although no worse than many, his tale evoked my own most unhappy memories of the Cultural Revolution; listening to it brought that familiar bitterness sharp to my mouth again. So many millions had suffered that many people saw their experiences as commonplace, part of the ordinary nature of human experience. Some even thought it would be presumptuous to expect anyone to listen to the retelling. Peng Ming knew better the importance of remembering the past.

Fortunately, the remainder of Peng Ming's story made these harsh memories more bearable. He had come through his personal nightmare amazingly well. He had met and married a woman willing to love someone who had endured so much hardship and disgrace, and now had a child, a big-eared young toddler who waved his hands in the air whenever music played, like Papa the conductor.

But Peng Ming derived happiness not only through his family: he was once again an active participant in political life.

For the first time, the deep love he had offered the "organization" had been requited. At last he had been admitted to the party. The notice had arrived only a few weeks before our visit, fifteen years to the day from his imprisonment. Even more extraordinary was this: Peng Ming had been appointed director of the television station's important drama division, and he sensed that he was being considered for the leadership of the entire work unit.

Peng Ming's self-confidence and ambition seemed boundless, much as in the old days. He even joked that he was fully prepared to become minister of culture if called on to serve. As a composer, he said, he had known the terrible difficulty of getting something performed, the layer after layer of bureaucratic inspections and permissions, the endless revisions demanded by the "musical illiterates" in power. Although the new post meant he would have far less time for his own compositions, he felt that if he and people like him did not become leaders, the uneducated old ideologues would remain. "I'm willing to give up my chances to write," he said, "if it means that with me as their leader, ten composers will have their freedom." He smiled broadly. "I'm not afraid of the censors anymore. The censors are me!"

I sat listening in a state of amazement; I could hardly believe my ears. Joined the party? Become a leader? True, I could not remember a time when Peng Ming was not writing an application for party membership. His commitment to Marxist ideals was equaled by none. True too, I had heard that the reformers were actively encouraging intellectuals to join the party. Still, I was astonished that he still believed in the organization after all he had suffered at its hands.

Peng Ming laughed at my expression of shock. "Answer me this," he said. "If not for the Communist party, who can lead China? The truth is, there is no alternative. What use is it to speak of other parties and elections? At least the reformers are trying to build the kind of party that I can believe in, one in which its members live by communist principles."

I had my doubts about whether Peng Ming's joining the party would do anyone any good. During the latter years of the Cultural Revolution, most of us had become utterly disillusioned with everything the party stood for. Almost half of its members had enrolled during the Cultural Revolution, when political conformity and "class background" mattered above all else. Many had climbed to power by grinding others into the dirt.

Close to a third were said to be all but illiterate. By the time I was admitted to the university, I had learned to stay as far away from the party and its activities as possible. Those applying to join were usually hated hypocritical "activists" and class spies, and the party members who had any decency often regretted their affiliation, knowing why people shied away from them and fell silent in their presence. I would never have guessed that the party could still attract people of the integrity of a Peng Ming.

Peng Ming agreed that the party's image had become tarnished almost beyond recall. "Ever since the Cultural Revolution, people have said that the only place you can find communist ideals practiced is outside the party; those within it care for no one but themselves. And the leaders are truly the worst of all, ignorant ideologues who know nothing of professional work and take up people's time in 'political study' with long-winded documents which are printed in the newspapers anyway." Peng Ming paused, as if giving me a revolutionary education as he had in the old days. "The socialism in China under Mao was fascist feudalism, which oppressed the people and made them serve the party as slaves. But now people who have experienced China's terrible capacity to distort ambition and power are becoming party members, people who have had the time to think about how we went wrong during the Cultural Revolution. We have a chance to build a party in which once again every member serves the people with heart and soul." Peng Ming smiled, suddenly self-conscious. "My ideas haven't really changed much, you see, after all these years, because China's problems haven't really changed much. But I've recognized that mass political mobilization isn't the answer."

With such a large majority of party members of such poor quality, I wondered what Peng Ming could do against so many. However, he said he felt that a purge was not the answer. The reformers had a far more interesting solution, one radically different from the destructive methods used in the past. They were trying to dilute the strength of the uneducated bureaucrats by encouraging skilled and educated people to join them, rather than launching another movement that might easily turn into yet another phase in the cycle of revenge. The party "rectification," he explained, was being used primarily as a tool to make leaders fall in line behind the reforms, except in a very few cases in which true criminals were in positions of great power.

I remembered Old Chen's story of the Shaoyang leftists, and told it to Peng Ming. If a journalist had encountered such great troubles in reporting on policies firmly backed by Beijing, how many greater difficulties was an outspoken visionary like Peng Ming likely to encounter! It seemed impossible to me that a party with one of the worst records of the century could transform itself into the democratic and open party Peng Ming wanted. It could become more lively, perhaps, be led by better-trained people. And it could certainly profit from the mistakes of the Cultural Revolution. But, especially after my years in the West, I believed that without checks the absolute power of a single party could always be turned to antidemocratic purposes.

Despite our many differences, I left Peng Ming's home feeling cheered. If even a few people like him were entering the system, it was a sign that China's leaders were succeeding in one of its most difficult tasks, improving the image of the organization that conferred their legitimacy. This was essential if national wounds were to heal. Still, perhaps it was my own experience of too many shifts in the political winds that made me fear that intellectuals, raised so suddenly from the "stinking ninth" category to what could easily be called the "fragrant first," might be punished all the more severely if the cycle came around again.

I found Peng Ming's love of China deeply moving. The old Red Guards had not given up after the failures of my father's generation. Another attempt was being made, as I was sure others would be should this reform movement be crushed. China would rise again, like the eternal phoenix, shaking the tears from her wings and flying out in still another, perhaps better direction. As I wished Peng Ming luck from the bottom of my heart, that was the only thing of which I felt entirely certain.

TAO SEN

I COULD NOT HAVE RETURNED to Changsha without crossing the Xiang River to visit the Hunan Teachers College, although my relationships there were even more complicated than those with my family. My student years had been fraught with struggle, each incident leaving me more notorious and controversial than the last. At the Hunan Teachers College I had met Judy, and our courtship and marriage became one of the most talked about, and to some, scandalous events of the year; at the Hunan Teachers College, too, I had proposed myself as a non-Marxist election candidate and thereby fueled a student movement that put most of the universities in the city on strike and nearly closed some factories as well.

Judy and I were well aware that whatever we did in Changsha would soon be spread as gossip throughout the city—already several people had told us they had heard about the pointed questions we had asked during a visit to a local prison. To return to the college would be like dropping a cold sweet potato into a pan of hot oil. The last time I had been there, loudspeakers were still blaring criticisms of my "thought," and I was spared a term in labor camp only because I was leaving the country. The other leader, Tao Sen, had no such escape. Yet a return to the school was necessary if I was to pay my respects to the professors who had meant so much to me. Several had taken great risks by giving me private instruction in subjects it was then still unsafe to treat in class.

The trip across the bridge was also, I had to admit, a display of defiance to those who had wished me ill. Even before we were married, small-minded xenophobes had spread rumors that Judy would "sell" me on the streets of New York. After we left, my friends wrote me that they had heard a story that she was met at the airport by her "first husband" (she had none). Reports of our "divorce" appeared with predictable regularity, one even reaching a Berkeley professor, an acquaintance of ours, who telephoned us in alarm. As if the idea that I could find happiness in the capitalist West was an unbearable threat to what the leftists believed, some college leaders informed people that I was wandering the streets penniless, washing dishes so as not to starve. After Judy and I got used to such tales, they didn't matter much to us since we didn't have to live in China anymore. But they were painful for my family, who used to write asking for recent photographs of the two of us to use as evidence that we were together. Now here was our chance to help my family save face and prove the gossips wrong.

We took bus Number 9 across the river, as we had so many times before, and decided to walk from Rongwan Town to the university rather than brave overcrowded bus Number 5. We soon turned off the main road onto the quiet footpath that led up into the Yuelu Hills. This was a route that few people knew about: we had used it often when we were courting secretly. I found it as pretty as ever, as it led among old brick peasant homes and plots of cabbages; it afforded a good view of Orange Island and of the city of Changsha on the opposite bank, today shrouded in winter mist.

Our unconventional approach allowed us to make an inconspicuous entrance to the school, so that we came down from the hills above like local folk. This gave me an eerie sense of the past, as if we still lived there and nothing had changed. We were soon among the first cement-block apartments for professors, each with its cement balcony hung with laundry. We looked automatically up at what had once been our own balcony, and it seemed we could recognize one of the scraggly potted evergreens, a gift from one of Judy's students. At the time, Judy had been the only foreigner at the university; now, we had heard, there were so many that a special compound had been built for them, complete with high wall and gatekeeper.

We descended toward the foreign languages department, the same route we had taken every day for so long, stopping at the garage to visit with a driver who had been unfailingly good to us. As we moved on, we noticed that a deep hole into which Judy had fallen one dark night five years earlier had been covered over; later we learned the leaders had at last been spurred into action when, a few months before, a freshman roused from bed for predawn exercise and unfamiliar with the lay of the land had jogged in and broken his neck. The foreign languages building had been given a face-lift, and farther along one of those decorative landscapes had been built: a pool of water ringed in cement, with a large porous rock dotted with miniature pavilions set in the middle. I hoped that the other changes at the university were more than cosmetic—I had heard that most of the college-level leaders had been transferred, and that now a former physics professor was president. That sounded like a sign of hope.

As we walked, several people stared sharply at us, as if not believing their eyes, and Judy was greeted joyfully by one of the English professors, who said it was only after we left that the department came fully to appreciate the extent of her contribution. She had been sorely missed. But we did not wish to put this good-hearted professor in an awkward position by talking with him too long in public. Judy too was a controversial figure at the college, by association with me, and her feelings had already been hurt when, a few days before, we learned that one of her favorite students was afraid to come see us. It seemed that some people had been warned.

We passed now through the chemistry building and into the student dormitory area. Dressed as ever in blue drab, the students looked fresh-faced, ill-nourished, and incredibly young. Most of them had come to college directly from middle school, and had never participated in a political campaign or lived in the countryside. My own classmates had been so different! I was overcome by a rush of nostalgia for them, for their questing worldliness. That kind of student had been a product of a particular period and set of political circumstances, and would doubtless never be found in Chinese universities again.

My grade, known as the 1977 grade because that was when we were enrolled, was famous in China. Since we were the first to enter college through examinations in more than ten years, among us were China's best and brightest, most troubled and thoughtful. From intellectual families, many of us, we had been despised and beaten, yet had dared to study secretly. Some had broken into boarded-up libraries, others begged ex-teachers for clandestine instruction. Even while we were in the countryside, planting and hauling, hardship could not drive the thirst for knowledge out of us. If anything, the questions crying for answers seemed the more pressing. The 1977 grade was ancient with the troubles of the world. Many of us were fully grown adults in our mid-twenties when we came to college; we had been turned into men and women many years earlier by political upheaval.

For me and my classmates, the opportunity to study at a university was a dream come true, a privilege we could never have imagined for ourselves while Mao was alive. Yet after we arrived at the Teachers College, a number directly from the harsh countryside with their bedrolls on their backs, many of us found the paternalistic education system a grave disappointment. Marxism—Leninism—Mao Zedong Thought governed every class from world literature to aesthetics. Political pressure seemed to have scarred our teachers permanently; it was as if they were apologizing for their knowledge even as they dutifully imparted it. We could hardly trust even one another, for we knew little about those with whom we lived, eight to a room; friends who seemed to be agreeing with us most fervently might well be making "small reports" on our "thought" to the department leaders who would ultimately be assigning us jobs for life. We didn't even blame them—it was a question of survival.

Hunan, as Chairman Mao's home province and early revolutionary base, was notoriously leftist; its passive resistance to Deng's pragmatic policies became food for criticism in the newspapers when it was among the last provinces to reject absolutist Maoist principles and carry out public discussion of Deng's pragmatic slogan, "Seek truth from facts." Our college was considered more leftist than most: it was run largely by old Red Army leaders whose only claim to power was their early participation in the revolution. Assignment to university leadership was considered an untaxing reward for unskilled revolutionaries in the sunset of life. As the familiar expression had it, "the relationship between the party and the masses was tense." The judgment of teachers assigned to Hunan from other provinces was often flat: "This is a bad place," they would say, and they were in a position to know.

In the autumn of 1980, just before the democratic election movement, several things exacerbated our hatred of the leaders. The college-level officials were building themselves and their families a new apartment building, with huge suites, but apparently they didn't think it important to plan for the thousand-odd new students in the 1979 grade, who were being forced to sleep fifty to one hundred students in large classrooms. Infectious diseases were said to be rampant, and many of us, although accustomed to seeing officials enjoy special privileges, were shaken to see the abuse of power quite so blatant. Student tolerance was also being stretched to the limit with the often inedible dining hall food, which was generally fried squash and chunks of pork fat for lunch and dinner, and for breakfast, all too often, sweet potatoes and gruel. Diarrhea and vomiting were common. Another issue was the lighting in our dormitories and classrooms, which was so bad that at night we had to go out and study beneath the streetlamps; and hot water was available in the student bathhouse so rarely that some went for an entire winter without taking a bath. Meanwhile, the leaders sat in their offices all day, reading party newspapers and drinking tea. Few could see any reason for their existence beyond receiving gifts. There were always unfortunate professors to be attended to—people were trying to transfer their husbands or wives to Changsha so that they could live together, hoping to move to a larger apartment, or politicking for a raise in salary. The other thing the leaders were good for was criticizing us students in political study meetings. Of course, they always claimed they did so because of the party's concern for our welfare.

Then one day we were told there were to be democratic elections for representatives to the local People's Congress, the lowest level of the largely powerless National People's Assembly. The Hunan Teachers College made up a district, and four delegates were to be chosen from six candidates. Primary balloting would determine the six names. Of course, the university's election committee had its own agenda; we were simply to cast our votes in approval. But a lot of us saw things differently.

Many of us believed that some Central Committee leaders were just as frustrated with local bureaucrats as we. Here at last was our opportunity to make our voices heard, to exercise some control, to help the top put pressure on the middle by squeezing it from below. And I was in a special position: married as I was to an American, I was protected as none of my classmates were. I believed I owed it to them to speak out when they could not. One afternoon in one of the Chinese literature department's grade-wide political study meetings, on what was perhaps a reckless impulse, I found myself standing up and offering my own name for candidacy. The other self-nominated candidate was Tao Sen.

Tao Sen, at thirty-three one of the oldest students, had a kind of backing of his own. His father had been a high-ranking cadre with old comrades-in-arms in the Central Committee. The man had been "persecuted to death" during the Cultural Revolution, but after his friends' return to power Tao Sen had managed to have his bones moved to a martyrs' graveyard in Xiangtan, his hometown. Tao Sen had several times visited Beijing to plead the cases of other persecuted cadres as well. Although we were in the same department, Tao and I had not known each other before the dramatic events of the months to come. However, we soon became locked together in a course of action as dramatic as it was ultimately dangerous.

Although we both said we supported the current leadership in Beijing, Tao Sen attacked the privileged class of party officials, and I, drunk with the thrill of speaking the truth, denounced ideologues who took Marxism-Leninism on faith like some kind of revolutionary religion. We gave our campaign speeches in the evenings, with borrowed megaphones, on the sportsground where hundreds were gathered, sitting on little bamboo stools they had carried from their dormitories, to see the weekend movies. Film showings quickly became political rallies. The same notice boards in front of the dining hall that Judy and I were now approaching had been plastered over and over, to a thickness of hundreds, with posters debating our positions. It had been in the style of Democracy Wall, although putting up "big character posters" had already been forbidden and the Beijing activists arrested. Today the notice boards were covered with colored advertisements for everything from toothbrushes and eye drops to swansdown parkas and truck tires.

Tao Sen soon became the number one candidate, speaking out

for freedom for students to find their own jobs, for better dormitory conditions, and for an end to the elitist practices of the new bureaucratic class. Tao was organized and high-strung, a real political leader.

Enraged university election officials tried everything to diminish our influence. They announced our placement in the semifinal elections according to the number of brushstrokes in the characters of our last names (this put Tao Sen fifth and me sixth, although in fact he had come in first and I third); they called Tao Sen into secret meetings, warning him not to be led astray by a non-communist like me. They interdicted public speeches; they forbade us to publish position statements. Finally, hoping to draw votes away from us, they added a seventh candidate of their own choosing, the leader of the college's Communist Youth League, claiming that this was in response to "the overwhelming demand of the masses."

It was this last that set off the students' fury. Many had not supported me, for they did not think it appropriate that a non-Marxist-Leninist represent them, but these machinations to distort the outcome of the "free" elections were in obvious contradiction to the national election rules. The university leaders' announcement about the new candidate came over the loudspeakers late on a Sunday night; even from our apartment in the professors' quarters, Judy and I could hear the roar of anger go up from the distant dormitories. Fifteen minutes later, thousands of students had circled the administration building less than two hundred yards from our balcony, demanding to speak to Su Ming, the seventy-year-old Red Army veteran who had been put in charge of the elections in the college president's absence.

Su Ming himself was responsible for what happened next, for he simply cursed the students as "Cultural Revolution hooligans" and declared he was going home to bed. And it was Tao Sen who led the angry students to join arms and march to the Hunan Provincial Party Committee offices many miles away across the river. They returned at dawn with the announcement of victory: an investigating team would be sent to look into the college's conduct of the elections.

In fact, it was no victory at all. The investigation never took place, and more petitions had to be presented at the gates of the committee. Election day was approaching fast. One Sunday morning when Judy and I were still asleep, Tao knocked on our door with a plan: we would take our names off the slate in protest, thereby leaving the school with an insufficient number of candidates.

But the college leaders ignored our withdrawal, continuing with their plans for a seven-candidate race. Soon eighty-seven of us, from Hunan University as well as from our own college, lay on hunger strike at the gates of the Hunan Provincial Party Committee.

It was already bitter cold in October, but we stayed outside the gate for three days and three nights. Tao Sen led our chanting draped in a faded blanket some sympathetic professor or factory worker had contributed, and appealed for doctors for the large numbers who had fainted. The students from the Teachers College, Hunan University, the Hunan Mining and Metallurgical Institute, and the Hunan Medical College were all boycotting classes; several factories looked as if they were about to join the strike.

As we hoped, the incident grew so big that Beijing had to take notice; although the *Hunan Daily* was silent, reports in the international press and over the Voice of America made it impossible to ignore. At last we got the investigating team we had been demanding, but not before a freezing rain and tactical disagreements left us weeping with exhaustion. I favored a lawsuit against the university so we could test the promised legal system as we were testing the promised democracy; Tao favored demonstrations to the bitter end, and even led a small group of the most confrontational students to Beijing.

The investigators, three men from the National Election Committee, spent two weeks at the college talking with people on all sides. Then they went back to Beijing to make their report. After weeks of anticipation, the committee issued a document that pronounced the Teachers College election invalid because of insufficient voter participation. University leaders were ordered to make a public self-criticism for polarizing the situation and distorting the election rules. The document came down in December of 1980. We believed, foolishly, that we had won.

I had been so lost in my memories that I had hardly noticed that Judy and I had reached my professor's home, one of the red brick buildings in the hilly part of campus that melded into Hunan University. I brought myself back to the present and knocked. A stranger answered the door and, staring curiously, told us that my teacher had been assigned one of the new apartments. He didn't know which one.

This was a pretty problem! Here at the university, most people did their best to remain inconspicuous and avoid unnecessary social contacts. It was extremely unlikely that I would be able to find out where my professor now lived by asking around. It seemed that my only choice was to visit the very place I least wished to go, the Chinese literature department's Party Branch Office.

I had learned to hate that severe concrete room, with its newspaper rack and locked cabinets. It had first grown familiar to me as the place where I was reprimanded for cutting too many politics classes and political study meetings. I had also been ordered to go there when my relationship with Judy became public knowledge: my department leaders, ever concerned for my welfare, had called me in to "do political thought work" and urge me to break off with her. They threatened to visit my father, who at the time knew nothing about Judy, and later actually made a visit to the county town where he lived, frightening him nearly to death with tales of my involvement with a foreign spy. As

Judy and I retraced our steps, I remembered that it was also in that room that the political cadres mustered their counterattack against the students during the election movement.

They would not have been able to do so had it not been for a major change in the national political climate in December, the same month that the National Election Committee issued a statement in our favor. The regime that we had naively believed supported us turned against us. Deng Xiaoping may have shared our criticisms of corrupt officials, but he did not welcome our questions about the legitimacy of the Communist party. He may have needed us to help him put pressure on his opponents, but not to threaten the one-party system. He made a speech, later issued as Document No. 2 of 1981, attacking the "disorderly thought" of certain university students who had "lost confidence" in the party and socialism.

The National Election Committee's document was, in effect, overturned, belying the official myth that in China the government is more powerful than the party; now it was the students, not the leaders, who were vulnerable. College party officials marshaled their forces for revenge.

Their preparations took place during Spring Festival, when we were all away on holiday. All party members were summoned back to school a week early to attend meetings. They had to study Deng's document and similar editorials in the *People's Daily*. Even those party members who had supported the movement, and there were many, were hard put to defend actions that Deng Xiaoping now seemed to think were "anti-party and anti-socialism."

When the rest of us came back, classes were postponed for three days of "study." We listened with a growing sense of despair to the damaging information that had been collected on Tao Sen: it was said that he had connections with underground newspapers; he had met with cronies of the famous Democracy Wall movement activist Wei Jingsheng; he had given information to foreign magazines. The ups and downs of his love life (he had had more than one girl friend) were said to be proof of his evil nature.

Rumors were rampant. People were sure that Tao Sen and I would be arrested at any moment. Everyone was whispering and frightened, and my mother came every day to our apartment to weep and beg Judy to make me listen to reason and keep silent. Many students recognized that we were lost, and those in the 1977 grade became increasingly worried about the work assignments that would be determined by the leaders at graduation, now less than a year away. Fearing they would be sent to the countryside, far from relatives and friends, where life was primitive and there were no books to read, they went voluntarily to "confess" and give information on their fellows.

During the meetings, we were forced to stand up one by one and state our opinions. We were asked such questions as why we should uphold the Four Basic Principles (the leadership of the party, the people's democratic dictatorship, Marxism–Leninism–Mao Zedong Thought, and the socialist road). We had to say who among us hadn't upheld them during the student movement; whether we ourselves had done so; why this question should be discussed. And we had to state who, after all, was right, the students or the college leaders, and who, after all, was wrong.

Then one morning the leaders produced a wild card: Tao Sen's best friend, his main campaign assistant, was ready to tell all. The frightened boy stood up in front of a tense student meeting and said, "I had a secret purpose in infiltrating the elections. I wanted to find out as much as I could about those who were attacking our Communist party. Tao Sen had a lot of confidence in me. He let me see many letters and diaries. I wrote in my own journal every day, too, wrote down whom he saw, and what he said." The boy paused, steeling himself to pronounce the judgment. "Tao Sen is an individualistic conspirator."

The boy went on to accuse Tao of immoral womanizing. He

even provided what he called "conclusive evidence" of Tao's unscrupulousness, the words he had said in his dreams about his selfish political ambitions. During the next few days, we all had many opportunities to listen to Tao's bunkmate and most trusted ally's renditions of his nocturnal speech.

We were very angry at the leaders' use of us against each other. They were the ones using "Cultural Revolution tactics," not we. They kept playing the game of "discussing," although we knew full well there was no discussion at all.

It went on for days. In our department, an entire class in the 1978 grade refused to admit that they were wrong. One student even stood up and said that the real question was whether the Communist party had any good points. The leaders had asked for discussion, and they got it: did Chinese people really have rule by law, the students asked? Did we actually enjoy the freedom of speech, assembly, and democracy guaranteed in our constitution?

But the leaders got what they wanted, of course, perhaps not our minds but certainly our physical obedience. Tao Sen was expelled from school amid large-scale public criticism sessions. The public security bureau took him away. Tao was guilty of "counterrevolutionary activities," so the leaders never had to go through the law courts. He could simply be dispatched to labor camp for three years to be reformed. And I—that spring I was untouched, but only because of Judy. My name was never even mentioned on the loudspeakers, although everyone recognized whose "thought" was being criticized in political study meetings all over the city.

Judy and I had reached the Chinese literature department. It was a Tuesday afternoon, time for political study, and the building was quiet. The broad stairs were spattered with gobs of mucus and saliva, just as they had always been. We took them two at a time, turning toward the Party Branch Office on the second floor. The painted red characters by the door hung drearily on the familiar sign—everything was as if I had never left. I had to pause and remind myself that now these people had no power over me whatsoever. I knocked hard, Chinese style.

Inside, lounging around the coal burner, were ten or twelve cadres. I filled the doorway. They all froze, staring. It was as if I were an apparition dropped from the sky.

"It's me, Liang Heng," I said, to break the silence.

All the ultraleftists were there. The reformist shakeup might have reached the college level, but it certainly hadn't come to the Chinese department yet. There was Old Gong, one of the men who had threatened my father, with his messy hair and swollen face, ever in his Mao-era cadre's jacket, his cigarette stilled in the air halfway on its journey to his mouth. By his side was the man who had organized the Chinese department's mass criticism meetings of Tao Sen. I spotted only one ally in the room, a woman, one of the typists, fatter and grayer now. During the election movement, she had secretly passed me the key to the department's mimeograph room, where I spent a long late evening running off copies of my campaign platform.

She now leaped joyfully up and took my hand tightly in both of hers, exclaiming, "Liang Heng! Really, it's you!" It was as if she were the only warm-blooded living thing in a room full of statues. Ignoring the others, she asked warmly after my situation, smiled at Judy, gladly looked up my teacher's new address for me. If she had not been there, I don't know what would have happened. During the few minutes that I stood there in that office, Secretary Gong never moved, and his eyes, full of suspicion, hate, envy, and embarrassment, never left my carefully polished black leather shoes.

When I found my teacher at last, he confirmed what I had already heard through letters. Many of my classmates had indeed received poor job assignments, as they had feared, and nothing the professors could say could prevent it, for the final decisions were in the hands of the party leaders. Many of the best students had been most outspoken during the movement. By rights, they should have been among those to stay on at the university, which had many openings for new teachers. Instead, those given the coveted positions were usually those "trusted by the organization," while the activists were sent off to teach in obscure middle schools in the far corners of the province. Some were given assignments so dreadful that they refused to go, preferring to stay at home with their parents rather than face the isolation to which they had been assigned. One brilliant English student had passed an excruciating battery of national examinations to go abroad and was preparing to depart for Canada, when university leaders suddenly informed Beijing that her "political thought" left something to be desired.

This was the situation in the first few years just after the graduation of my grade; however, my teacher told me, now there was greater freedom for people to negotiate their own jobs, and more emphasis on expertise. Many of my classmates had passed examinations for graduate schools; others now had good positions as editors, administrators, and professors. The black mark of the election movement seemed gradually to have faded from their files. My teacher could tell me nothing of the fate of Tao Sen, however, other than that it was rumored that he had been released from labor camp.

About a week later, as Judy and I were preparing to go out, the hotel telephone rang. A soft, dignified voice said, "It's me, Tao Sen. Someone told me you were asking for me."

I was stupefied. This polite tone resembled not at all the hoarse cries I remembered him by, the shouted slogans to answering crowds of thousands, "Down with the bureaucracy, down with feudalism, long live democracy!"

"Where are you?" I asked, controlling my excitement.

He was only a few minutes away.

I waited with greatest anticipation, standing nervously at the window, watching, fearing he might be followed by the public security forces. There was a light snow. I dared not go to the gate to meet him, and worried what he could possibly say to the gatekeeper to gain entrance. Surely not that he had come to see that other notorious troublemaker, Liang Heng.

The knock came; I leapt to my feet. I pulled Tao into the room, checking nervously to see whether the floor attendants at the end of the long corridor were paying undue attention.

He looked well. He was wearing a Russian-style fur hat and a heavy wool coat. Underneath was a Western-style jacket. The top of a blue silk tie just showed above his sweater, and a small black leather document case hung from a strap on his wrist, matching a pair of well-shined shoes. He hardly fit the image of a man recently released from labor camp.

We shook hands warmly, and he looked me up and down with admiration. When he took off his hat, I saw that his receding hairline was about where it had been four years before, his forehead gleamed with the same limpid skin. When he spoke, his wide, angular jaw moved at the old machine-gun pace.

"I was supposed to go to Qingdao today," he said, "but I put it off as soon as I heard you were in town." His manner was utterly matter-of-fact, as if he had been making trips to the northeast every day of his life. "I've been so busy since we started the company."

Company? It was natural that Tao Sen come to see me after all we had been through together, but I hardly recognized him in this strange new incarnation. The atmosphere of intense anticipation I had created was apparently completely off-base. It turned out that Tao had come not to talk of human rights or democracy but to ask me to help him find foreign connections and capital!

With excitement, Tao described what he had been doing. First, with the cooperation of the remaining relatives of the famous painter, Qi Baishi, who had been a native of his hometown, he had collected many of Qi's scrolls which had survived the Cultural Revolution. He then established a Qi Baishi Cultural Corporation. He proposed to build a small tourist hotel with an attached museum, and in a shop sell reproductions of Qi's paintings and souvenirs embossed with the elegant shrimp that were his trademark. He also hoped to send exhibitions abroad. The project had the blessing of the Xiangtan District Party Committee, Tao said, and also, as he showed me with pride, of the Hunan Provincial Party Committee, which had given him a letter of introduction stamped with its official seal.

"What about labor camp?" I protested, when I could get a word in edgewise.

"I've been out about half a year. I got out early," Tao answered, briskly zipping the letter of introduction back into his leather bag. "There's not much to say about it. At first it was pretty rough, a hundred of us sleeping in one filthy room. Hard labor and a lot of thought reports. But the longer the reform winds blew, the more relaxed things got. Pretty soon I was being invited to help out with the camp accounts. Then they let me out." Tao smiled beatifically.

"But how can you do business? Aren't people nervous about your past?" Judy asked, apparently as amazed by the turn of events as I.

"All that's over," he said. "There's no stigma at all. Everyone knows we were right. I'm even going to graduate from college, after I make up the final exams that I missed while I was in labor camp."

I could scarcely take in this sudden switch from radical democrat to entrepreneur. From my father to Peng Ming and now to Tao Sen, the changes in people's lives came too fast, were too unpredictable. People shot to the heights and plummeted to the depths in the space of a moment. Sometimes it seemed one could never be certain of anything in China. It wasn't until Tao Sen and I had spent several hours talking that I began to understand the consistency in his behavior.

When Tao was released from labor camp, China's economic

reforms were just spreading from the countryside to the cities. In order to resolve the problems of the many unemployed youth waiting for work and to improve economic efficiency in factories and enterprises, the government was actively encouraging the formation of individual and collective businesses. Now huge numbers of people had become involved, like thousands of winter-bound insects climbing out of their hideaways into the warmth of the season.

At first, because he didn't want to accept the position arranged for him by the labor camp (Chinese teacher at a factory middle school), Tao Sen went home to Xiangtan to live. He thought he wanted to write; he had a lot to say, after those years in which to think things over. But no one could remain oblivious to the excitement of what was happening all around, even if it was only to notice the liveliness of the produce markets and the new clothing fairs, or the clean family restaurants and noodle stands. Tao found himself restless staying indoors all day with his mother and thinking about abstract questions of political change.

The failure of our election movement had led him to reconsider many of his ideas. Like Peng Ming, he had come to the conclusion that political democracy in China could not be realized through a radical mass movement. The Chinese people were still poor and uneducated, and the feudal tradition of obedience to a strong central authority ran deep in their souls.

In Tao's view, the economic reforms were making changes no political campaign could, moving China gradually toward a more liberal system. With the emphasis on economic life, the authority of the party seemed to be weakening. In order to permit these small, lively companies to exist, the party could not exert absolute control over them. The new economic organizations thus had the potential for balancing the Communists' excessive power.

Another reason Tao was interested in entering the economic sphere was the political ambition which had never left him. He

felt that he had learned a lot from organizing our student movement; could he not learn that much more from organizing a new
company? He could "observe life through practice," as the saying
went, in preparation for his future political career.

Thus resolved, he had interested several old friends and supporters in his project. Of course, it wasn't easy. Their group of
four or five people was typical of the risky, experimental new
"briefcase companies," so nicknamed because their "offices" were
located in the leather bags they carried with them. They were
more like brokers than anything else, as they negotiated among
various groups for the trade of properties that were not their
own.

Ironically, the young man who had fought so hard against
corruption and backdoorism was forced to fall back on his father's old comrades for support. Without them, he could never
have gotten the official permissions he needed or the bank loans
for start-up capital. Like the son of the vice-governor of Hunan,
the leader of another briefcase company now building hotels in
Changsha, Tao found himself riding about in taxis, renting fancy
hotel rooms for meetings, eating banquets with Hong Kong
businessmen, and taking airplanes to distant cities. All his articulate speech-making skills were now being put to use around the
negotiating table.

It was hard for me to tell how much of Tao's motivation was
financial, how much for the sake of political ideals. But no matter
if Tao Sen had his own interests at stake in this, or if he secretly
enjoyed the high-rolling life he was leading. What was fascinat-
ing to me was that, for whatever reasons, a political dissident had
become so actively involved in business. I wondered how tolerant
the party would be someday when this new economic class grew
into a political force far more powerful than our student democratic movement could ever have been. Would Tao and his
fellow businessmen then be punished for their economic success,
as we once were punished for our political beliefs?

Tao Sen's quick embrace of the climate of the times made me think of how different he was from Peng Ming. All those years in prison had not made Peng reject his Marxist values. It would have been difficult for him to contemplate abandoning the ideology in which he had invested so much. Instead, he thought he could save the old values by leading the life of a good, clean official. But after two and a half years in labor camp, Tao Sen's life had taken off in a new direction. Of course, Tao was from a different generation, my generation, the searching generation. The more bitterness he was forced to swallow, the greater his willingness to try something new.

Tao and I were both well aware that not all dissidents were so lucky as to be able to experiment with the new economic freedoms. Many remained in labor camps and prisons. However, Tao told me that there were fewer people now being imprisoned for political offenses, and he claimed to be far from the only activist who had decided to throw his weight behind the reforms. A number of leaders of Beijing's democracy movement had gone to the Special Economic Zones on the coast, he said, and they were pioneering the liberal policies there. Some months later, I myself heard that the democratic thinker Wei Jingsheng, still in his labor camp in desert Qinghai Province, spent his days writing opinion papers on the economic reforms.

I found that I agreed with much of what Tao had to say. I too believed our country's main problems could be traced to the feudal past. China's lack of an effective legal system, our fanatical worship of Chairman Mao during the Cultural Revolution, the corruption and backdoorism that characterized so many of our dealings—these were all consistent with thousands of years of patriarchal central government. If free national elections were held in China today, I too feared that yet another dictator would be chosen.

As I escorted Tao out the door, now walking fearlessly past the floor attendants to the elevator, I thought once again about those early years after Deng Xiaoping's return to power, when there had been a similar fit between party reformers and democratic activists. After the unofficial magazines and democracy walls were shut down and so many arrested, few of us would have predicted that dissidents and reformers would work together once again. But this time the situation was different. This time the masses were not being used to shore up one faction against another, but were experimenting together with the leaders, searching for the way to lead China out of its stagnation and failures.

We were at the gate. The rare Changsha snow was falling heavily. Young men and women rode carefully by on shaky bicycles, plastic raincoats over their brightly colored clothing. "Don't forget to look for foreign investors for me," Tao said, smiling and shaking my hand. He walked quickly down the street in his Russian hat, disappearing into the free market, where the vegetable sellers stood patient and undismayed under their umbrellas, and the steam from the sweet potatoes rose all the thicker for the frost.

THE
GUO
FAMILY
VILLAGE

*I*T HAD BEEN RAINING for days. The bus, packed with a hundred damp peasants, bounced along the rutted roads, spattering itself with mud. Judy and I had been unable to purchase seats. A place had been found for her among the passengers squeezed onto the metal engine cover beside the driver, out of courtesy for her foreignness. I was standing on a step at the exit door so I wouldn't have to bend down under the low ceiling, and from a broken window the cold rain lashed my old blue Chinese jacket.

The rain was just this heavy when Father, my stepmother, and I came to the countryside to learn from the "politically advanced" peasants in 1969. With hundreds of other intellectuals and their families, we had been packed into overbursting open-roofed trucks. We had said good-bye to our city lives, as we then thought, forever. Rain streaming off the eyeglasses that marked Father and his colleagues as despicable bookworms, wet ropes holding together what was left of our sodden possessions, we arrived three days later in southern Hunan's Guanling Town to wait for local peasants to take us to our assigned Production Teams. Father had just been released from Mao Zedong Thought Study School, for he had fully disclosed his elitist errors and been deemed worthy of further reform; at the time, we believed the move to the countryside was a happy occasion.

Sixteen years later, as I covered the same ground again, the only signs of the past were occasional slogans from the Cultural Revolution, not yet worn away by the elements, in large white painted characters on the sides of mud-brick peasant homes. Judy and I made a game of collecting them, trying to distract ourselves from our discomfort. "Earnestly Carry Out Struggle, Criticism, Reform!" I read on the side of an isolated dwelling. "Put Politics in Command, Let Thought Take the Lead!" she called, spotting another. "In Agriculture Learn from Dazhai!" "Plant the Fields for the Revolution!" "Carry Out the Great Proletarian Cultural Revolution to the End!" How fortunate we were that we could laugh about it!

Years ago, living by those slogans was no joke. Father's many talents had been turned to the grueling task of "putting politics in command": he declaimed the works of Chairman Mao to illiterate peasants as they toiled in the fields, led them in Chairman Mao worship, evaluated the worth of their day's work by their political attitudes. The peasants "learned from Dazhai"— the famous model village in Shanxi—about the insidious dangers of the individual economy, and the last privately owned pigs and ducks were slaughtered by commandos "cutting off the tail of capitalism" in the night; on bellies empty but for sweet potato leaves, we planted the fields for the revolution. If the Cultural Revolution had really been "carried out to the end," I thought, many of us would have plunged from subsistence into starvation.

Guanling was greatly changed. Outside the bus station, peasants sold wonderful sweet tangerines which fell open at a touch; big smooth yellow apple-pears; roasted peanuts and raw ones, shelled and unshelled, salted and boiled; and fluted round egg cakes bigger than the palm of your hand. The old cobblestones had been paved over, and the street seemed much wider now, lined with low new shops with red wooden roofs. Dangling from ceiling racks were large red birthday candles, decorated with brightly colored wax dragons spiraling from base to wick. They were apparently a folk tradition that I had never seen before. Drawn in for a closer look, we bought sweets for the Guo family children, choosing, from among a wealth of almost ten varieties, the little bags of candy that came with toy plastic wristwatches, testaments to the now permissible materialist ambitions of a new age.

The route into the countryside was exactly the same as the one we followed that unbelievably black night years before, with Father and me carrying our heavy wooden bed through the paddy fields, trying to keep up with our peasant guide, a nine-year-old boy. Now, the five-day rain had turned the narrow, raised path into a slippery mudsnake. My big feet seemed unfairly clumsy. After I had slid once or twice into the paddies, I was soaked to the knees with frigid muck.

But without hesitation, I remembered the way.

Everything had been washed clean by the rain; the intervening years were gone and the past shone crystal clear before me. Low blue ridges beyond the open, watered fields, pretty thatched adobe homes half-hidden in groves of pine and bamboo—it had looked like this for centuries. Our progress marked by the barking of dogs, each one picking up from the last, we passed family wells, wove between two backbones of mountains, crisscrossed from rice field path to mud road and back among the fields again. An hour passed, two hours, nearly three. So many years later, the Guo family was still this difficult to reach. We slid across the exhausting miles as peasants with empty baskets dangling from their shoulder poles stared curiously, often overtaking us on their own barefoot journeys back from the village; young girls pounding wet clothing at the mud-yellow ponds looked up at us, startled. Sometimes the residents of a whole compound of joined homes, sensing strangers, turned out to watch us—the giant in city clothes and glasses, and the woman with the pointed nose and big green eyes.

The closer we got to the Guo family village, the faster I

walked. There was "our" plot for growing sweet potatoes, I showed Judy excitedly. And there was someone hoeing at it! It was a young man, and he recognized me immediately.

"It's Old Liang's son!" he cried.

I recognized him, too. This strong, thick, barefoot man with a hoe had once been that small boy who sang mountain songs to lead us in the dark. I wasn't the least surprised that it was he; the Guo family had planted this land for centuries and would doubtless continue to plant it for centuries more.

Without pausing to shake my hand, Young Guo, Guo Guifu, threw down his hoe and took to his heels, running surefooted in the mud, shouting out the news. "Old Liang's son has come! Old Liang's son has come! He's brought a foreigner!"

By the time we had crossed the last hillock, all the Guos were waiting for us in the open courtyard between the wings of the familiar compound. Standing in front was a sea of new children. They made a wall up to my knees. They stood staring, snotnosed, in silent rows. All the adults were there; I recognized them one by one. There was Guo Lucky Wealth, in whose dark kitchen I once had a bed; there was Guo Laoda, the unfortunate duck-raiser who tried to avoid slaughtering his "capitalist" ducks by claiming he planned to present them as a gift to Chairman Mao; there were Guo Xiangling, Guo Xiangchun, Guo Dezi, Guo Dexi, Guo Guichun, Guo Delin . . . and their wives, who never seemed to have names of their own. Many of the women were strangers to me, evidently brides for the Guo clan within the past sixteen years. Some had one child in their arms and another on their back.

The first to step out to greet us was Guo Lucky Wealth's wife. Childless because of an accident during the illegal removal of an IUD, she had treated me as her own son. She looked much older, her skin coarser and darker, but her braids were still black. She took my hand in her two parched thick ones. "Heaven blesses us, that you remember us," she said, tears in her eyes. "In our dreams we never thought we would see you again." She looked shyly at Judy. "You are welcome to our family." If not for my past intimacy with them, such humble people would never have dared to play host to a foreigner. Many generations of Guos had never seen one, and now there stood my thin-faced, round-eyed wife, with mud up to her knees.

Perhaps Guo Lucky Wealth and his wife had no way of grasping how very far we had traveled, what it meant to come from another country beyond China. A guest from Hengyang, the district capital and the nearest place linked to the rest of the country by railway, would have been from an equally unknown world. They seemed to accept my grateful remembrance of their kindness to me in the same spirit that they accepted the irregularities of nature. An early frost or an unusually rich harvest was fate and had to be dealt with calmly, as did unexpected guests who fell from another world.

The boys who had been my playmates had grown up now and made children, so many children, one family with nine, two with seven each. Now there were twelve households in the old Production Team, 108 people in all. All these small new peasants now crowded into Guo Lucky Wealth's kitchen and stood staring at us from a safe distance with their big silent eyes, coming close only to grasp a piece of candy in a dirty chapped fist and run away again, as we sat by the faint heat of the charcoal burning on the floor and drank strong bitter tea.

Guo Lucky Wealth's wife had big news. Her suffering from the IUD disaster was over. The tear between her uterine wall and her bladder, which had once made her leak urine constantly, had at last been repaired. In fact, it had been a simple procedure, one that could have been done years before except that there were no real doctors for miles around. Otherwise, life was the same, she said cheerfully. She seemed as busy as ever, chopping a huge mountain of leaves and vegetables for the pigs as she talked, then cooking it over the sooty kitchen stove. Guo Lucky Wealth sat close to the floor, feeding dry grass into the fire below. It would be well after dark before his wife washed the pot and prepared their own supper.

After we had rested, the children followed us in a huge crowd as our host took us to visit each of the Guo families to present our gifts.

Most of the rooms were the same as I remembered, dark and earthen-floored, with humble furniture and sandy yellow walls. On the tables were cracked kerosene lamps, flickering now in the dusk. Although this spot lay in the heart of one of China's richest agricultural regions, far from impoverished West Hunan, the Guos' lives were very hard. The rooms were all but empty of anything of value; there was no sign even of the pretty blue and white ginger jars that Judy sometimes collected when we visited the countryside.

The bedrooms of the elders were most tattered and torn, giving a general impression of blackness and poverty, with filthy dank quilts losing their stuffing and gray mosquito netting in rags. Then there were the slightly better appointed rooms of the middle-aged. The young newly marrieds' rooms were most comfortable, decorated fresh for the Chinese New Year with posters of house-protecting demons wielding fearsome swords, grotesque pink babies descending from the sky, plumply embracing peaches of longevity, and colorful opera singers with painted faces and long feather antennae. Some crudely cut drinking glasses might be arranged around a water pitcher on a tray, and clean new cotton comforters folded neatly on straw-laid wooden beds. Judy had remarked before on the sharp generational differences among the rooms in the countryside, surprising in this land believed by Westerners to have such a strong tradition of collective ownership. The explanation is simple enough. For most peasants, the gifts they received at their weddings had to serve a lifetime.

But some things in the Guo family village were not the same. The Chairman Mao worship room in which Father had once conducted the "Three Loyalties, Four Worships" ceremonies had been turned back into an ancestor worship room. Faded black and white photographs of the dead, adorned with red ribbons, hung on the walls; before them stood jars of incense sticks. Where there had once been only empty pens, now pigs were grunting noisily behind nearly every household; there were so many chickens that it was easy to trip over them. Two families had bought transistor radios, and one a foot-powered sewing machine. Some would have bought even fancier appliances, we were told, but the village was one of a few in the area that still had not been wired for electricity.

The most important change of all was the big brown vats of unhusked rice, standing where I remembered only piles of sweet potatoes and limp leaves. "Look at all this!" boasted Guo Lucky Wealth, taking a woven cover off one of the many vats and letting the rice fall in a rush from a bamboo ladle. "Now even girls can eat rice! Do you remember when Chairman Mao sent you to us? We hardly knew how we would feed you! But now, you could stay here half a year and we wouldn't even feel it!"

Indeed, when we returned to the kitchen there were big steaming bowls of white rice on the table, several kinds of fried cabbage, and even a plate of small dried fish. In the past, the Guo family had eaten like this only at Spring Festival, or when some government cadre showed up unannounced and had to be banqueted, lest the family's work points be docked for inadequate warmth toward the Communist party.

The reason for all the rice was the "responsibility system," the agricultural policy that had revolutionized Chinese agriculture and was creating a stir in socialist countries all over the world. The collective land had been divided up and assigned to each family according to size and labor power (men of laboring age got more than women). There was a government quota of grain to be grown on each *mu,* but what was produced beyond that could be sold on the free market. This system sparked their enthusiasm as no political sloganeering had; in only a few years, government warehouses were overflowing, and the peasants themselves had more rice than they knew what to do with.

Hunan Province had been late to introduce the responsibility system, Guo Lucky Wealth told me. In their team, it had begun in 1982. The peasants had been terrified at first. How could they "contract" for land to treat as their own? How could they keep whatever they produced above a quota? How could they grow their own vegetables, and in their homes raise pigs, chickens, and geese to sell on the free market? Wasn't this the capitalism and individualism supported by that counterrevolutionary who had been done away with, National Chairman Liu Shaoqi? They had never dared imagine that official policy would permit this, not after they had been forced to slaughter their animals and close down the markets during the ultraleftist years.

But for thousands of years orders had come from above, and for thousands of years the peasants had obeyed. This time, as they did so, they discovered that the new system worked to their advantage. Their fear gradually turned into joy, and then anxiety that these welcome policies might not endure.

Their average local crop yields of 400 *jin* per *mu* had almost doubled, for the lazy old ways were gone. Peasants nurtured each plant like a baby and were glad to work long hours in the fields. They no longer feared the cadres, who had no control over them now. The old Production Team had even been dissolved. Accountant Wang from the Wang clan across the way occasionally called them together to listen to a document on birth control, but that was about all. Now the Wangs and Guos were called a "villagers' group" instead.

The only problem was that the new system was working a bit too well, and the government didn't need to buy all that subsidized grain anymore. The state was even going to end its control of the grain market and turn that whole area of the economy over to the private sector, purchasing grain only if it was the peasants' last resort, at reduced prices. That was all well and good for peasants who lived near the big cities, but what was the Guo family to do? For miles around, everyone was a peasant; they all had their own huge piles of grain, their own chickens, eggs, and vegetables. How were they to raise their living standards now?

Without a market for it, rice is only rice. The fish on the dinner table, I suddenly realized with horror, were intended for us alone. Guo Lucky Wealth and his wife were slipping off to another room to eat their usual meal of pickled vegetables! Only when I insisted did they sit down with us, adding the pickles to the dishes on the table; only when I forced the tiny dried fish onto their bowls would they share them with us.

As we talked, the children from the other households were finishing their dinners and coming back to watch us again, as if we were rare animals that had been captured in a mountain country far away. They were losing their shyness. I was curious to know if they were any better educated than the children of sixteen years before, when almost everything was Chairman Mao quotations.

It seemed that most of them had had some primary school education, with some math and Chinese, but Guo Lucky Wealth said that with the responsibility system, the adults needed their children at home to help in the fields more than before. Even their small contributions could make a difference to the family income. The teachers, themselves local peasants who had completed lower or upper middle school, also wanted to be in the fields, since the Wang-Guo villagers' group had no money to recompense them for their teaching. By common consent, then, there were constant vacations. An older girl with thick black braids named Lianhua explained that school was expensive, too, over five *yuan* a semester for primary school, for books and supplies. When there were seven or eight of you, she sighed, that was a lot of money. And it got more expensive the higher you went. She herself had gotten as far in her studies as the first year of middle school, she told us, but, like most of her classmates, she had not passed the examinations that would have permitted her to continue. But anyway, her parents had been planning to spend the money on her younger brothers.

So many children, produced like so many eggs! If the population here kept increasing and the children were not taught to do anything but live off the land, eventually not even the responsibility system could save them from greater poverty, and even starvation.

Suddenly the children, giggling nervously, vanished into the shadows. Guo Laoda had come in, the bachelor seeking the company of the childless. I remembered the cranky old gentleman well, the very last to kill his ducks. He was still as dirty and ugly as ever, and now his eyes didn't look so good, red and teary, one half-closed. He did indeed look fearsome.

"Still not married, eh?" I joked. "This year you'll make a lot of money on your new ducks and find yourself a pretty bride yet!"

"To hell with marriage," he said gruffly, pulling up a bamboo stool and squatting by the warm coals. "My ducks have died the last two years in a row. Every *fen* of my savings I spent on special feed for them, and then they got sick before they were big enough to make a meal."

Guo Laoda had been waiting many years for the new freedoms, I reflected sadly, but it seemed they had come too late. When he had been young and vigorous, raising ducks was not permitted. Now that it was encouraged, he was old and forgetful and lacked ability. Here in the Guo family village there was little transport or information, no way to learn agriculture and husbandry techniques. It was not laziness that held the peasants in this backward state, but ignorance.

In the blackness outside came the sound of doors opening. Kerosene lanterns announced the arrival of the other adults to

Guo Lucky Wealth's kitchen, one by one, and the children were scolded off to scatter like so many chickens. The men set down their stools by the charcoal burner and lit their pipes, the women stood to the back, and we all settled in for a good long chat.

An outsider's arrival was still a valuable occasion for getting news. We were their radios, their newspapers, their television. But whereas sixteen years ago I had spun tales of the grandeur of Changsha and Beijing, tonight I spoke of the world.

The peasants, too, seemed better informed than they had been —they had heard rumors that in the "imperialist" West, the peasants were better off than they. What they could not fathom, however, was how a single Western peasant family could plant land the size of their entire Production Team and fly in an airplane to fight bugs.

The peasants were bursting to speak of their good fortune since the introduction of the responsibility system. Deng Xiaoping got all the credit. Who Premier Zhao Ziyang was, or General Party Secretary Hu Yaobang, they seemed less clear. Once, they had known Chairman Mao, and before that, Chiang Kai-shek, and earlier still, the Emperor. Now they knew Deng, but with an important difference: the peasants referred to him affectionately as "that short guy," whereas if they had mentioned Mao's baldness they could have been shot. The danger in making verbal errors was obviously a thing of the past; Deng had not only given them as much rice as they wanted, but had freed them from the constant threat of punishment by local leaders.

Before, they had feared beatings on the least provocation; now they did not. They could go to the fields when they were ready, do what they liked when they got there, come home when they wished. The only time they saw the officials was to pay the taxes to support the brigade and commune administration—only they weren't supposed to be called that anymore. The old terms, "village" and *xiang,* had been revived, although no one could get used to them.

Many of the Guos asked after Father. They had never understood why Chairman Mao brought the intellectuals to learn from
them the taste of hardship and teach to them the principles of
political study, but they had found Father to be a sympathetic and
kind man. They recalled now how often he had lent them money
for fertilizer, for clothes, for salt—in the days when no private
trade was permitted, Father, still drawing his old editor's salary,
was the only person for miles who had cash. He rarely refused
anyone, they said, no matter how many requests there were.

I had not known how very deeply Father had been loved, but
the peasants' warm memories did not surprise me. They had
known his energetic and generous true self. When I told them
of his illness, they blamed themselves and the bitter life he had
lived here with them. Guo Xiangling said, "Please tell Old Liang
that his sacrifices will never be forgotten. My son is grown and
married now, because of him." He told us how Father had lent
him two *jiao* to buy medicine when the child had a high fever,
thus saving his life.

Speaking thus of children now grown, I suddenly noticed
that I hadn't seen one of my old playmates, Guo Heizi.

I was told that Guo Heizi had a problem. He had married
after the one-child policy had begun to be enforced more strictly
in the area, and his wife had given birth to a useless girl who
would no doubt eventually marry into another family and leave
him destitute in his old age. Heizi was so angry that finally the
woman conceived again, slipping off to her parents' home in
another district to avoid local officials during her pregnancy. She
gave birth there, so that not even hospital authorities, who might
have forced her to have a late abortion, knew about it. She
returned in triumph to the Guos with a three-month-old baby
boy.

According to local policies, there was now a fine of 400 *yuan*
to be paid to the *xiang* Planned Birth Office. Although this was
low because the region was poor and the population not as dense

as in some areas, Guo Heizi's entire savings amounted to only about 200 *yuan,* which he turned in. Then officials ordered his relatives to carry his furniture and other possessions to the *xiang* to make up the rest. But how could they take away the belongings of their own flesh and blood? the peasants asked, still outraged. In fact, they were all filled with rejoicing at the birth of the little boy! Finally the officials came themselves and took everything—beds, wardrobe, even Heizi's household wok. All this had happened just the week before our visit, and now Heizi and his wife were away at her family clan, borrowing the basic necessities until they could get the money to replace them. The child, however, was right here, the peasants volunteered proudly, pushing a shy-looking woman forward from the outer circle of watchers. By the hand she held a fat toddler, naked from the waist down, the evidence of his maleness clear.

In the opinion of the peasants, Heizi had come out of the affair quite all right. After all, the second child had not been a girl, and the fine did not really matter, especially to someone who had little cash and few possessions in the first place. It was worth it. Even in wealthier areas, where the fine was said to be as high as 2,000 *yuan,* people often preferred to pay; one family was said to have nicknamed their extra son *Caidian,* "Color TV," for he had cost them just as much as one. All the newlyweds the Guos knew were waiting for boys. The situation was very clear: under the responsibility system, the more labor power you had, the wealthier you would be. As it was being applied in their district, you got more land each time a child was born, but lost some when a girl married off and left you. If you had only a single daughter, you would have to work in the fields for your rice until you died, poor and lonely.

Not everyone had been as fortunate as Heizi, the peasants said. In another village, the Yang clan had consulted fortunetellers for months in order to find a bride who would produce a boy for one of their sons. They finally found one, and the marriage feast was as lavish as any that had been seen in many years. Even the Guos had been invited, from several *li* away. All the old customs had been followed. The red-clothed bride had been fetched from her home, with the plaintive, festive sound of the *suona* horn in accompaniment; in a long train, the relatives carried the new bedding on shoulder poles to the bridegroom's home. There kowtows were made to the images of the ancestors, and a huge banquet was served, for which five pigs were killed. Glutinous rice cakes were consumed in abundance, and rice wine flowed. It was as if the Yangs were already celebrating the birth of the new baby boy.

Perhaps the fortune was poorly told, or perhaps the pregnant young wife encountered a spirit, a peach ghost. The birth was a tragedy.

The baby girl was ignored by her father; the clan spoke of revenge. Some threatened to beat the soothsayer, others to send the woman back to her family. Then, quietly, the problem was resolved. The baby disappeared during the night. The Yangs let it be known that she had been taken away by the same ghosts who had entered her mother and robbed her of the boy that was hers by right.

Then the county officials came and made an investigation. To everyone's surprise, the unfortunate father was taken off to spend a year in prison for murder! It was so unfair, the Guos complained. What else could a man in his position have been expected to do?

It was very late when at last we retired. Guo Lucky Wealth and his wife yielded us their bed. They had done their best to make it comfortable, but the bedding, of handmade coarse cloth, had never been washed, and the straw on which we slept was crawling with fleas and bedbugs. I felt as if we were sleeping on a platform in the middle of a chicken coop, hens scratching underneath us, cackling and pecking all around, roosters letting out ear-blasting shrieks. My skin itched all over, and I was freezing cold. How could anyone, I wondered, think of sex in a bed like this?

I finally slept near dawn, and awoke again very late, sometime midmorning. Everything was quiet, and I assumed that the peasants were all out in the fields. But no, I heard stirring from up near the roof, and Guo Lucky Wealth and his wife climbed down from the storage shelf on which they had spent the night. They too had been sleeping in, as had nearly the entire compound!

This was incredible to me. When I had lived in the countryside, Father blew his whistle well before daybreak, and everyone assembled for Chairman Mao worship, rubbing the sleep from their eyes as they bowed to an inspirational poster of his face. Then all the Guos would march off collectively, laboring four or five hours before returning for the first meal of the day. Now they were lying abed, with no one to order them awake or criticize them for insufficient proletarian consciousness.

While we were breakfasting on more or less the same menu as the night before, there suddenly came a great clattering of gongs and indecipherable songlike wails. We rushed out to see what the commotion was. Two men were approaching the compound, one leading a frozen, flea-bitten monkey, the other carrying two boxes on a shoulder pole.

They were outsiders, folk artists, they said, come all the way from Anhui Province on foot. "Monkey playing" was a local tradition there, only recently permitted again. For two *yuan,* they would give us a show.

Most of the Guos had never seen a monkey before, and the children were very excited. It was clear, however, that their parents could not afford to pay two *yuan* (about 70¢) for anything that would not feed or clothe them. We were glad to treat everyone; it seemed a fortuitous way to thank them for their hospitality.

Because it had begun to rain again, the whole clan spaced themselves around the walls of the central ancestor worship room. None of us could understand a word of the local Anhui opera, recited in a rhythmic falsetto to the sound of deafening gongs, but the hapless and diligent monkey fulfilled her task with resignation, circling her master ceaselessly at the end of a rope, putting on various hats and masks as the story required, playing sometimes a beggar, sometimes an official, sometimes a landlord, sometimes a thief. She climbed to the top of a long bamboo pole, turned somersaults and flips, walked on her hands, carried a miniature shoulder pole with two little pails. The masks gave her a particularly woebegone expression, and she was clearly very cold.

The drama seemed long, repetitive, and cruel to me, but the peasants were entranced. In their world, except for the occasional movie, there was little entertainment. This elemental slice of ancient culture, this din of gongs and chants and cries, today brought them joy, where once there would have been rainy day political study, lessons on preparation for war, or criticism of the renegade Liu Shaoqi.

ONE MORNING EARLY, we announced regretfully that we had to go. The peasants did not try to stop us: if we had appeared from the sky once, fate would doubtless arrange for us to come back again. I pressed ten *yuan* onto Guo Lucky Wealth's wife; Judy left her a roll of toilet paper, the only one she had ever seen. The whole Guo family turned out to see us go, some forty of them crowded together at the front of the courtyard. It was drizzling again, and the road was very bad, making it impossible to follow the old route through the paddy fields. It had been decided that we should go back the long way around, on a vehicle road that led from the old brigade to the *xiang*. The girl named Lianhua, the one who had told us she hadn't passed the examination for the second year of middle school, had been chosen to lead us there.

It was a half hour's walk through the fields to the road, and along the way we asked Lianhua about her life now. She was a talkative girl, very sturdy, about sixteen, with a plump round face, full mouth, upright chest, and strong braids. She walked with an assured bounce. She hadn't wanted to waste the trip, and was carrying a small handbasket in which to put some kerosene and salt.

She missed the lively classroom atmosphere and her old class-mates, she confessed shyly. She liked learning things and found her present life dull. But her friends lived far away, and there was no custom for young girls to go about visiting each other when there was work to be done at home. Now she was marriageable, too, and her parents couldn't have her running about. They were eager to have the question settled. She had already caught a glimpse of her prospective husband once, peeking at him from behind a door. All the arrangements were in her parents' hands.

What if she didn't like him? we asked.

Lianhua smiled and sighed. "Then there's nothing to be done."

Did she want to leave home and start a new family? we wondered.

The girl blushed fiercely, looked down at the path, and shook her head.

What she wanted, it seemed, was to know about life outside, about Changsha, about how girls in the cities lived, what they wore, what they thought about. She would love to see Changsha someday, she said with longing. To her, that provincial capital was as far away as paradise.

With Lianhua in the lead, we had climbed to the top of a small hillock planted in tea bushes. Now the pebbled vehicle road lay below us. Farther away were the mountains, covered with mist, where we were going. "Here you are," the girl said, with regret she could not hide. "You'll be going that way. I have something to do at the brigade."

"Come along with us," I joked, half serious. "A lot of peasant girls are getting jobs as housekeepers in the city."

Lianhua shifted bashfully from one foot to another. In her heart, she surely wanted to, but how could she? So many generations of her ancestors had grown up and died on this land, or if not here, then on land very much like it. To be a peasant woman was her destiny, as it had been the destiny of her mother and her mother's mother before her. The rest of her life would be spent like Guo Lucky Wealth's wife, chopping pig food, cutting dry grass, carrying water, spreading fertilizer, sowing grain, transplanting shoots, harvesting, binding, threshing, hauling; cooking, wiping, mending, sweeping; the ceaseless labors of the Chinese peasant woman.

If Lianhua was very, very lucky, she would give birth to a healthy male child right away. Her husband's family would not reject her, and she would live out an old age blessed with her son's filial obedience.

SHEKOU

*F*ROM THE MOMENT WE ARRIVED in the Special Economic Zone of Shenzhen, on the border with Hong Kong, we could spot the northerners. They were serious-looking, men most of them, dressed too warmly for the southern heat in conservative blue cadres' suits. Strapped around their wrists were the usual zippered black leather document bags. They stood awkwardly tall among the wiry local hipsters, who wore scrawny jeans and loud Hong Kong T-shirts brought to them by fathers and uncles who had swum across the river to freedom years before. Traveling in self-protective little groups, they stared at the high buildings and neon lights, at the electronic equipment displayed in the shop windows, at the Walkmans, color TVs, cameras, watches, and calculators they longed for but had little means to buy. They spoke round-toned, bell-like Mandarin to the locals, who yipped back at them in bad-tempered, incomprehensible Cantonese.

There were said to be 200,000 so-called *neidiren* here, "people from the interior," come to sign contracts with foreign companies, to open offices for their factories and provinces, or perhaps simply to purchase or sell in a one-time-only deal. Chinese had to have a special border permit to come. Most of the resident outsiders had been carefully selected because they had skills; they contracted to work for several years, often in construction. Their salaries were much higher than they were at home, but never really adequate in this society—not exactly China and not exactly Hong Kong, but some third invention between the two. Chinese *yuan* were all but worthless: as far as the locals were concerned, even the usually precious Foreign Exchange Certificates, FECs, in Chinese denominations but backed by hard currency, were second-rate. What counted were Hong Kong dollars, which could be used by relatives to buy things across the border, and the most active black market was in those, not in FECs as in the rest of China. I had never seen so many Chinese smoking high-status imported 555 brand cigarettes in one place before.

We met a number of *neidiren* on the three-hour train ride south from Guangzhou. Sitting opposite us, sharing a table, was a minor peasant official from Kaifeng. His wife, who had never before left her village much less been on a train, was leaning red-faced and queasy against the window, rail-sick. The peasant, reticent at first, told us they were going to Shenzhen to buy a color TV. For help they were counting on a relative who lived there. They had never met him; he was so distant that only a Chinese would have considered him a relation at all. The couple seemed to be unaware that in Shenzhen their *yuan* could buy almost nothing, and their anxiety when I told them so confirmed my impression that they were a bit frightened by their trip, as if they had embarked on an adventure that they now regretted.

What the man had to say about his yield per *mu* did not seem to account for his wealth, but he stuck to this story as his sole explanation. I felt sure it had more to do with his post as accountant at a village grain-purchasing station, which would have put him in an excellent position to accept bribes. Two other northerners, engineers from Tianjin, had been eavesdropping into our numbers games from across the aisle, and they joined the entertainment, pointing out with good humor and occasional hilarity the contradictions in what the peasant said. I liked them for their willingness to make the peasant, not us or themselves, the center of attention. This was an early indication to us that some of China's most worldly and sophisticated people were to be met in Shenzhen.

We saw the engineers again late that night, standing in line at the public telephone station. They had been trying without success to reach their local contact from a pipe-fittings import company. In one of the usual bureaucratic mishaps, someone had neglected to send a telegram, and no one had met them to take them to guest quarters. Now they had no way of notifying their business associates that they had arrived.

Earlier in the evening, while trying to register for the night at a "reception station," we had befriended another pair of northerners. These were strapping Beijing girls struggling with a huge number of bags and parcels, which they were carrying on shoulder poles. None of it was theirs, the girls told us with resignation. These were all gifts from fellow workers for the homesick comrades from their factory, part of which had been temporarily transferred to the Shekou Industrial District, a 2.14-square-kilometer stretch of land a mere forty-minute boat ride from Hong Kong. The girls had arrived too late at the already full hostel and were going to have to fend for themselves, although it was extremely unlikely that other inns would have beds at that late hour. Our own problem was that I had allowed too many people to shove their way in front of me in the registration line, for I had grown accustomed to a more civilized queueing etiquette.

After Judy came out of the shadows (we had been afraid of being packed off to an expensive and dull foreigners' hotel), the impatient and very rude hotel workers, yelling bad Mandarin like seals, finally agreed to find us beds. We couldn't imagine leaving the worried-looking girls standing there with all those bags, and insisted that the hotel workers not use a double standard in their treatment of foreigners and ordinary Chinese. Judy ended up sharing a room with the girls in a local hospital clinic that was taking advantage of the paucity of hotels to make some easy money. My own roommate was already snoring beneath the glaring light bulb, but every time I pulled the cord and fell asleep he managed to awaken and pull the light on again. Perhaps he was trying to drive away the mosquitoes.

I couldn't help feeling a bit sorry for these alien northerners we had met, these peasants, intellectuals, and workers, although I knew that they considered themselves privileged to have been given permits to come here. It was almost as if they had come to a foreign country for the first time, without ever leaving China.

Judy and I had come to Shenzhen to meet some of the most important architects of the economic reforms. A Hunanese friend who was studying at Princeton had written ahead on my behalf to members of the Research Group on the Problem of China's Rural Development, the group that could take most of the credit for the recent transformation of China's countryside. Although most of them were based in Beijing, many of them had come to the Shekou Industrial District, a few hours from downtown Shenzhen, for an important meeting. The focus of the reforms had shifted from the countryside to the cities, and Shekou was their strategic southern base, their experimental laboratory. During the Cultural Revolution, Shekou was a land of shark-gnawed, rotting corpses, as thousands risked their lives to wade out at night from the deserted beaches to swim to the just visible glitter of the high rises of Hong Kong. Now, at a happier time, its very barrenness had made it the perfect tablet on which to write a very different story of freedom.

We were luckier in making contact than our engineer friends. When I came at last to the head of the line and placed my telephone call, it was answered immediately by Ho Weiling, a friend of my Princeton friend. He had been expecting us, he said, and our timing was perfect. He would see us in Shekou the next morning.

Why was I, a critic of the Communist party, being treated

with such friendliness by these policymakers, when so many others had tried to meet them and failed? The answer lay both in the power of personal relationships in China and in the unusual character of the reformers we were about to meet. Even the most dogmatic party ideologue can be charming if approached with a letter from someone with whom his "connection" is binding, and I had a first-rate personal introduction. Matters of official attitude toward my writing or my involvement with the democracy movement therefore became irrelevant. Ho Weiling trusted my friend, so he trusted me; this was crucial because the reformers' political situation was still extremely sensitive. But perhaps more significant in this case was my role as chief editor of a magazine devoted to the exchange of ideas between China and the West. These reformers believed, as I was later to hear, that openness to the West was not only important to China's future, but the decisive factor in whether the reforms would succeed or fail.

The next morning, our ears still ringing with the love songs of Deng Lijun, Taiwan's most popular singer (the shuttlebus driver had kept the Toyota's quadraphonic cassette player on full volume for the duration of the hour-long ride, to the apparent pleasure of everyone but ourselves), we had our first view of Shekou. It lay sparkling, quiet, and subtropical along a bright green bay; the broad main street was bordered with expensive-looking restaurants and apartment houses built with obviously imported construction materials, in blessedly varied design as compared with the monotony of the rest of China. A Western supermarket, its stainless steel turnstiles shining, stood empty of customers but fully stocked with Baggies, boxed breakfast cereal, and peanut butter, as if their mere presence would summon customers. Along the beach, cookie-cutter gray stone bungalows seemed to be pushing up through the sand, multiplying practically before our eyes.

We found Ho Weiling in the living room of a thoroughly modern suite with synthetic wall-to-wall carpeting and a glass coffee table. In the bedroom, floral drapes matched twin bed-spreads; a pea green American Standard washroom had a West-ern-style sit toilet with clean water in it, a rust-free bathtub, and a sink with hot and cold faucets, both of which worked. After our days with the Guo family, I found the rooms unbearably, almost tragically civilized.

Ho seemed delighted to see us. He was an informal, sophis-ticated, and exceedingly talkative man originally from Shanghai, in his early forties. Vibrant with nervous energy, he spoke a highly educated standard Chinese full of economic terminology and literary references. I could imagine how persuasive the re-ports he wrote for internal distribution to the Secretariat must be.

My Princeton friend had told me that Ho came from a long line of distinguished scholars, among them Xu Fang, the famous private teacher to China's last emperor, and several other Hanlin Academy officials. His parents were graduates of China's top universities, Yanjing and Beiping. Before the revolution, his father had been general secretary of Shanghai's enormous Yong An Company. Ho himself had attended Beijing University, in applied physics, and was now teaching international politics there.

If it was surprising that a hard scientist had become a re-former, he was not alone: also among the new policymakers were statisticians, mathematicians, biologists, and economists. The other thing they all had in common was their victimization during the Cultural Revolution, and their long exile among the Chinese peasantry.

Ho Weiling answered our questions frankly. His manner was so casual, and I felt such a rapport with him, that it was often difficult to believe that someone as open-minded as he was in-volved in policymaking for a country that had so distinguished itself for totalitarianism.

His intellectual development had been similar to my own, but, ten years my senior, he had come to many of his conclusions much earlier than I. He described his doubts about Mao's socialism as dating from 1963, when, like the other college students, he first went to the countryside to carry out the Four Cleans movement, a national campaign to correct abuses of power and to educate local cadres. "It was a revelation," he remembered. "When you asked the peasants about their greatest hardships, they spoke of those brought to them under the red flag. The power of the party officials was absolute. If they disliked someone, they could refuse him even the right to beg. In comparison, the peasants remembered some of the old landlords as having been kind, but in the mythology of the time, there was not a single one who was not a monster."

The following year, he went to the countryside again, this time far from Beijing, to a Yi minority area in the Little Cool Mountains in Sichuan. The barbarity and poverty he found there overwhelmed him. The peasants told him that only a few years earlier it had been common to punish thieves by cutting off their fingers and throwing them, arms and legs tied, onto stinging anthills. Because of the starvation during the "three hard years" of natural disasters following the ill-conceived Great Leap Forward of 1958, about half the population had died. All the old and young were gone: there was no one left over the age of forty-five or between the ages of two and five.

All this confirmed Ho's sense that the worst problem in the rural areas was not class struggle, as Chairman Mao claimed, but the feudal, oppressive relationship of officials to peasants. Chinese society was like a forest, he said. The higher up in the trees you climbed, the brighter it seemed. Down below, all was primeval darkness.

When he returned to Beijing University, he was convinced that the Communist party no longer represented the people, and that the cadre system had to be thoroughly reformed. In the innocence of the times, he did not understand the dangers of speaking out. "The new-born ox does not fear the tiger," he told us, ruefully remembering his naiveté.

He welcomed the Cultural Revolution as an opportunity to

transform the party, and organized a study group to explore which aspects of Chinese political life were inconsistent with Marxism. His writings went too far when he rejected the cult of Mao worship. Almost immediately, his group became infamous for opposing Lin Biao, Mao's second-in-command and architect of the Little Red Book–waving sessions. In public criticism sessions attended by thousands, he and his friends were given "airplane rides" with their arms tied and lifted painfully behind them. "It was our great privilege to be criticized together," said Ho, with the irony typical of many Chinese who have undergone persecution. "The relationships we established then have helped us make the reforms today."

After a year in Gongdeling, a jail in northern Beijing, Ho was sent to a labor camp in the nearby countryside. Living conditions there were even worse. He stayed there for nearly eight years.

One of Ho's college roommates had been Deng Pufang, son of then-disgraced Central Committee leader Deng Xiaoping. Young Deng had slept on the bunk below him, and like him had been one of the university's outstanding students of applied physics. When the Cultural Revolution degenerated into factional violence, Deng was seized by members of a Red Guard group. Because of his father, his captors' cross-examinations of him were particularly cruel. He was always blindfolded so he could not identify them, for some were nervous about what they were doing to the son of such a high leader, even though Deng Xiaoping was the country's number two "capitalist roader" after National Chairman Liu Shaoqi. Deng Pufang was ordered repeatedly to expose his father's "conspiracy" against Mao, and in fact, he knew a great deal about his father's attitudes that he was not prepared to reveal. One day, he tried to escape Red Guard torture by throwing himself from the fourth-floor window of the physics building where he was being held.

He snapped his spinal cord in the fall. The doctors at Number Three Hospital, where he was taken by some merciful classmates, refused to treat him. Only when his younger sister came, begging them to save him from death, was he given the operation that he needed.

From then on, he was paralyzed from the waist down.

In 1977, Deng Xiaoping became China's most powerful leader, and in his son Ho had a very influential friend. It was Young Deng who helped him return to Beijing University. In China, Ho said wryly, everyone needs a "backbone." I sighed wearily. It seemed that these new reformers had not departed from the feudal tradition of relying on personal connections in their rise to power.

When I asked Ho about his ideological position today, he answered, "To me, any 'ism' that interferes with the people's prosperity and happiness should be thrown out. When visitors come to the Special Economic Zones, they usually ask whether the SEZs are socialist or capitalist. We always answer indirectly, saying we are searching for a road for China's future, not following one 'ism' or another."

In fact, Judy and I knew that the SEZs had departed very far indeed from the orthodox centralized system that had governed China for over thirty years. Joint ventures using Chinese and foreign capital were encouraged, and market forces dominated the economy. Businesses had the power to sign contracts with foreigners without central approval. There was a free market for labor. If workers' applications were accepted, they were given contracts, not lifetime guarantees. They could quit or be fired. Unlike the rigid wage hierarchy to be found elsewhere, salaries were flexible, based on a system commensurate with responsibilities and performance. Most of the Chinese managers were elected for a set term, and were highly educated: of 793 cadres in Shekou, 494 were university graduates, an extraordinary statistic. Even private ownership of property was permitted here, and workers were encouraged to purchase housing on the installment plan. The reformers were extremely clever, I reflected. By putting the emphasis on the economy, they could shift attention away from politics and thereby limit the power of the ideologues, forcing them to become servants of modernization in spite of themselves. In fact, these economic changes had enormous political and social ramifications.

It was nearly noon, and Ho Weiling suggested that we join him in a luncheon to be held in a local restaurant. The director of the Research Group, Chen Yizhi, would be meeting there with some of the local reformers. We accepted immediately. My Princeton friend had mentioned Chen to me, but said it was extremely unlikely that I would be able to see him. He was so busy that he slept only three hours a night.

Outside, the sea breeze had blown up salty and clean, and the air was warm but dry. Ho walked with energy, as if he had been refreshed by the morning's conversation. He spoke tirelessly. The restaurant, he informed us, was a famous one, from Shanghai. The entire staff and operations had been transplanted to Shekou, for like all the major cities, Shanghai was promoting its most attractive resources as a way to earn foreign currency.

The screens, lamps, and scrolls in the busy restaurant were indeed in the "South of the River" style, and from the heavily laden tables came the sugar-and-vinegar aroma of Shanghai cuisine. We were led to a section of the floor made completely private with a tall lacquer screen. A few others were already seated around a circular table, many, it turned out, graduates of Beijing University like Ho and Chen. It seemed the reforms were being carried out by a "Beijing University mafia": the Chinese old-boy system was firmly in place. Chen wasn't there yet. I couldn't help feeling nervous about meeting him. After all, I had never liked officials, whether my old factory managers or the university bureaucrats who had caused me so much grief. Chen would be the highest leader I had ever spoken with face to face. To my mind, he must surely have those familiar, speechifying, fat-bellied airs, no matter how much of a reformer he was.

When at last he arrived, he walked directly to a seat between me and Ho, greeting everyone briefly and shaking hands all around. Contrary to my expectations, he was a sickly-looking man, thin to emaciation, with a yellow, tired face, a modest manner, and severely short hair. He wore a black cadre's jacket buttoned tightly to the neck. Although he was in his late forties, he looked much older.

When Chen spoke, his air of illness disappeared completely. He was a bit stiff and controlled, but sometimes became quite animated. He was clearly not one to waste time on pleasantries. He seemed quite willing to be engaged in private conversation with me, and the buzz of other voices and the click of chopsticks seemed to fade far away.

Chen told me that many believed that the Special Economic Zones were simply marketplaces for attracting foreign capital for China's modernization program. In fact, just as the reformers' long-range strategy was to use the countryside, with its freer economy, to put pressure on the more rigid city bureaucracies, they were using the coastal areas to urge the interior forward. The SEZs would show by example the prosperity and advantages that could be gained by adopting an efficient and rational economic system. Although the reformers were not advocating that the innovations of the SEZs be transported bodily to the whole of China, many lessons could be useful. Indeed, ever since Deng Xiaoping had given his official blessing, the SEZs had become showplaces, where inspection tours were given for recalcitrant bureaucrats in an attempt to open up their minds.

As he spoke, Chen put down his chopsticks and gave up all pretense of eating. The reformers were changing the system in select coastal areas, he said, while moving educated fresh blood in all over the country. There were already experiments with applying some of the successful SEZ experiments to certain interior cities such as Chongqing and Wuhan, as well as to some factories and enterprises. The elections for managers, for example, now common throughout China, had first been tested here.

Chen and his colleagues were now working urgently on the reform of the cadre system, and on the related question of party reform through the separation of party and administration. The party should interfere less, said Chen, from the top levels all the way down to the grass roots, allowing professionals, technicians, and scientists to take care of day-to-day affairs. The party should concern itself only with enforcing regulations and supervising the party members themselves.

I applauded these sentiments from the bottom of my heart. I had been ruled for six years in a lubricating oil factory by leaders who had no idea what a ball bearing was, and I had seen illiterates running universities. In Changsha, I had witnessed the beginnings of the changes Chen described, as my friends became leaders and the old guard was squeezed into advisory positions. However, it gave me a special thrill to hear these views from the mouth of one of the men behind the policies, which now seemed real to me in a new way.

The space of a meal passed quickly. I ate only what others placed directly on my plate. It seemed Chen felt, as I did, that we hadn't finished our conversation. Quietly (apparently even the reformers didn't fully trust each other) he arranged for Ho, Judy, and me to meet him elsewhere.

We were led to a large conference room on the seventh floor of a modern building with plenty of glass. The atmosphere was so natural and professional that it was an effort to remember the alternative. Where were the political slogans in tall red characters? Where was the pantheon of the saints, Marx, Lenin, Engels, Stalin, and Mao? Where were the red flags, the banners, the framed certificates of commendation? Where were the rows of narrow benches, the beat-up podium at the front? We were simply in a clean and spacious room with plenty of tables and sofas for a comfortable meeting. Outside the window was the azure bay, and beyond that, the hills of Hong Kong.

Prominently featured in the front of the room was a panoramic mock-up of the Shekou Industrial District, on a large glass-covered table about ten by five feet in size. As they stood around it telling us of their plans, Chen and Ho became as excited and proud as parents. Here in papier-mâché were the images of their dreams. The future Shekou was a modern-looking little city, with low-pollution, high-tech electronics assembly plants, ornamental parks, hospitals, theaters, apartment complexes, little white sailboats, and even an amusement park with a roller coaster and a Ferris wheel. In only a few years, they told us, half of these paste buildings had already become realities.

"Shekou was built on the lives of hundreds of thousands," said Chen, with sudden emotion. "It grew directly out of the lessons of the Cultural Revolution. China paid a great price, but perhaps history will prove it was worth it."

"It hasn't been easy," added Ho. "We've encountered almost more resistance than support. One Central Committee leader accused us of starting a second Opium War, a second wave of imperialism. Another one, a powerful old Red Army man, took one look at Shekou and burst into tears of rage. 'If I had known that this would be the result of the revolution,' he shouted, 'I never would have joined the Red Army.' "

We all laughed at this, well aware that such attitudes were no joke. Then Chen commented seriously, "Most of those who once slept with landlords' oxen and ate bark and leather belts on the Long March will never understand Shekou. Their political careers have been based too long on hating everything it stands for."

The afternoon had grown warmer, and Chen got up and went to the windows, opening them one by one. The task put him in mind of a metaphor, and he stood looking out over the bay, the sun in his face. "After Liberation, the party locked all the doors and windows and sat in the stifling darkness, congratulating themselves on China's greatness. Almost thirty years later, the windows have opened and the fresh breezes and light come pouring in. All of a sudden, some of them feel very uncomfortable." He turned, smiling, to look at us. "Their breath catches in their throats and they begin to sneeze. 'Who opened the windows?' they ask. 'Close them again, quick!'"

Chen returned to his seat. Now that the Chinese people knew something about other countries, he said, they could never again be fooled into thinking that China was not backward. Their understanding of how far behind the rest of the world it was, including even Taiwan, could only be a good thing, for it raised urgent questions that needed to be answered.

Ho agreed that at least part of the solution to China's troubles lay beyond its borders. He told us, straight-faced, that there were three cornerstones to their policies: number one, opening the door to the West; number two, opening the door to the West; number three, opening the door to the West! Although Chen and Ho knew that the Western and Chinese heritages were too far apart for the Western system to be transplanted to China, they believed that Western and Chinese culture could supplement each other, helping build China into a legalistic, democratic, and efficient modern country.

Our new friends complained that although even the Soviet Union had moved away from its early patterns, many of China's leaders seemed to think that China's problems would be solved if it returned to the situation of the fifties, when the two countries had been closest. China had much more in common with the Soviet Union than the West, these people thought; after all, both were socialist countries that revered Karl Marx.

Chen did not try to hide his own negative views of the Soviet system. He described the importation of the heavy industry-oriented model to backward, agrarian China as "like putting vinegar on biscuits." It hadn't solved China's problems, but the centralized Leninist system of rule by a party elite fit in all too well with Chinese feudalism, and brought out China's strongest antidemocratic, totalitarian tendencies.

Ho mentioned another kind of opponent of the reforms, in

his opinion the most daunting of all. These were the millions of workers used to the "iron rice bowl," the fixed salary guaranteed for life. They had never had to work under pressure in their entire lives, and they disliked the new emphasis on efficiency and talent. The unskilled and lazy, in particular, were unhappy about reform. This was a problem even in the SEZs, for the Hong Kong managers expected a much higher level of productivity and competition than the Chinese were used to. The workers complained that their bosses were inhumane. Sometimes disputes even had to be mediated by the "Labor Service Company," which handled their contracts. This was ironic, Ho thought—in the past, the party organized the workers to struggle against the capitalists; now it was teaching them how to cooperate with them!

We laughed, and a serving girl appeared to refill our teacups with hot water. The afternoon's conversation had grown more informal and relaxed. We began to talk more about ourselves and our personal experiences.

I was fascinated to learn that Chen's paternal grandfather had also been a reformer, in the short-lived reform drive of the late Qing dynasty. Then, too, intellectuals had raised the need for active interchange with the West and for using what they learned to overturn the entrenched feudal system. At the time, however, their strength had been too weak, that of the Dowager Empress Cixi too strong, and the reforms had lasted only one hundred days. Many of the leaders were executed, others escaped abroad; Chen's grandfather had lost his position and been exiled to Sichuan. In a sense, as Chen himself pointed out, he and his colleagues were trying to complete an unfinished task, begun in the late Qing, and continuing with the aborted May Fourth intellectuals' movement of 1919. What was happening in China today belonged to a long, hitherto unsuccessful tradition.

From the time Chen had been small, he told us, he had been devoted to the socialist cause. At eighteen, he joined the party, and after entering Beijing University in 1959, became an important student official. At first, like Ho, he had been in physics; after a two-year break on account of illness, he had transferred into literature.

Chen had become a party member with a pure heart, and carried out its regulations and abided by its standards. But he discovered there were great gaps between ideals and reality. The biggest question, to him, was why the masses were afraid of the party. The Anti-Rightist movement of 1957 had left a stifling atmosphere at the university, in which relations among people had become distorted and no one trusted anyone else. Many of those who had been labeled rightists were, in Chen's opinion, loyal and honest people. They had been called on to express their criticisms freely and had then been punished for doing so.

One day, in a meeting, he took a step that radically changed the direction of his life. He spoke out on behalf of a student who was being criticized as a rightist. He not only failed to protect the student, whose fate he never learned, but was himself attacked, in 1963, as an enemy of the party. He lost his powerful position and was thrown briefly into the whirlwind of criticism/ self-criticism. Then he was sent to the countryside to carry out the Four Cleans movement, as was required of most college students at the time.

What he saw there affected him deeply. Relations between the peasants and the cadres were so tense that when peasants appealed to their leaders' superiors for justice, the cadres cut off their food supplies in revenge. Thin, tattered peasants said to the young Chen, "In the past, when the Communists were fighting the Nationalists and the Japanese, it seemed that everything they did was for our sakes. Now, it seems as if everything they do is against us."

From the countryside, Chen returned to Beijing University rather than going to work, for with the commencement of the Cultural Revolution, the job assignment system had come to a halt. Once again he was made a target, this time a major one.

His girl friend, a "reactionary" professor's daughter, was forced to watch while he was nearly beaten to death three times. Unconscious, he was dragged along the ground for such great distances that he lost most of a toe. "I lay in a coma for six days," he said sadly. "There were times when I knew how easy it would be to give in to death. If only I had recovered earlier, I might have been able to stop my fiancée from killing herself."

There was an awkward pause in the conversation. I thought that I would never understand how the propaganda authorities could ask the Chinese people to put the Cultural Revolution out of their minds and focus on a glorious, sunshine-filled future. I had heard about hundreds of such tragedies and witnessed many of them. Almost every urban family had had its unforgettable experience of political violence. Perhaps it was the unexpected way in which the tales sometimes came to light that gave them the same force as if I were hearing them for the first time. I saw Judy fighting tears.

Chen broke the silence with a bleak joke. "The Gang of Four made their biggest mistake around then. They forgot to finish off Deng Xiaoping and the rest of us when they had the chance."

In 1970, after most of the violence was over, Chen was at last permitted to take a job assignment. He indicated that he wished to go back to the countryside. He was given work in Henan Province, near the Anhui border. There, no longer a target of criticism, he rose quickly to become a commune party secretary.

In that position, he told us, he learned how, by its very nature, the system of "carrying out policies according to documents" transmitted from Beijing made the peasants hate the officials. The documents were written by leaders who had not the slightest idea of the actual conditions in the countryside, and were more concerned with ideology and their own political survival than with how to feed and clothe the peasants. The local cadres, obliged to enforce the policies, became nothing less than the peasants' oppressors.

Chen continued to rise in the hierarchy. He was promoted to County Education Department leader, and became acutely aware of the desperate lack of resources for country schools, and of the high incidence of illiteracy.

In his official capacity, Chen had frequent occasion to return to the capital. In 1975 he became friendly with future General Party Secretary Hu Yaobang, then still in disfavor. Another subsequently powerful associate was future Propaganda Chief Deng Liqun's son, Deng Yingtao, who worked as a Production Team leader under Chen while Chen was commune party secretary. These personal relationships were extremely important to Chen's political future.

In 1976, when Mao died, Chen felt that at last his time had come. "In a totalitarian country, when the dictator dies, there is always a moment of hope," he said. A great many other talented people were coming forward to express their belief that China had gone astray. At the same time the new party leaders were groping for new ideas. It was a unique moment in history.

But few were looking to the countryside. It had been for too long a place for punishment, a spirit-breaking ground for sinners against the revolution. Because of its tradition as a place of insult and exile, and because of its poverty and backwardness, few sought the opportunity to work there. Even at the top levels the prejudice was evident: those put in charge of agriculture were often the least capable. There was a kind of feudal scorn for anyone connected with the countryside. "While I worked at the commune, whenever there was a film during meetings in town," Chen recalled, "we commune leaders were always assigned seats in the back rows, behind the city officials."

There was thus a vacuum of power just where, in Chen's view, it would be easiest to begin to redeem a bankrupt system. In 1978 he made his move. He wrote letters, both to his well-connected friends and to the Central Committee itself, describing his background and abilities. At the time, this kind of self-recommendation was most unusual. But as it turned out, the Academy of Social Sciences was being reopened after a long hiatus, and Chen was invited to work in the Agricultural Economy Research Institute there.

But he found he could accomplish little. The old Soviet-style bureaucracy had been restored, with its system of endless meetings and document readings. Few dared to discuss the systemic reform that Chen believed essential. One of the first tasks he was assigned was to do research on the people's communes. "How could I 'do research,' " he asked us, "when the communes' very existence was a historical mistake?"

The following year, with his old friend and fellow well-known counterrevolutionary Ho Weiling, Chen began to go his own way. He organized a small, unofficial group of middle-aged intellectuals to discuss "What our generation can do for the country." Even with this patriotic title, the participants were highly nervous, for groups assembled outside the watchful eye of the party were often considered potentially subversive. Many of the invitees, strangers to one another, feared there might be spies in their midst and would come only on condition that there be no photographs. But the participants included a large percentage of high-ranking cadres' children, and there was little to fear. By 1980, with over thirty members, about 80 percent of them well connected, the infant Research Group on the Problem of China's Rural Development was quietly beginning to do its work.

Listening, I remembered that at the time struggle within the party between the reformers and the orthodox Maoists had been intense, and the situation in society had been volatile as well. At first, just following the fall of the ultraleftists, days had been heady, because many people blamed the Gang of Four for China's troubles and thought that now all their problems would be solved. Soon, however, leaders realized their ambitions for quick modernization had been overoptimistic and called for a belt-tightening "economic retrenchment." The people went through a period of anger and disappointment that expectations were going unmet and injustices unredressed.

Meanwhile, we activists had been trying to find answers by working outside the party, many calling for a multiparty system. I recalled this to Chen now, and he said that in his view, people like myself had been politically naive, especially about the intricacies of the leadership struggle. He believed that for the foreseeable future there was no alternative to the Communist party. "If left to their own devices, the Chinese people would tear each other to bits," he said. "We all saw that during the Cultural Revolution. Democratic foundations have to be built gradually. If you handed democracy to the Chinese people now, they wouldn't know what to do with it."

Chen's group had its own way of circumventing the bureaucracy. They established an academic label for their activities, by making an agreement with the Academy of Social Sciences to carry out agricultural research, and used some elderly, well-respected scholars as figureheads. They kept their real purposes secret from all but a few; their members had other jobs at universities, research institutes, and publishing houses. Meanwhile, through the cadres' children, who were essential to their success, they avoided all the usual channels and passed their position papers directly to the powerful.

"What did you write about first?" I asked, impressed by the circuitous measures they had been forced to adopt.

"The countryside, of course," answered Chen. "The responsibility system."

Many Westerners seemed to think that the responsibility system, which we had seen carried out in the Guo family village, began in Sichuan Province. We learned that day that the seeds were sown in Anhui in 1977. It all began in Guzheng County, a poor, drought-stricken area so isolated that its quiet departure from collective production went unnoticed for a time. The peasants returned to the practices advocated in the early sixties by "capitalist roader" Liu Shaoqi, restoring private plots of land, fixing grain quotas for each household, and trading freely among themselves. By 1978, after a second drought, nearly twelve hundred Production Teams, about 10 percent of those in the entire province of Anhui, had revived the pre–Cultural Revolution methods. When these new "capitalist sprouts" became the subject of public controversy, the Research Group went to make its own investigation.

They found a vital economy that stimulated the peasants to find their own solutions to their difficulties, and they were not afraid to say so in writing. The first report, written by Chen, was called "Dawn in the Countryside: China's Hope." Premier Zhao Ziyang, whose own successes in Sichuan had come through emphasizing productivity over ideology, read their reports and called them "an extremely clear account of the problems in the countryside." Zhao's comments marked a shift in the group's fortunes toward official recognition.

An open-minded future Central Committee leader, Wan Li, was then Anhui's first party secretary. He supported the Research Group's findings, and the first formal experiments began. They moved very carefully, beginning their work in new areas by permitting whole Production Teams to keep what was grown above a certain level. Later, the teams were broken into smaller groups, and finally into families. This was the future responsibility system.

"We were terrified, at first, that everything would go wrong," said Chen. "We had no guarantees that exploiting classes and grave inequalities would not re-emerge, that capitalism would not, indeed, be the outcome. But we told ourselves not to worry too much about ideology. We worked very quietly, so that our success would become an unshakable fact before anyone could denounce our methods on theoretical grounds."

As young, unknown scholars, Chen and his group were extremely vulnerable, always "walking along the brink of counterrevolution," knowing they could be used as scapegoats at any time. In the beginning, before top officials dared become too openly associated with the new policies, they were often trotted out to explain the responsibility system to those who opposed it; this was the case at one harrowing meeting of provincial governors, nearly all of whom were against it.

There were times when members of the group could not escape personal attack. When Chen's health failed because he never slept, when he had marital troubles because he never came home, he had something like a nervous breakdown. An enemy saw his chance, said Chen had gone insane, and called for him to be institutionalized. Fortunately, Chen's supporters arranged a two-year rest instead. Ho Weiling had been criticized too, to the point that he was once nearly forced to withdraw from political life.

Sometimes, the high-ranking cadres' children who supported the group did not see eye to eye with their more conservative fathers, and this created another kind of problem. During the campaign against spiritual pollution in the autumn of 1983, for example, Propaganda Chief Deng Liqun tried to clamp down on "laxity on the ideological front." The group became handicapped by its association with his son, although most of their members expressed strong opposition to the campaign. During that time, because of their own conflicts with Deng Liqun, neither Zhao Ziyang nor Hu Yaobang was able to work closely with the group. "We were like a ship without sail or rudder, floating on a sea of struggle," Ho sighed.

Meanwhile, things in the countryside were going more smoothly than they could have dreamed. The land still belonged to the state so it could not be sold, and this restriction seemed effective in preventing the collection of too much wealth in one place. Although some peasants got rich faster than others, nearly everyone was better off, and the wealthier peasants were stepping in to help the poorer ones. Chen and his group had also feared that peasants would choke the already overcrowded cities when they were permitted greater mobility in doing business, but they found that county seats and smaller towns could be developed and attract peasants. In this way, many peasants could "leave the earth but not leave the countryside."

Gradually, the responsibility system became an incontrovertible success. It spread from the sparsely populated mountain areas in which collective production had been obviously unsuitable down to lower-lying areas. News spread of the enthusiasm and increasing prosperity of the peasants working under it, and despite the reluctance of grassroots cadres to give up their power, more and more regions followed suit. The central government began to do its part to reassure the peasants that the new policies would not change. Soon it seemed that the only question was how to maintain dwindling government coffers, as government-subsidized purchases of the tremendous harvests enriched the peasants and drained the state's cash resources.

In 1982 the group formally got the support of the Secretariat, the most powerful administrative unit in the Central Committee. "Until then, we were a 'shadow group,'" commented Ho, describing the way they had always avoided the limelight. With the Secretariat's recognition came the national shift of attention away from the countryside, for which the basic policies were now successfully established, to the cities. For this far larger task, some members of the group were reorganized into a new body called the National Committee on Economic Systemic Reform, and Chen was appointed director of the Research Institute on Economic Systemic Reform. A tiny, dangerous, unofficial group of intellectuals had become members of the most important policy-making organ in the entire nation.

The urban reforms were proving far less simple than those in the countryside, said Chen. After all, the countryside seemed very far away to most of China's leaders; it didn't affect their jobs or surroundings directly. In the cities there was more resistance, and the economy was far more complex. Many of the problems were primarily technical ones, such as the reform of the irrational price and wage systems, but there were also profound issues that promised to provide difficulties for many years to come. Chen named but three of these, and my head began to spin.

There was a tremendous conflict, he said, between traditional revolutionary values and the people's ever-increasing thirst for better material living standards. Here in Shekou, originally a blank slate, the problem was especially grave since there had been few native cultural traditions upon which to build. But the tendency was clear throughout China. Under conditions of freedom in a very poor country, the pursuit of wealth had come quickly to have an unfortunate prominence in people's lives, often to the exclusion of almost everything else.

Another big problem was how to implement the new programs. It was far from enough that the policymakers could write policies welcomed by the great masses of the people; the best plans were useless unless there was an administrative apparatus capable of carrying them out. In addition to the need to train capable administrators, it was important to find a way to decentralize sufficiently to enliven the economy, yet maintain government supervision at the same time. One problem for which the reformers had been totally unprepared, for example, was the question of whom the newly elected enterprise managers represented. Naturally, the managers were concerned about their popularity, so in the autumn of 1984 they had issued wild bonuses, essentially borrowing from the government to do so and avoiding government taxes. The state did not even have a viable inspection system, as most accountants simply reported whatever figures the managers gave them.

A final, and perhaps most important question, continued Chen, was the reformers' own lack of experience. "Nothing quite like this has ever been attempted, in China or anywhere in the world," he explained. "We are trying to build a Chinese-style socialism which is neither feudalistic nor capitalist, modeled neither on the Soviet Union nor on the West." He smiled modestly. "Sometimes we feel as if we are groping for stepping-stones to cross the river."

After listening to all this, and after the long, full day we had spent in Shekou, I felt almost as if I too shared the great burden of charting a new course for China. We were all silent for a moment, staring out the big plate-glass window. On the darkening blue bay, the Hong Kong ferry had docked and the visitors in their Western clothing were already indistinguishable from the natives. Seagulls floated on the sea winds, and beyond was the twinkling skyline of Hong Kong.

"It isn't easy," I said. "I wish you every success."

"Deng Xiaoping has given us the opportunity to do a little something," said Chen, "but he's very old and we haven't much time. We hope to accomplish so much in the next few years that no matter who gains power later, they'll never be able to turn back the clock."

"What if you fail?" I wondered.

"We may well do so," Chen answered, as if the possibility was very real. "But if the reforms are aborted this time, future generations will continue to look for a way."

Perhaps Chen and his friends would indeed someday be executed, or end in prison or in exile overseas like the late Qing reformers or the intellectuals of the May Fourth movement. It seemed they had accepted the risks. But I knew they were right about one important difference between their movement and those of the past: before this one, there had been a Cultural Revolution. What had been our greatest misfortune was also our greatest hope, for it offered us a chance to understand, as a nation, the great urgency of liberating ourselves from our tragic past.

THREE
WOMEN
OF
GUIYANG

*I*T WAS LATE FEBRUARY, nearly the fifteenth of the first lunar month, and all Guiyang was dressed up with strings of paper lanterns. Some were as small and simple as a baby pumpkin, some as large and complex, literally, as a cow, for it was now the year of the ox. There were hundreds of variations on that theme, from pairs of solitary horns to full-blown bovines suspended plumply in the air, udders and all. There were airplanes, too, and rocket ships for the Four Modernizations, and every conceivable living thing, from fish, frogs, dragonflies, and birds to tigers and horses and the gods and goddesses of legend. By night they were all lit from within by electric lights, and the inhabitants of the city came out and strolled the length of them, reading the signature tags and commenting critically. This ancient event seemed a celebration of variety, creativity, and bounty, coming as it did, for the first time on this scale, after so many years of cultural barrenness.

The free markets of Guiyang seemed to have spilled over their assigned districts and into the whole city. On the sewing streets, you could buy a length of cloth at one stall, get your measurements taken and a pair of pants made up at another, and choose from a wooden box of heels of every size and height to fix your shoes at a third. You might also pick up a paper diagram of the ghosts of the heavens. The snack stands seemed infinite, vending dry rice noodles, wet rice noodles, wheat noodles, rice paste curd. Plastic juice-dispensers labeled "Made in Massachusetts" circulated fountains of suspicious-looking orange liquid through their bowels; tidy stalls of blue jeans and Shanghai-made jackets stood next to dry brown hill medicines spread on paper on the sidewalks, the efficacy of the poisons proven by the rows of enormous dead rats lined up beside them. There were small vats of the famous Guizhou fire liquor, crisp sheaves of uncured tobacco leaf, and blind fortune-tellers to tell every fate. The most exotic merchandise of all, however, was a carton of boxed Italian fettuccine, of a brand readily available at Zabar's in New York.

Guiyang had once been an ethnic minority town of the Miao, Buyi, and Muslim Hui. But, ironically, it was precisely Guizhou Province's cruel geography, its inaccessibility, poverty, and isolation that had attracted outsiders. They had come in four recent waves, each of which brought thousands of new residents to the capital city. The first was in the 1930s, when the Japanese invaded China and the refugees fled south. My father had joined the migration when the Changsha orphanage where he was growing up was bombed, and he was among those who passed through Guiyang. He went on to Kunming, but many stopped here, and even when the fighting was over did not go home again.

When Mao's Communists grew strong, the Nationalist army also retreated to the mountain fastness of Guiyang. With the army's defeat, only some made it onto the airplanes and escaped to Taiwan; many more were left behind, especially the wives and children.

Another, smaller wave of outsiders arrived not long after the 1949 Liberation, volunteers for relocation to the poor provinces and border regions. Many lived to regret their actions, feeling themselves exiles in a foreign land, but in the fervor of the 1950s there was a veritable orgy of self-sacrifice. These patriots were joined in the early 1960s by many more who were not volunteers:

After the Sino-Soviet split, when border disputes threatened to become full-scale war, Mao transplanted essential industrial plants into the mountains, hiding them in this barren, scrubby province amid the protective shields of rock. Reluctantly, the clever and sophisticated Shanghainese came, the proud and arrogant Beijingers, the engineers, scientists, technicians, and ordinary workers who had little choice but to obey "the needs of the state."

So terry cloth–turbaned Buyi shared the streets with lipsticked young women escorted by men in suits and ties; heavy-whiskered, white-capped Muslims sold shishkebab down the road from fat little ethnic Chinese girls frying pork. The people of one of China's most recessed, landlocked, interior regions were truly "from the five lakes and four seas." Here, Judy and I had no friends, relatives, ex-students, or friends-of-friends, yet it was never difficult for us to make new contacts. Within a single hour, we spoke to people from Jiangxi, Hunan, Shandong, and Anhui, some of whom had arrived fifty years before, others only twenty. Of the many new friends we made in Guiyang, there were three who left a deep impression, all of them women with stories to tell.

We met the first quite soon after our arrival. We were looking for a bowl of noodles for Judy, a longtime vegetarian who could rarely find much to eat in China, for many Chinese believe that only meat and lard can make a dish delicious. The problem was compounded by the fact that people seemed convinced that all foreigners lived in grander style than they. Time and again she would make her requests to vigorously nodding chefs, only to have them reappear some minutes later with meat.

Sometimes noodles were a good bet, though, so we went into a rickety wooden noodle shop on one of Guiyang's ancient side streets. It was doing a lively business for the peasants after the day's marketing. At the doorway, I tried to explain our request to the surprised chit-seller, a young man seated before an abacus at a table. As I began to repeat myself for the third time, from inside, amid the stream beyond a partition, an authoritative female voice called, "What's the trouble?"

The young man yelled, "Some Americans want to eat vegetable noodles. No meat, no MSG, no hot pepper, no lard. No anything."

The startled voice answered, "Americans? No problem, no problem." Out came a middle-aged woman in a blue cotton work jacket and flower-patterned protective oversleeves, wiping her hands on a long white apron.

She seemed immediately to understand our problem, and urged us to sit, guaranteeing that she could cook a delicious bowl of completely vegetarian noodles. As she walked back into the kitchen, we heard her say thoughtfully to herself, "Ay, when I was young, didn't I make a few bowls of noodles for Americans!"

Judy looked after her in surprise. Soon two ginger-fresh bowls of long white noodles with yellow-flowered broccoli came steaming back. The soup was a clear soy brown in the clean white bowls, and the sesame oil was pure and fragrant. The woman set our dinners down in front of us, and, without our asking her to do so, rinsed two pairs of chopsticks with boiling water. Then she fetched a narrow bench over and sat down beside us companionably. It was as if we were old friends come from a long way off.

As she sat chatting to us, I looked at her more closely. She must once have been a real beauty, for her features were regular and fine, and her eyes large. I could hardly believe it when she said she was over sixty. True, there were many lines on her face, but they were shallow and delicate, so as to give her skin a smooth appearance. Her hair was still black, and her back was straight and strong.

Her friendliness increased when I told her I was from Changsha. "A fellow countryman," she cried, "and married to an American!"

As we spoke, she sometimes looked quickly around her, as

so many who have lived through the Cultural Revolution do, to see who might be listening. The only remaining customers were a few brown-toothed peasants, loudly slurping down the last of their noodles. She seemed confident of the other workers, who treated her with respect. In fact, we learned, this was her shop and she was their boss.

Mrs. Yang, for that was her name, spoke eagerly of what she termed the goodness of Americans. She was in a position to know what they were really like, she said. Young people today had been taught first to hate them, then suddenly to respect their materialistic achievements. They admired the West blindly without any real understanding. "I lived through the war," she said. "When the Nationalist army could barely fight, it was the Americans who kept us alive. I had dinner at their homes, and sometimes they came to us. I made them noodles." She smiled at Judy. "So you see, I know what Americans like."

"Your husband was with the Nationalists?" Judy asked.

Mrs. Yang nodded briefly. A new group of peasants was heading for one of the tables that had just been wiped clean for the night, and she shouted, "No more food!"

"When did you open the restaurant?" I wondered, impressed with the good business she was doing. "Since your retirement?"

She laughed bitterly and answered with sarcasm in her voice. "Retirement from what, from labor reform?"

It was becoming obvious that this was not the place to talk. Mrs. Yang wrote down an address on the back of a receipt. "It will be more convenient if you come to my house," she said.

It was easy to sense a story behind her words. Her apparent eagerness to speak with me and Judy was familiar. Our foreign connection put us beyond many of the usual constraints of Chinese society, so many people trusted us more than they did each other. When we had lived at the Hunan Teachers College, all kinds of people had sought us out, sometimes in the hope that Judy's foreign "face" could help them redress injustices, sometimes simply in search of an outlet for their sorrows. Many times we were told we were the first people ever to hear their tale of abuse or secret grief. Although listening often made us sad or angry, we learned a great deal from such encounters, and felt too that it seemed to help people to speak their "hearts' words" out.

Outside, it was already dark, but the lanterns were lit. We went on a long stroll to give the woman a chance to finish up at the restaurant. She lived very close to our hotel, off a narrow hill street above a small river. At the top stood an old wooden pagoda, grassy and broken with age and lack of attention; on the other bank of the river shone the massive Soviet-style monstrosity in which we were staying, outlined in colored lights for the New Year, its neon name flashing purple.

Mrs. Yang welcomed us warmly. She had laid the table with yellow cakes and sunflower seeds, oranges and hard candies. Tea leaves lay in white porcelain cups. There were cigarettes, too, Kents from the free market. She held out the pack to us and, when we refused, lit one herself, inhaling deeply. Chinese women seldom smoke, and Mrs. Yang looked unusually tough and independent.

She told us that the house had once belonged to her husband, both floors of it, but that during the Cultural Revolution two other families had moved in, and she had been squeezed into this single small room. As she spoke, she gestured about her, and I saw that the furniture was old and some of it lovely, but that it looked as if it too had been through a struggle. The teak wardrobe had a new leg in raw wood, pieces of the carved work under the small square dining table were missing, and the mirror over the washbasin stand had a long jagged crack across it, bandaged with thick white tape.

Mrs. Yang noticed my interest. "They've slowly been returning some of the things they took away," she said.

It was unnecessary for her to explain further. All over China, wherever the Red Guards had catalogued the "reactionary" old and "capitalist" things taken during search raids of the homes of intellectuals and other bad elements, efforts were now being made to restore the items to the original owners. Of course, most things had been irreparably broken or destroyed, and only a tiny percentage of the most durable ever came back. Nothing had been returned to my own family, but then, we had never been so wealthy in earlier generations as to have antiques or real valuables. We lost books, mostly, and a few scrolls, all of them deliberately burned in a metal basin one terrifying night. I could still remember the black brushwork of my favorite horse's tail going up in violet flames. When we moved Father back to the newspaper, I had realized that not a single artifact was left from the days of long ago.

I took a deep drink of the fragrant green tea and asked Mrs. Yang about her family.

She hesitated. "There are some things that can't be returned," she said at last, with deep bitterness.

The story came out, as we knew it would. Mrs. Yang was originally from Changsha, and when young had been married, through a matchmaker's introduction, to a young man expected to have a great future, for he was the son of a prominent landlord. Her husband joined the army, and from then on he was always away somewhere, fighting the Japanese, fighting the Communists. Mrs. Yang lived the life of a widow. During those years, because she had so much time to herself, she managed to give herself something of an education.

When Changsha was burned in 1938, she was left to face alone the cruelty of the Japanese. Many years later, she still spoke of the invaders with hatred, her face twisting in naked expression. Although she didn't say so, I had the impression that she had been raped.

After the anti-Japanese war, her husband was promoted to the rank of general and assigned to Guiyang. He sent for his wife. The city was filled with Nationalist families, and at last Mrs.

Yang thought she could be happy. For a few years, she moved in nothing but the most elegant society, and all her reading became quite useful in the sophisticated international life of the day.

When the Nationalists were defeated, her husband's battalion was among those to surrender voluntarily. For this, she and her husband were treated better than those who held out, and they lived fairly peacefully even after Liberation. She bore a daughter, Xiao Hua, who gave her great joy. However, her husband was not permitted to work, and to support the family, she had to endure the insult of wiping tables in a government restaurant.

Far worse humiliations were yet to come. On May 16, 1966, the Cultural Revolution began. "How could I have known then that our great tragedy was upon us?" Mrs. Yang asked, shaking her head. "How could I know that I would have to bury a ten-year *qi* [anger] forever in my heart?"

Her husband, who had fought the Communists for so many years, had a better sense of what a campaign against reactionaries could mean. While Mrs. Yang went off to the Neighborhood Committee to listen to documents about the proletarian dictatorship over "class enemies," he stayed at home to nurse a bad cold and listen to the transistor radio. When she came back, she found him still sitting at the table, white-faced and sweating, clutching the radio. "It's all over," he told her with a look of terror. "Oh my God in heaven, it's all over for us now."

Ever in frail health, that night her husband became horribly ill, delirious with fever. He was finished by sunrise. Before the storm hit, he had been literally frightened to death.

Mrs. Yang sighed. "He was lucky, of course."

She and Xiao Hua, then a sixteen-year-old middle-school student, were quickly spinning from criticism meeting to criticism meeting. For Mrs. Yang, things were a bit easier than they were for her daughter: she was able to stay at home for the most part, appearing at meetings when called upon, and making the required self-accusations. The heart of the Cultural Revolution beat among the students, however, and the pressure on her daughter was enormous. Every day Xiao Hua was told to "draw a clear line of separation" between herself and her Nationalist mother. "She was crazy with hatred for me," said Mrs. Yang, betraying her sorrow for the first time. The girl was set to work every night writing articles exposing her mother for her school and for the Neighborhood Committee. Relations at home were so tense that mother and daughter, sleeping in a single room, were often unable to speak to each other.

This lasted several months. "Every evening I could hear her tossing in her bed, crying out in her dreams," Mrs. Yang told us. "Sometimes she would wake up shouting. At first, I tried to soothe her, but that only made her angry. She would denounce me in her sleep." Mrs. Yang drew deeply on her cigarette, and stared for a moment out the window toward the purple lights of the hotel across the river. "Eventually, I became afraid of her.

"Then one evening, I awoke suddenly. The room was strangely still. I sat up very quietly to see. Her bed was empty, the quilt folded neatly. The floor was still covered with all her crumpled papers, her confessions from the evening. The window was open. And on the desk was an empty bottle of liquid pesticide." Mrs. Yang wiped her eyes angrily. "I spent the night searching the riverbank for her, calling her name. No one would help me. Her body washed up against a factory sewage pipe the next day."

Judy reached across the table to put her hand over Mrs. Yang's. The woman seemed to take some comfort from the touch, and spoke again with tear-filled eyes. "I blame myself, you see. I've been over the events of that night a thousand times in my mind. Why didn't I wake up earlier? Why didn't I know that she was so desperate? Why didn't I stop her? It's like a bad dream that plays again and again. Each time I get into bed I remember that neatly folded quilt, and that open window."

Mrs. Yang looked shrunken and tired. My sisters and I, for

reasons that were hard to know, had not made the same choice as her daughter, but I had treated my so-called counterrevolutionary mother, my so-called bourgeois journalist father, in much the same way. The nightmare was over and the terror was past, but how could Mrs. Yang's scars and those of thousands of Chinese families ever truly heal? The love we should have received, the understanding and support we should have given, these were gaps too great ever to be filled.

During the following ten years, Mrs. Yang told us, she had lived the life of the constantly humiliated. The Neighborhood Committee organized the family members of bad background who had not been sent to the countryside into garbage-picking brigades. While young students and workers fought each other on the streets with tanks and grenades, she spent her days in filth, pawing through the rubbish for reusable glass bottles and scraps of metal. Most of those with her were also from Nationalist families, but she could trust no one. "Ten years," she sighed. "A stomach full of ten years of *qi* and nowhere to put it! You couldn't move, you couldn't speak, you couldn't show with a tic of your face the least emotion. Everyone was spying on everyone else. At night, they broke my windows and urinated onto my bed, shouting, 'American bitch!' "

Guiyang's fighting during the Cultural Revolution was famous. It must have been worse here than in Changsha, for people at home rarely brought up the subject, whereas even at our hotel, the floor attendant had mentioned it with casual horror. How many had died in Guiyang, ten thousand or a hundred thousand? I feared we would never know. It was unlikely that even the current regime would investigate the tragedy seriously, for too many of those now in power had children who had been Red Guard radicals.

I was moved that Mrs. Yang dared treat us with such trust after what she had suffered because of her Western contacts, but I was afraid to allow her to sink too deep into her memories. The evening was getting on and I didn't want to leave her depressed. I shifted the conversation to her prosperous little restaurant.

"What's a noodle stand to me?" she exclaimed, with a hint of her pre-1949 pride. "I, who once ate banquets with generals, serving noodles to peasants. What does an old lady over sixty know of getting rich?"

Mrs. Yang conceded that since the end of the Cultural Revolution, life had indeed been much better for the Nationalist families. In addition to the furniture, the salaries that had been confiscated had reappeared. Special movie tickets were now distributed to them on holidays, and the official judgment that her daughter's death had been a counterrevolutionary "suicide to escape punishment" was changed to make it one of the thousands of "persecutions to death."

The business fever was quite recent, Mrs. Yang told us. Guiyang would never take the lead over other cities, but it was good at sensing the winds. The breeze out of Beijing had blown a new face onto the Neighborhood Committee. Instead of hunting down counterrevolutionaries, it was busy organizing young people "waiting for jobs" into their own collective shops. At first, many residents had been afraid of going too far to the right, but when they read enough newspapers and saw what other streets were doing, they grew afraid of being too far left. Some opened tea stands, others gave permanent waves or sewed clothing. Mrs. Yang's specialty had always been noodles, so she decided to invest her windfall accumulated salary in a shop. It was not so much to make money, she said, but to keep busy, and to help by employing some of the youth. Her assistants were like a family to her, many of them orphans from bad backgrounds. Without Deng Xiaoping, she said, what would their future have been?

Wasn't it sad and predictable, I thought, that the economic reforms were being understood as yet another political movement that had to be supported or else one might be considered backward! The conformist instinct was profound in the Chinese soul, and although Western analysts sometimes liked to repeat the cliché that the emphasis on the collectivity contributed to social harmony, conformism could also be extremely dangerous. On Mrs. Yang's street, people did business as if they were sheep, just as, like sheep, they had once waved Little Red Books and danced the dance of loyalty to Chairman Mao.

It hadn't been easy for Mrs. Yang to go into business. To get a license, she had to go through the back door—and it wasn't enough to decide to curry favor, she had to figure out how to get the gifts into the hands of the right bureaucrats. She had an acquaintance who knew a relative of a man in the local commerce office, so she began inviting her acquaintance to dinner, mentioning the problem with proper indirectness; her acquaintance began mentioning the matter to her friend, and passing on some well-chosen gifts from Mrs. Yang. The friend finally began working on her bureaucrat relative. The whole affair was a complex relationship net that took many months to build.

After the shop opened, trouble came again: Mrs. Yang's delicious black bean and garlic sauce, warm attitude, and clean tables got such a reputation that customers flocked to her, leaving the nearby government-run restaurant nearly empty. She was soon earning 200 to 300 *yuan* a month, after taxes. Then someone wrote a secret report to the commerce department accusing Mrs. Yang of trying to prove that capitalism was superior to socialism. They "exposed" her flexible prices, which were higher at times of greatest demand, as a "dangerous tendency," and called for a full government investigation. It was a clear case of jealousy, the "red eye disease."

Mrs. Yang had read the newspapers and was not afraid. When the inspectors came, she prepared her noodles for them as if she didn't know who they were. "It must have been my bean sauce," she said proudly. "Not only didn't they criticize me, but they issued me a commendation. I framed it and put it on the shop wall. There hasn't been any trouble since."

She smiled. "Aiya," she said, shaking her head. "I've seen war, famine, every form of political humiliation and hardship. Just to have survived was a miracle. Now, at last, I am having a few good years."

To me, these words were even more affecting than Mrs. Yang's earlier tales of trouble. China had truly survived countless tragedies. Deng Xiaoping had brought it the first respite in many years. But how long, I wondered, would the gentle spring rain continue?

It was time for us to go. Outside, all was silent except for the sound of the river water against the stone ditch walls. We bade farewell to Mrs. Yang, standing outside in the doorway with her for a few moments and watching the sharp neon lights of the hotel flash from across the river onto the mossy old pagoda. So many centuries that ancient edifice had stood there, I thought, that symbol of traditional culture, since long before the Soviets had built their heavy monuments and brought Marxism-Leninism to our feudal land. It had endured through Mrs. Yang's greatest sorrows, and now, at this late hour, it was witnessing her prosperity and peace as well.

SOME YEARS AGO, while exploring Kunming, Judy and I came across a festive-looking building decorated with streamers in Arabic writing, and learned it was a mosque of the local Hui Muslims. We walked in and were warmly received by bearded, intense young men who spoke emotionally to us about the travel restrictions that made it all but impossible for them to visit Mecca. It was startling, especially so soon after the Cultural Revolution, to find people so outspoken and visibly angry; most Han (ethnic Chinese) were better skilled in the arts of self-protection and ambiguity. I wondered then whether the special treatment accorded to minority nationalities, which had been restored in 1979 with the revival of official guarantees of "freedom of religion," exempted them from the usual limitations on freedom of speech, or whether they simply had more grievances than the rest of us and a different cultural tradition for expressing them.

When Judy and I learned that Guiyang had a small Hui population and a mosque, we decided to track it down and see whether these Hui would be equally outspoken.

After we had been given many wrong directions by helpful but ill-informed locals, we finally saw the big blue dome from some way off. The wooden entrance door lay off a short lane called, curiously, Brotherhood Alley. I wondered when it had been renamed. The door was locked, and we rang the bell many times before a little girl of about five opened it a crack. Imam Wang was sick, she told us, and there was nobody else home but her father. Only after much persuasion did she finally let us in.

A stone corridor open to the sky led into a courtyard; the girl's father, who turned out to be Imam Wang's son, was seated on a two-inch stool before a metal basin of soapy water, washing a button-down shirt. He was a young man in his late twenties, completely "Han-ized," as the phrase went, without even a skull-cap. He stood up in confusion and, when we explained that we were foreigners, gladly volunteered to give us a tour of the prayer room and the main building. As we followed him, he told us proudly that the provincial Minority Affairs Department had allocated 240,000 *yuan* toward the restoration of this mosque, which was being rebuilt according to the design of their own Hui architect.

We were disappointed in what we saw, however, for in comparison with the colorful mosque we had visited in Kunming, the place seemed sterile and deserted. Perhaps this was because the restoration was still under way, but the already completed prayer room was also utterly devoid of character. The main five-story building, which would eventually be an inn, promised little better. We wondered who could possibly be induced to visit the ambitious reception room for foreign visitors, its heavy new leather furniture covered with a thick layer of dust.

As we stood on the balcony of the top floor, looking out over the city, the young man told us he had been called back to Guiyang from the military because of the work on the mosque. He knew very little about Islam, he explained apologetically, except that the Hui did not eat pork. Now the state needed him to prepare to succeed his aged father. He was willing, although he knew no Arabic. In his opinion, his lack of background wouldn't matter too much, since his primary work would be the administration of the hotel.

I heard in his words a member of my own generation speaking. Both of us had grown up in an era in which religion was considered evil, and Islam probably meant almost as little to him as it did to me. Even when I was a child, religion had been no more than a curiosity. In my family, only my grandmother had religious beliefs, vague Buddhist ones that involved incense burning and occasional trips to sacred Heng mountain. In the movies religious leaders were usually depicted as black-caped international spies.

During the Cultural Revolution, my older sister's Red Guard group was among those to go to the mountains and smash the ancient temples, for Chairman Mao said they interfered with the rebirth of the new revolutionary man. Once I saw a monk being publicly criticized and beaten and, in later years, when I was a worker, had friends who worked in factories that had been converted from old temples and churches. A tenth-century Confucian academy near my college had been turned into housing and a woodworking shop, and brick additions were built up against the ancient walls with unabashed practicality. At the time, such things seemed quite natural.

When we had completed our tour of the building, we asked Young Wang whether there was any discrimination against the local Hui. He answered readily that sometimes he felt the special considerations they were supposed to be given were very superficial. For example, a Han family was living on the second floor of one of the two Hui restaurants in town, the largest one. Every day, they went shopping and carried their offensive pork through the Hui dining hall and up the stairs to their room. Many of the customers were visitors from other provinces and didn't understand that this was not the fault of the restaurant. They often stood up angrily and left, insulted.

The Han family would have been more than happy to move out, Wang continued, but they had nowhere to go. Over and over again, the Hui had written reports to the Minority Affairs Department asking them to settle the problem, but they were always given a bureaucratic runaround. "If the mayor were Hui, he would see to things," Wang said with a sigh. "Here everything is done mechanically, according to the letter of the document, nothing more and nothing less. They give us coupons to buy cheap beef because they're required to do so, and for no other reason."

We had taken a lot of the imam's son's time, and we refused his offer to see if his father felt well enough to meet us. If he didn't mind, we said, we would spend just a few more minutes here by ourselves, enjoying the tranquility. He bade us good-bye and disappeared into one of the ground-floor rooms, where we could see through the window his little daughter practicing her Chinese calligraphy.

As we rounded the corner back into the courtyard, we saw a woman wearing a white cap such as is required of restaurant workers in some provinces. She was sweeping the flagstones with an old rush broom. We were surprised that we hadn't noticed her when we came in.

She stared suspiciously at us, but we nodded and smiled. When she slowly nodded back, we walked over to say hello.

"If you aren't here to worship, why have you come?" she asked bluntly. I recognized her accent as from Yunnan Province. She had a worry-lined, middle-aged face, and her eyes were red and watery, perhaps from the dust she had stirred up, or from rubbing. "You don't look as if you're from around here," she persisted, staring at the blue swansdown parka I had purchased in Changsha. She seemed even more confused by Judy, who was dressed as a simple Chinese. Perhaps she took her for a Uygur.

When we said we lived outside China, her eyes grew bright. "Have you ever been to Mecca?" she asked.

Judy and I looked at each other. "Not yet," I answered, and Judy added, "But maybe we will have the chance someday."

The woman suddenly grew very friendly. At her invitation, we sat down on wooden stools and drank the hot water she poured from a thermos. Imitating her Yunnanese accent to diminish the distance between us, I asked her about herself.

She told us her surname was Ma, and she had come here to see relatives. But as soon as the words were out, her voice shook, and she changed her mind and said that she lived here. Sensing another story, we chatted casually about ourselves and our interest in minority nationalities, to build her confidence in us. In fact, she was most eager to talk.

She was really from Shadian Town in Yunnan, she confessed. It was in an almost all-Hui area in the southwest part of the province. Her ancestors had first come to China's Great Northwest from Central Asia, then traveled south to trade along the Burma Road. For generation after generation, they had been muleteers, independent and loyal to their religious traditions. After the great Han slaughters of the Hui during the nineteenth century, when sixteen million Yunnanese Muslims had been reduced to only six million, the Hui had learned it was useless to look for trouble. In Shadian, they had lived peacefully, according to their traditional customs and beliefs.

But the Cultural Revolution had been a disaster for them, beginning when Mao raised the cry "Combat the Four Olds" (old thought, customs, morals, and culture). The religious groups were fiercely attacked, which meant that the greatest burden fell on the minorities, almost all of whom had strong religious traditions. The Shadian mosque was burned by a group of Red Guards. All the religious objects in the village were destroyed or carried away, and their imam was humiliated and taken off to the city. They never saw him again. Then the propaganda teams came, to teach everyone to carry out the revolution. "It was as if they wanted us to become identical to the Han," said Mrs. Ma, "even in our souls. Outwardly, we had to dress exactly like them. But we resisted silently, praying at home and keeping our hearts pure."

Year after year, the Hui did not give up their struggle against ultraleftist policies. Quite late in the Cultural Revolution, in 1975, the situation reached a crisis. They were pushed beyond endurance when the party secretary, a woman whom Mrs. Ma described as a collaborator and a traitor, tried to force them to eat pork. When they refused, she had bleeding pigs' heads thrown into their courtyards and then into their wells, so that their water became contaminated. They had no alternative but to act.

A group of men went to the party secretary's office and threatened her. She escaped. When she returned, she brought Han soldiers with her, to intimidate them into obedience. The villagers became only angrier and beat up the soldiers and scared them away. Then, without any attempt to negotiate, the party labeled the whole town of over eight hundred families as counterrevolutionary. The People's Liberation Army arrived, a whole infantry division, fully armed with tanks, grenades, and machine guns.

The Hui, conveniently close to China's supply routes to North Vietnam, then fighting with the United States and the South, had long ago begun to build up a cache of stolen weapons. Still, the townspeople's quickly dug trenches were poor protection against the professionals, who tried first to cut off the Huis' food and water, calling with megaphones for their surrender. These exhortations were no use. "We had made up our minds to die," Mrs. Ma told us, almost matter-of-factly. I could well imagine, if she had such conviction now, what fearsome warriors the Shadianese must have made at the time.

"The battle was swift and bloody," Mrs. Ma said. She spoke

as if she were reciting an oral history for future generations. "My husband and sons were killed on the first day. Many hundreds lost their lives to bullets, but almost as many sacrificed themselves. They ran with grenades toward the enemy, then fell on top of them and died. Young and old, all of them were religious martyrs. Because of them, the enemy's losses were great."

The battle of Shadian sounded infinitely worse than the Red Guard skirmishes I had seen. It was astounding to me that such extreme violence could have occurred so late in the Cultural Revolution, after most of the rest of the country was relatively quiet and Mao so close to death. Mrs. Ma's story spoke worlds of our ignorance about what had gone on in the far corners of China during the Cultural Revolution. It explained much, too, about the anger of the Kunming Hui with whom we had spoken years earlier.

Only a few escaped from Shadian, Mrs. Ma told us. Nearly the entire town was wiped out, as were neighboring villages. It was said that a thousand Hui had died. She herself, now alone in the world, was among the refugees. Afraid she was being pursued, she didn't know where to go. At first she traveled only at night. She begged food from the peasants, and the kind ones gave her sweet potatoes and pickled vegetables; others set their dogs on her. She slept hidden among the threshed rice bundles in the fields during the day. Slowly she found her way to Kunming, the provincial capital, where she joined the beggars who haunt restaurants, waiting for leftovers from others' bowls. Once, a fellow beggar tried to sell her, but she escaped again.

After the death of Mao and the fall of the Gang of Four in the autumn of 1976, she dared to take a train to Guiyang, where she had a cousin. Although it turned out that her cousin had long since been imprisoned as a counterrevolutionary, his family was good to her. They hid her for several months, until they were confident that the Guiyang authorities were not looking for her.

It wasn't until after Deng Xiaoping returned to power in the summer of 1977 that she knew she was really safe. The Shadian Incident, as it had come to be called, was officially no longer "counterrevolutionary," and the party secretary who had sparked it was sentenced in criminal court. Still, it infuriated Mrs. Ma that the Communist party had conceded only that the Hui had been manipulated by evil people, not that they had been right to defend themselves.

Mrs. Ma sighed. "There is a great gap between promises of freedom and the practice of it," she said. "It's a very good thing that our mosque is being restored. It's a good thing, too, that young people are being recruited to replace the imams, for we have lost a great many through old age and persecution. But the traditions have been interrupted, and many of these young people will never be able to make up for lost time. Young Wang, for example," she said, glancing toward the future hotel. "He's a good boy. But it frightens me to think that someday he will be our imam."

I knew there were many other problems and limitations for religious groups as well. All religious organizations had to be approved by the party, and no proselytizing was permitted. Party members were strictly forbidden to hold religious beliefs, as was anyone under the age of eighteen. Life was perhaps most difficult for groups seen as threatening the supremacy of the party. In Tibet, where the old religious organization was also the primary political one, followers of the Dalai Lama were frequently treated as potential insurgents. Among Christian sects, those loyal to the pope had the greatest difficulties, for the Vatican's ties with Taiwan and unbending position on birth control and abortion made the Catholic Church particularly unwelcome in China. A number of priests unwilling to switch their loyalty to the Chinese Catholic Church remained in prison even today, nearly ten years after the end of the Cultural Revolution. For the Hui too, it seemed there had been many problems, for their religion was deeply connected with independent nationalistic sentiments.

The party granted limited religious freedom to four officially recognized groups, Buddhists, Christians, Muslims, and Daoists. I sometimes felt that it did so as much because of the important role of the minority nationalities as because of any respect for beliefs and customs that differed from those of the ever-chauvinistic dominant Han. Fifty-four of these somewhat arbitrarily identified groups were officially recognized, and they occupied about half the land area of China, including most of the sensitive border regions. Since the government could not afford disruptions there, it played a delicate game, giving enough freedom to keep the minorities relatively content, but controlling religious activities so that they would never provide a base for rebellion.

"This mosque, today, is my whole life, my consolation," Mrs. Ma said, gesturing toward the prayer room. "Hosting Hui visitors from other provinces, doing whatever small things are useful. I have nothing else, but it is enough. If you asked me fifteen years ago to predict the future of our people in China, I would never have dreamed of the good treatment we are getting today." She paused thoughtfully. "Still, for me, the blood ditch will never run dry."

I had once been too young and too fanatical to understand what religious persecution was, and the vast suffering it had caused. Maoism had been China's all-encompassing religion, and it left no room for any other belief system. Today, ironically, many of the young people who were once Mao's greatest worshipers were now most curious about religion. Mao had been like a god to our generation, and when we lost our faith in him, we began to look for something else to believe in. Some turned to their families, others to materialistic pleasures—but many others were attracted to organized religion, both Western and Chinese. I shared their curiosity about what we had once been cut off from, and now felt even more drawn to understand the complex world of China's religious life.

We promised Mrs. Ma that we would do everything we could to tell Beijing about the Hui people's desire that the Shadian Incident be reevaluated. Just before we left, she asked us for one more favor: "When you go to Mecca, bring my heart's spirit with you." We made our way out of Brotherhood Alley, and when we came to the corner of the main street, I looked back and she was still in the doorway, a slight figure with a broom, standing in the shadow of the light blue mosque.

WHEREVER WE WENT, we sought out dance parties, not so much because we liked dancing, although we did, but because the dance climate was as good a barometer as any for the general state of freedom of expression. National and local policy about whether dances were to be permitted not at all, occasionally, or frequently; whether they had to be work unit–organized, or could be private as well; whether only traditional ballroom dancing was suitable, or "disco" could be called "good exercise" too; whether the floor had to be flooded with bright lights, or a little atmosphere, even a mirror ball, was okay—all of this could change by the month or even by the week. In early 1985, reflecting the liberal economic situation, China's cities seemed to be in the grip of a dance mania, and there were even, if briefly, lessons given on television.

In Guiyang, posters announcing balls seemed to be everywhere. We chose one being held at the Provincial Song and Dance Troupe, because Judy, herself a dedicated ballet dancer, had a long-lasting friendship with the sister Hunan troupe. After we paid our two *yuan* each and entered, however, it was immediately apparent that the darkened floor was full not with professional dancers but with workers and other nonintellectual types. To the leaden wail of the band, made up of musicians from the troupe's music division, the merrymakers pushed each other gravely about, looking past each other's shoulders with slightly glazed stares. There was no central heating south of the Yangtze River during winter, and many wore the heavy overcoats, scarves, and gloves in which they had arrived. Below were tight jeans and high heels, on men and women both, and many of the women wore bright red lipstick. By Western standards, it was an odd mixture of extreme formality and everything goes: among the demure couples there were men dancing with men, women with women, young parents dancing with toddlers, old ladies with children. I knew that the same-sex dancing partners were probably not homosexual—it is usual in Chinese society to have a great deal of physical contact between members of the same sex, but very little between unmarried members of the opposite. Many find it embarrassing even to touch someone's hand. However, I looked curiously at one slender young man in a heavy beard and spiked high heels, dancing intimately and exclusively with a male friend.

The band was playing what is known as light music, tunes with romantic themes that Judy said resembled bad organ music at Western skating rinks. Such music was controversial in China, and during the campaign against spiritual pollution in the autumn of 1983, it had been attacked as "weakening the revolutionary ardor of the young." In this case, Judy joked, it had been misnamed: "heavy music" was more like it. The lugubrious beat seemed to be driving iron spikes into the ground.

We took two inconspicuous chairs near the band, but Judy had already been spotted as a foreigner. A middle-aged woman came up and asked her to dance. Her face was round and fat, and her hair, although permanent-waved like the other women's, was streaked with gray. She wore an artificial leather jacket with one of those prominent Chinese zippers, and jeans that stretched tight over her rather plump hips. According to Chinese etiquette, Judy couldn't refuse, and soon they were whirling in a low, balanced waltz. Judy was a graceful ballroom dancer, Chinese style, having picked up the steps during her stint in Changsha. The two of them looked as if they had been dancing together for years.

I barely saw Judy the rest of the evening. Hardly would she begin to walk back over to me than another person would approach. Everyone, it seemed, wanted to dance with a real foreigner. The woman who had first invited her came and sat down next to me instead, asking questions. At first, she assumed I was Judy's escort from the China International Travel Service. When I told her we were married, she grew very excited: it turned out she had read about us in one of the Chinese leisure magazines, *After Eight Hours*.

I recognized her as a bit of a lowlife: it was rare for a woman of her age to be dressed as she was, and it was unusual too that she seemed to have come to the dance unescorted, although many people greeted her. She had an aggressive, excessively animated manner that put me off a bit. I told myself that I could learn from almost anyone about the recent situation, however. And anyway, although I had learned to dance avidly to Western pop music, I had never learned to waltz, tango, foxtrot, or rumba. I bought Mrs. Xiao a beer.

For a Tuesday night, it was no small crowd willing to pay the high price of a ticket. If the dancers in the other work units holding parties that evening were as numerous, that made a great many dancers indeed. Shouting over the din of the music, I asked the woman how long there had been this much dancing in Guiyang.

She told me that it had been only in the past year or so that they could again dance freely. The situation was constantly "loose" and "tight" in a never-ending alternation. "During the anti–spiritual pollution movement," she said, "they arrested a lot of people for little more than what's going on here right now!"

How often had I heard that campaign mentioned with that same mixture of black humor and bitterness! A full seven years after the fall of the Gang of Four, it had been a brief but terrifying echo of ultraleftist xenophobia. It had quickly been nicknamed the "twenty-eight-day Cultural Revolution," although in fact it had lasted somewhat closer to two months. The notion that "spiritual pollution" should be combated had its origin in the summer of 1983, in the Central Committee's conservative Propaganda Committee. Then in October Deng Xiaoping made a major speech about party rectification and ultraleftist criminals still in positions of power, also giving a nod to the Propaganda Committee's concerns with a few sentences about the need to combat "laxity on the right." In the deeply instilled, almost reflex belief that it was always safer to be left than right, officials hurried to be first to carry out the movement, interpreting Deng's phrase as it suited their own ends. Middle- and lower-level cadres, discontented with his good treatment of intellectuals and with his economic reforms and open-door policies, saw their chance. Before long, enthusiasts were putting on red armbands and raiding people's homes, tearing reproductions of Botticelli's Venus out of art books, and confiscating light music tapes. It was said that in some divisions of the army only two songs were permitted, "Without the Communist Party, There Would Be No New China" and "Socialism Is Good."

Here in Guiyang, complained Mrs. Xiao, you couldn't walk down the street in a pair of wide-legged pants, or public security officers or self-appointed vigilantes might attack you with a pair of scissors. Men with long hair went out at great risk to their coiffures; they couldn't wear wedged shoes, either, or the heels might be broken off. Blue jeans were considered signs of spiritual pollution, as were makeup, perfume, and neckties; almost anything influenced by the West was no longer safe.

I asked whether anyone had been arrested for showing "yellow"—pornographic—videotapes, a major target of the campaign in most of the large cities. Mrs. Xiao answered ironically: "fortunately" Guizhou was a backward province. In the autumn of 1983, the VCRs had not yet come in from Hong Kong, so no one in Guiyang had the opportunity to be arrested for that. However, Mrs. Xiao confided, she herself had almost been in serious trouble.

She said she had been one of about two hundred friends who liked to dance together. What was the harm in that? They held private parties, mostly in meeting halls of work units where they knew someone influential. It was a good way to meet people, and anyway, there was nothing else to do in the evenings except watch TV or go to one of those predictable movies. Dance parties were much more interesting, and good for the health, too.

Most of her friends were couples, affianced to be married or already married. But still, the authorities accused them of dancing too close together, and in rooms too dark. Sometimes, Mrs. Xiao conceded, some people had "black light parties" and "did some bad things" there.

"I don't know why the leaders are so frightened," she complained. "After all, we are only human beings. Anything that they can't control they think will create a climate for overthrowing the Communist party." She laughed cynically. "What they call pornography probably wouldn't surprise a ten-year-old child in the West. But here, everything is political."

She and her friends were investigated as a *jituan*, a clique, a group operating on its own without the blessing of the organization. Many were arrested, and the "leaders" sentenced to prison. One man, a driver who had allowed the backseat of his unit's car to be used for after-party activities, was executed. "Deal quickly, deal severely," had been the slogan for the anticrime sweep begun a few months before the anti–spiritual pollution drive. The driver and the three others from their group who were shot with him had hit the wrong political moment.

"Just imagine executing someone for that!" the woman exclaimed angrily. "Most of them were probably engaged to be married and didn't have housing yet, or not permitted to marry because they were still college students."

I had heard many other stories about this anti-sex aspect of the anti–spiritual pollution movement. In Changsha, one acquaintance from the Provincial Sports Commission, a swimmer, had been arrested for sneaking into the pool with four or five other men and women and going for a midnight swim. They were naked when they were caught. He was still in labor camp. One of my other friends from the Sports Commission had been in even more serious trouble, for he was involved in a "ring" to show yellow videotapes that a high-ranking cadre's son had gotten through his Hong Kong connections. My friend had borrowed the Sports Commission's VCR and was thus guilty of "providing the conditions," an extremely grave offense in the Chinese criminal code—if someone was raped in your house, you were considered almost as guilty as the rapist. Fortunately for my friend, there were enough public security bureau personnel and high leaders' children involved (one the son of a provincial vice-governor) that the investigation was an extremely embarrassing one. There was a lot of cooperative foot-dragging and back-door negotiating. By the time the case came to court, the campaign against spiritual pollution had been called to a halt, for the wild interpretations of it were influencing the modernization plan. The drive against "pornography" had also lost its momentum. Otherwise, my friend told me, he certainly would have been shot. He was set to sweeping the walkways and halls of the Sports Commission, and most people, he said, went out of their way to be nice to him. In China they often "kill the chicken to scare the monkey." Instead of him, others less lucky had been used to strike fear into the hearts of potential wrongdoers.

Such stories were very sad to me, further examples of China's tendency to go to extremes. I knew that Chinese people usually became involved in such things out of curiosity, because they had been forbidden for so long, rather than out of any moral depravity. In New York, one of the first things visiting Chinese scholars would often ask was to be taken to Times Square to see an X-rated film. When the lid has been on so tight, how could they not be interested? Within China, when social controls become looser, sometimes people lack the ability to set their own limits because society has always done it for them. My friend who provided the VCR had told me he was simply looking for excitement and a chance to supplement his meager salary.

I was interested to know where Mrs. Xiao worked, but she

grew embarrassed when I asked. "The 'three door knocks,' " she said bitterly. " 'What's your unit, what do you do there, what's your salary.' " She changed the subject abruptly. "Did you bring any magazines with you from America? I'm very interested in fashion."

The band was taking a break, and Judy had escaped her captors. She suggested that we go. I was ready too, but Mrs. Xiao wouldn't hear of it.

"Why don't I walk you back to your hotel," she suggested finally, after prolonged discussion, and I could see that unless we wanted to hurt her feelings, we would have to let her come with us.

She fetched her bicycle and walked it along the deserted night streets. It seemed she had something on her mind, but didn't quite know how to bring it up. Although she was not someone I wanted as a friend and there was something vaguely disturbing to me about her, I was curious to know what she wanted from us. I decided to invite her to our room.

But how to get her past the registration desk? It was already past nine, the deadline for visitors in most hotels in China. We made a plan.

I went in first and approached the friendly young man. I offered him one of the imported 555s that I always kept in my breast pocket (although I had stopped smoking years before), and said, "I haven't seen a newspaper for days. Have you got any?" With alacrity, he accepted the cigarette I held out and went off to his bedroom to fetch the papers; as soon as he disappeared, Judy and Mrs. Xiao slipped in and went up the stairs to our room.

When I joined them a few minutes later with a stack of *Guizhou Dailys*, Judy had already poured our guest a cup of tea and given her one of our precious postcards of New York City at night, which she was examining with delight. With such small gifts were many relationships cemented.

Now Mrs. Xiao grew loquacious, her story bursting forth like a fountain. Once she had been married to a worker in a small paper-box printing factory. During the Cultural Revolution, everything printed there from toothpaste containers to cigarette cartons had quotations from Chairman Mao. In 1967 someone made a tragic mistake. The patriotic slogan of blessing for Chairman Mao, *wanshou wujiang,* "ten thousand years of life," was misprinted. Instead of the character 万, "ten thousand," one that looked very similar— 无 —was chosen. The slogan was now counterrevolutionary, for it wished Mao "no years of life."

Although the investigators never found out who was to blame, Mrs. Xiao's husband, as the man then on duty, was held responsible. He was locked up and criticized—it was only because there was a shred of doubt that he was not shot. Mrs. Xiao refused to divorce him, so she too lost her job. She became a member of "black society," the limbo of those without organizational membership. She collected refuse, kept bees, another uncontrolled occupation, and at times, during the winter, allowed herself to be picked up for begging, just so she would have food and shelter. Two years after he was imprisoned, she was told that her husband had died. She had no way of knowing if he had died of illness, committed suicide, starved, or been beaten to death.

She gave up all hope of a government job and had never considered remarriage. How could she have found a mate, she asked, when the "three door knocks" had been sufficient to make anyone lose interest? And even if she had found someone, who could have guaranteed that he too would not turn out to be a counterrevolutionary? "That's all behind me now," she said. "What I want to do now is to go into business and make some money!"

I realized how radically the economic reforms had changed the situation of people like Mrs. Xiao. The strength of the individual was being unleashed, the power monopoly of the work unit being broken. Mrs. Xiao was now on a more or less equal footing with other individual and nongovernment entrepreneurs, and it no longer mattered much what her political history had been, or what class background her ancestors had been from. The fringe members of society were moving into the mainstream. How very different than when I was growing up! Then, a person without a unit was like a ship without water, but Mrs. Xiao should no longer need to dread those questions about her job. To some people, her lack of affiliation would even seem enviable, for sometimes, if someone considered very useful to a work unit requested leave of absence to do business, the request was denied.

"What kind of business do you want to go into?" asked Judy, sensing that Mrs. Xiao had come to the main subject of her visit.

"I've been thinking about it for a long time," she confessed. "I'm very interested in foreigners. I've decided I'd like to be a tourist guide."

Of all the impractical ambitions! The tourist business, which was one of the state's main sources of foreign currency, was still tightly controlled. Furthermore, Guiyang was hardly a tourist center, and it was unlikely that many foreigners would be visiting here for many years to come, if ever. Jobs in foreign trade and tourist organizations were usually reserved as rewards for high-ranking cadres' children or university foreign languages department graduates, not for middle-aged ex-vagrants with no language skills!

For the next hour, we tried to explain how the tourist system worked in China, but Mrs. Xiao refused to believe we couldn't help her. If she couldn't be a guide, she said, then maybe she could be our agent to help us export Guizhou's precious hill medicines. We protested that we weren't in business, but she insisted that in that case we should consider going into it. Just as I was beginning to find Mrs. Xiao's obstinacy infuriating, I had a flash of brilliance. Why didn't she sell souvenirs! We told her about Westerners' fondness for T-shirts, which she found amusing and peculiar, and about their interest in the weaving, dyework, and handmade clothing of minority nationalities, which she found simply amazing. Why would anyone want to own cotton hand-work when they could buy synthetic clothing made by machine? However, we had pointed her in the right direction, and now she was bursting with ideas and excitement.

She could print "Guiyang" in nice calligraphy, and set up a booth in front of the foreigners' hotel! She could go to Guizhou's Yellow Fruit Tree Waterfall, the largest in China, a Yi minority area, and sell both T-shirts and ethnic clothing! She could even travel to the main tourist cities, to see what they were selling there!

For all her lack of experience, Mrs. Xiao seemed to be taking to business as naturally as if she had never been told that the individual economy was counterrevolutionary. She was full of imagination. I reflected that this third woman of Guiyang found consolation not in personal relationships as the noodle-shop owner Mrs. Yang did, nor in religion as the Hui woman Mrs. Ma did, but in the excitement of exploring the many avenues of life that had once been forbidden.

We felt exhausted by our conversation, but delighted to have been able to suggest a possible solution. It was already two a.m., and the purple lights of the hotel had long ago stopped flashing outside our window. The main entrance was doubtless locked and chained for the night. We had to take another risk and let Mrs. Xiao sleep in our room. On the way out the next morning, when many people were about, it was less likely that questions would be asked.

As soon as she had crawled into bed, probably the softest one she had ever lain on, Mrs. Xiao's breath grew heavy, as if she were already whirling in another world of T-shirts and cash. Judy and I, uncomfortably squeezed together on the narrow bed opposite, were slower to rest. Before I fell into my own oblivion, I remember hoping that someday Mrs. Xiao would realize her dreams.

THE
RED
ARMY
SPIRIT

THE ZUNYI TRAIN STATION was disproportionately large; or, depending on your point of view, it was suitably grand. Although Zunyi was only a Guizhou mountain town, it was a place rich in revolutionary significance. (The railway station in my hometown of Changsha was also incongruously magnificent, because Hunan Province had spawned Chairman Mao.) Here in Zunyi, in 1935, during the Long March, the "Great Helmsman" had won political victory over the wing of the Communist party taking its orders directly from the Soviet Union, the so-called Wang Ming faction. Mao's supremacy was rarely challenged from that time on. Was it not only appropriate, then, that the train station be huge?

Even in the freezing cold, Zunyi's entrepreneurs were out and busy. We bought ourselves face washes—the use of a kettle of warm water and a metal washbasin; we eschewed the much used towel. Then we went to buy tickets to our next stop for the following day. Judy held our place in the long line while I went to look at the chalk-written schedule on the wall. When I came back, she was engaged in conversation with a middle-aged woman. My heart sank: it was undoubtedly some overzealous foreign affairs bureaucrat or public security bureau officer, making sure we had the proper papers and were on our way to the foreigners' hotel.

"Spend tonight with us," the woman was saying in a low voice. "It's inexpensive and convenient. Just a five-minute walk away."

That didn't sound so bad. I was relieved to be spared the official inquiries, and Judy was eager to see what a private hostel was like. There had been none, of course, when we lived in China before, and if they were anything like the private restaurants, we thought we could expect far better treatment and living conditions than were provided in the slovenly state hotels. Government workers would certainly not have been out rustling up business! We followed the woman and her squarely built husband, who appeared out of nowhere and whisked up our bags. I wondered whether they knew that there were national regulations about where foreigners could stay; usually we had to argue to be allowed to sleep in Chinese hotels. In this out-of-the-way town there was probably only a single government hotel that met all the criteria for receiving foreigners: sufficiently comfortable to satisfy Chinese hospitality standards, sufficiently secure to guard against theft and incident, and sufficiently isolated to ensure the proper separation between insiders and outsiders.

The couple took us up a long flight of stairs past a cement-block high rise; behind the building, completely hidden from the road, lay a group of ramshackle homes leaning against each other for support like wooden playing cards. Apparently we had arrived in the private hostel district, for we saw at least ten crudely drawn signs with arrows pointing to the "Come Again Inn," the "Honorable Wealth Inn," the "Li Family Inn," the "Satisfaction Inn," and our own, "New People's Inn." It seemed only our hosts had gone out to find customers, for the rest lay quite silent. It was hard to imagine how anyone would know that rooms for rent lay hidden up here.

The innkeeper told us he had once been a government cadre in the town of Maotai, source of the famous liquor. He thought he could do better by going into business, and in 1982 had withdrawn from his post, adopting the unitless status that had once been the great humiliation of Mrs. Xiao of Guiyang. He borrowed money from the bank to rebuild this small cottage and now earned close to 500 *yuan* per month, after taxes, an excellent sum. He and his wife met every train until all the rooms were full; it seemed that even in revolutionary Zunyi, where I had expected the Maoist dislike of the individual economy to be deeply entrenched, government cadres agreed with the slogan "It's glorious to get rich!"

Inside the inn it was very dark, and much dirtier than we had expected. Our host led us up the stairs and across a narrow open ledge that had no railing and slanted precariously toward the cement courtyard below. Our room was tiny, with two hard beds and a table. Along the table were arranged, perhaps for decoration, empty bottles labeled with the names of the various brands of local liquor, most of which, we had been told, were very hard to buy even here. A chipped metal cup was half full of someone else's wet tea leaves; the sheets and pillow towel could have been washed no more recently than a month earlier. When I tried the bed, I feared I would be unable to sleep at all until Judy suggested I try putting my head at the higher end.

Though we could no longer say much for the superiority of private hotels, we were pleased to note how few questions we had been asked. We had been invited to sign our names into a guest book, but nobody demanded a letter of introduction, travel permission, or work permit. In the past, such documents were essential. Even if you slept at a friend's or relative's, you were supposed to register with the local public security bureau. Such restrictions had been basic to government control.

The following morning, when we explained we had come to visit the revolutionary sites, the innkeeper seemed surprised. That sort of thing appeared to have fallen out of fashion. Too bad we hadn't come a few weeks earlier, he said, for the fiftieth anniversary of the Zunyi Conference. Some old Red Army leaders now in the Central Committee had returned, and there was a parade. Ordinarily, not much happened in Zunyi.

His comments about the parade made me remember how, as a child, I was fascinated by anything "revolutionary." Few things distressed me more than having been born too late to run underground messages for the Red Army. I knew from the comic books that I read, two for a *fen* in the open-air street corner libraries, that little boys and girls evaded Kuomintang capture better than grown-ups, even though they too usually died heroically. Whenever my father reprimanded me or told me I was still too young to understand, I would go throw stones into the river and think angrily about how much he would respect me when the next war came and at last I could sacrifice myself for the revolution.

In those days, one of my favorite daydreams was about how I too would have joined the 6,000-mile Long March from the Jiangxi mountains to the Shaanxi caves, overcoming snowy mountains and treacherous boglands, and eating boiled leather belts and grass all along the way. I would have braved the iron bridge above the perilous gorge with the rest, never faltering in the face of enemy gunfire, falling silently, perhaps, as the bullets hit me, and disappearing in a blaze of glory into the icy water below.

I had heard living Red Army survivors speak: they came to our classroom in the *Hunan Daily* primary school, pulling up their shirts and rolling up their trousers to show off their proud scars. The Red Army taught us to live tough, to "temper" ourselves like iron in the fires of hardship. Through them, we knew how to be in the world; through them, we understood the makeup of our universe. They gave us our aspirations and values, and showed us the meaning of the revolution in its most concrete form.

However, I had not been permitted to live according to the spirit of the Red Army, for my mother was a rightist. With relentless inevitability, all my classmates were slowly accepted as Young Pioneers, but not I, because the party didn't trust an offspring of one of its "enemies." The Pioneers had been chosen to bear the torch of revolution for the next generation, they were the elite whose "thought" and ability to bear suffering were held to be superior to mine. When they were lucky, their bright red membership bandannas were tied about their necks by real Red Army veterans. How deeply I believed myself to have been misunderstood!

My childhood dream of joining the Red Army came true, in a sense, in the autumn of 1966. For a few months, almost all of us young people from the cities, those of good and bad background alike, had the chance to join the Cultural Revolution. In response to Chairman Mao's call, we dressed in imitations of Red Army uniforms and laboriously hiked along the route of the Long March, sharing in spirit the Red Army's hardships and pain, matching—we hoped—the revolutionary zeal of an earlier generation.

As one of fervent millions, I walked from my home (Chairman Mao's home!) in Hunan all the way to the Red Army's birthplace in the Jinggang Mountains. I cherished the sweet taste of cold, hunger, and illness. But my experience was limited as compared with that of many. There were five major revolutionary sites: the Jinggang Mountains, where the March began; Ruijin, from which another branch of the army set out; Zunyi, here, where Chairman Mao became supreme leader of the party; Yan'an, where the Communists regrouped their forces; and Beijing, the liberated capital. I had visited only the first and last. Now, almost twenty years later, when my feelings about the revolution were so different, the chance had come to improve my record.

Leaving our innkeeper, we took a bus to a park at the outskirts of the town, where we had been told there was a monument to the martyrs of the revolution. It was a chilly, drizzly day, but the schoolchildren were there, playing their after-class sports. Many of them were at just the age I had been when I loved the Red Army most. A small girl in a dirty red Young Pioneers scarf, with a big pink bow crowning her mussed-up hair and a drippy nose, came running in our direction. She did not notice our unusual appearance until she was nearly upon us, and she stopped short with a little shriek, staring up at my foreign camera with big eyes. It was a perfect opportunity.

"Little ghost," I said humbly, "can you help me? Can you tell me what the Red Army is?"

The little girl was dumbstruck, both at the sight of us and at my strange query. We were gathering a small crowd of children. I repeated my question for the general audience. There was much giggling and prodding, but finally a boy pointed courageously into the wooded hills where the white top of the monument could be seen. "There," he said.

"Not where is it, what is it?" I asked.

In a great burst of recitation, another boy announced, "The Red Army were martyrs of the revolution!"

The children were growing lively now. One volunteered that he had seen the Red Army soldiers in the movies, and that they had five red stars on their caps; then he had an animated argument with a playmate about whether any still existed in real life. (We learned later that in fact the city was full of veterans.)

"What about your father, was he in the Red Army?" we asked the big-eyed, snot-nosed little girl.

She immediately hid behind a taller child, peeking out to see if we were still looking at her.

"If he was, we would have moved into a new apartment by now," answered the older girl, apparently her sister, tartly scornful of my ignorance.

"We should learn from the Red Army not to be afraid of sacrifice," interrupted a tall boy, educating me as his teachers had educated him. "The Red Army teaches us the spirit of serving the people."

Clearly, in Zunyi the language of revolution hadn't been reformed out of existence. We walked on. It occurred to us to make some grown-up inquiries. Riding on the bus, we had noticed a large red billboard exhorting citizens to "Propagate the Spirit of the Zunyi Conference, Carry Out the Urban Economic Reforms Well!" Since we could not discern any connection between what we knew of Zunyi and the current reform policies, we hoped that local residents could enlighten us.

We walked for more than two hours, the whole way back to the hostel, stopping all kinds of people along the way. Did they remember the Red Army? What was the "spirit of the Zunyi Conference"? Could they please explain the relationship between the Long March and Deng Xiaoping's reforms?

Many people laughed outright at our questions—then a few, smiling broadly, gave us a stock answer: since Mao had gotten power here in Zunyi, "the spirit of the Zunyi Conference" meant "resolute determination in the face of all obstacles." "The Long March spirit" was needed for any long and difficult project that involved great self-sacrifice. That was why it was necessary for the reforms.

A small group of young men selling cassette tapes of Taiwan love songs at a makeshift sidewalk stand responded to our questions with particular hilarity. Then one of them grew grave and stated flatly that of course that slogan on the billboard made no sense at all. The Zunyi spirit was one of abnegation and absolute egalitarianism; the Long March was the very symbol of glory achieved through suffering and poverty. But the urban reforms encouraged a consumer economy and individual initiative. Under Deng Xiaoping, it was no longer counterrevolutionary to want to live better and enjoy life. We confessed that was what we thought, too, and walked away feeling a bit guilty at having feigned ignorance.

We tried again, in a magazine shop, in an old and twisting wooden lane, in a dry goods store. Everywhere, we met the same responses: giddy hilarity; embarrassment; fragments of remembered stock phrases; bafflement. Two fashionable young women from whom we bought an orange remembered something about the Red Army—that there was a roller skating rink at the base of the Martyrs' Monument. Heaven knew why we were asking such weird questions about the spirit of the Zunyi Conference!

Judy and I left Zunyi late that night, feeling that it might be impossible to resolve the paradox implied by that slogan, "Propagate the Spirit of the Zunyi Conference, Carry Out the Urban Economic Reforms Well!" Perhaps, in this transitional period, it was understandable that the two share the same strange space. The balance between them was not constant and would doubtless continue to shift, sometimes one in the ascendant, sometimes the other. The Chinese people would have to keep guessing from one day to the next how much ideology would be governing their lives.

Our departure was near midnight, in a fine rain, the lights of the train station so dim that they seemed to give off no illumination. The sleeping car was already dark, for it was after ten o'clock. Only a pale row of lights shone along the floor of the corridor, revealing swaddled, still bodies in layers of three up to the ceiling, as if at a crematorium. A weary female conductor showed us our bunks with a flashlight, her beam flickering past an overladen luggage rack that stretched the length of the car. Beneath hung a tidy row of tattered facecloths on a slender metal bar, each one folded over once and once again, an echo of the disciplined, militarized life of communal living and forced relocations. The heavy air of stale, sweet cigarette smoke, accumulated through long hours of diligent inactivity, was tinged with the moldy dampness of old terry cloth and carbon monoxide from the coal-burning water vat.

This was a so-called hard sleeper, a second-class car. First-class would have offered us four people instead of six to a section; heavy gray upholstery instead of hard, narrow bunks; a lace doily and perhaps a plant on the table; attentive hot-water pourers; a door that closed and even locked; and shorter lines at the toilet in the morning. But one of the functions of the class system on trains was to separate the elite from the masses, and we always found it more interesting to travel with ordinary folk than with high-ranking cadres, military men, or foreigners. With practiced movements, we tucked our shoes under the bottom bunks and climbed the metal ladders to our berths beneath the ceiling.

As was usual, the loudspeakers went off at 5:30 a.m., first an electrified pop tune, then the "news." This was followed by glass-splitting local opera in falsetto, with plenty of gongs and static. It was still pitch-dark outside, but all the lights in the car blazed with a vengeance. I groaned. The man sleeping diagonally below me put his pillow over his head. The two on the bottom began resignedly to collect their tin cups and toothbrushes, and to pull their frayed facecloths from the rod. There would already be a line for the toilet and sink. I turned to the wall, outrage fighting with exhaustion.

It was hopeless. I wriggled my trousers on over my long underwear and climbed down. The occupants of the two lower bunks, unshaven men in their mid-thirties, had returned from the washbasins. One wore a black turtleneck sweater, its shoulder closed with a big clumsy zipper. His companion, a long-haired man in dungarees, had a gray sweater-vest on over a white shirt which was bright and shiny at the back of the neck with old sweat and oil. They had already lit their morning cigarettes, and nodded to me in a friendly way, holding out the pack. When I returned from my wash we chatted, and I learned they were purchasers for a machine tool factory in Chengdu, returning from a trip to the Shenzhen Special Economic Zone, where they had tried to buy a certain piece of imported equipment but failed because their factory wasn't authorized to change enough *yuan* for hard currency.

The men had bought breakfast tickets while I was fighting off the loudspeaker, and when a dining hall worker wheeled a cart of *song fan,* "sent meals," down the corridor, they exchanged them for oblong metal containers with noodles and meat, and two pairs of wet chopsticks. They ate fast, chewing up the bones and gristle, then spitting them out. I decided to go to the dining car, where there would be more choice and slightly better food, including rice porridge and steamed white *mantou* buns. Judy was prepared to take care of herself with her usual instant coffee and milk powder.

In the din and chaos in the meal car, someone unusual caught my attention. At first, I wasn't sure if she was a woman—she was —or a man. She was about twenty-five, nearly six feet tall, and very heavy and strong. She was wearing high leather boots and a tan and brown corduroy pants suit unlike any made in China, covered all over with pockets and zippers. Her hair was cut short. But it had been her voice that first made me turn and look at her table, for it was arrogant and distinctive, a voice used to commanding far more than just a cleaner pair of chopsticks. It was the voice of a unique breed of Chinese: the voice of a *gaoganzidi,* a high-ranking cadre's child. I saw what could be achieved with that voice: the head cook brought the new chopsticks himself, asking solicitously if she didn't also want a bowl of egg soup. She declined, in a tone that implied that eggs, usually considered a luxury for breakfast in China, were beneath her.

When, twenty minutes later, I returned to my section of bunks, to my surprise I found the woman standing there. She was leaning with her elbow on a middle bunk, her other hand on a thrust-out hip, talking with the Chengdu buyers, who had moved to the flip-down corridor seats by the window. Apparently she had slept on the bed below mine so I had not noticed her; perhaps the Spring Festival crush of travelers had made it impossible for her to buy a first-class "soft sleeper" ticket. She had her sleeve rolled back over her strong forearm to reveal a complex digital watch, and she was showing off its many functions, toting up sums on its calculator face. "This way," she boasted, "I'm always ready to make a quick transaction." She scarcely glanced at me as I squeezed by and found a seat by Judy, who was combing her hair on one of the bottom bunks.

I listened to the conversation with interest. Having seen all that the watch could do, the men proceeded to admire her outfit, praising it outrageously, feeling the rich corduroy while she demonstrated how well foreign zippers worked, zipping smoothly back and forth at her shoulder pocket, at her knee, at her waist. Then she sat down, her back to me, to show off the softness of her leather boots, and the man in the black turtleneck fumbled in his overjacket to offer her a cigarette. It was a Double Happiness brand, one of China's best, often passed out at weddings. The woman sniffed at it, and the other man, quick on the draw, produced a Zhonghua.

"None of your cigarettes are any good," she said impatiently. "I'll be right back. The trainmaster will be able to do better."

When she left, the buyer in the turtleneck turned to me, suddenly dropping his slavish manner. "Don't underestimate that girl," he said. "She's got incredible connections. Every buyer in Chengdu has heard of her." He told me that her name was Fu Weiguo, "Defend the Country" Fu, and that her father, a Long March veteran from near Zunyi, was a commander of a large military district. During the late Cultural Revolution years, when most young people were still being sent to the countryside, he had arranged for her to join the army. There, because of her height, she had become a volleyball star for one of the provincial army teams.

Nowadays, however, opportunities and requirements were different. It was not enough to be a volleyball star with a salary of less than eighty *yuan* a month. In the buyer's envious opinion, anyone in her position who hadn't switched to business would have been a fool. She didn't know anything about buying and selling, perhaps, but all she had to do was team up with some people who did. Her father's Red Army "face" combined with a little professional know-how made her a powerhouse. After all, her father's comrades-in-arms were all "uncles" to her when she was growing up, and today she had connections in charge of finance, banking, and economic planning, in both the Provincial and Municipal Party Committees. The party secretary of the machine tool factory in Chengdu to which the buyers were attached was among her father's old comrades: she would come in a chauffeured Toyota to make deals with him, and all the dining hall cooks were set to preparing a banquet. Her connections could be found in the SEZs as well, in the foreign trade and foreign exchange bureaus. Her company imported television sets, VCRs, motorcycles, air conditioners, and washing machines, all of them high-grade goods tightly controlled by the state, highly coveted, and exceedingly profitable in private hands.

The buyer broke off our conversation as soon as he saw that the young athlete was back, two packs of 555s in her hand. She unwrapped one and held it out to her admirers, ignoring us, perhaps to show that to someone like herself, foreigners were no big deal. The buyers now ignored us, too. They were doing their best to *la guanxi* with her, to "draw a connection." It was plain that they were willing to go to any lengths to do so. They brought out a bottle of imported Scotch whisky, which must have cost them dearly, filling their two glass screw-top jars and borrowing our metal cup for a third. Judy and I moved over to the corridor window seats to get out of their way. As the men toasted the Red Army daughter's success, we watched the lush fields of Sichuan roll by.

The woman was glad to have such an attentive audience and seemed to feel she had nothing to hide. She drank with the men in a way I had rarely seen a Chinese woman do, especially with strangers before lunchtime, and she accepted a handful of salted sunflower seeds with none of the usual obligatory pretense at refusal. The men were good drinkers, and the flush of liquor soon flooded the skin below their eyes.

Miss Fu, condescension, boredom, and arrogance never leaving her voice, told how, through her father's old comrades, she would obtain scarce local products that were usually under the jurisdiction of the state, like soybeans and maotai. She transported them to the SEZs, where she could exchange them for imported goods, which she would sell at a profit back in Sichuan. However, she complained, more and more well-connected people were getting involved in such projects. She guessed that 80 percent of all sports and film stars were now doing business. And some were the children of governors and ministers, whose names she dropped with an air of confiding privileged information. "It's not just a question of soybeans, for them," she said, "they control coal and lumber, steel and oil!"

As became gradually clear, she was also involved in another scam. She collected Chinese *yuan* from local customers in Sichuan —no problem, since many people were loaded with cash because of recent high bonuses, and had little to spend it on. Traveling to an SEZ, she exchanged the currency for Foreign Exchange Certificates on the black market, bought the goods (at a low price because she had hard currency), and pocketed the profits. She herself never took the risk of standing outside the exit where the Hong Kong passengers got off—she had underlings do it for her. If they were caught, all they had to do to evade further trouble was exchange some currency for the security bureau. By trading in currency, Miss Fu said, especially during the major tourist seasons and the Spring Festival, when so many overseas Chinese came to visit their relatives, she could quadruple her cash in a day's time.

"What about taxes?" one of the men wanted to know. (Taxes on imported goods could run as high as 55 percent of their purchase price.)

"Never heard of them," she responded, with a proud toss of her head. "My company is tax-free."

An expression of admiration bordering on worship crossed the faces of the two buyers. Obviously, her connections extended to the customs administration. "If I started a company, could you help me become tax-free too?" the black turtleneck wanted to know, trying to make a desperately serious question sound like a casual joke. But she avoided the question. Perhaps she thought the men had little to offer but the bottle of Scotch and the tin of salted pork they had taken out and were picking at to complement the liquor.

After several hours had passed there was a lull in the conversation. "Let's take a picture together," suggested the man in dungarees, suddenly inspired. "Meeting you is a great honor for us. We have 'long heard your great name.'"

I was pressed into service as a photographer, and the three squeezed themselves together for the formal iconization of their acquaintanceship, Miss Fu almost a head taller than the two men.

This ritual reminded me of the experience of a certain friend of mine, the son of an ordinary Beijing traffic policeman. He had a friend who was the son of a high party official. They had got to know each other when, as "educated youths," they were sent down to the countryside. Later, as a special favor, his friend had given him a photograph of his powerful father, which proved to be very useful when my friend, posing as an overseas Chinese, was trying to get into hotels or shops for foreigners in order to buy scarce goods. Whenever his disguise failed, all he had to do was pull out the photo as proof of his *guanxi*. He told me that gatekeepers were terrified of offending high-ranking cadres' children. Their "backing" was made of steel. If the police made the mistake of harassing them, their fathers were never far away. It was often the unlucky security official who ended up being criticized. Repulsive as was the sight of these two buyers toadying to their *gaoganzidi*, I could see that few people would be in a position to pass up a similar opportunity.

It was nearly lunchtime, and the trainmaster came to our car and asked Miss Fu if she would be eating with the first-class travelers. "I always take this train," she boasted to the buyers when he had left. "He knows me. I never have trouble with transport fees."

When she had been summoned to her meal, the man in the black turtleneck opened up one of the plastic bags on the table and brought out a small pressed duck. His manner had grown suddenly somber, even disgruntled. "She eats hers, we eat ours," he said. "But we don't necessarily eat any worse." He ripped off a fat leg and handed it to his friend, then urged me to have some too. It looked very good, so, after several invitations, I accepted with thanks. Later I would bring down the string bag of bananas hanging up by our bunks near the ceiling. Judy, having spent the morning accumulating an enormous pile of peanut shells, declined to join in.

"Didn't you say you've been to Shenzhen?" asked the buyer. "What do you think of her operations?"

I decided to be frank. I said that it seemed to me the back door played entirely too great a role in the "enlivening of the economy." Companies founded on little but *guanxi* and shady practices, I had the impression, were common.

The man sighed. Yes, he agreed, but what could you do? Apart from those out of work and waiting to be assigned work, many of those in business for themselves—and by far the majority of those playing for the highest stakes—were high-ranking cadres' children. "Aiya, how can we compete with them?" he asked. He threw the strong liquor down his throat, pursing his lips in bitter enjoyment. He seemed like another person, one full of pent-up resentment. "I've been a buyer since age eighteen," he confided. "I built my skills slowly. At first I didn't know how to drink or smoke, and then I slowly learned how to use liquor and cigarettes and wine to draw my connections. I learned how to carry different brands with me. One kind of cigarette for a driver, another for a factory leader." He grew defiantly proud. "I'm famous in my factory." He leaned heavily against his colleague and patted him on the shoulder. "He knows I'm not boasting. I'm famous in my whole district for my *guanxi*. If I want a long distance telephone line, all I have to do is ask for it. Out of seven operators, every single one of them recognizes my voice." He told us how each time he came back from the SEZs, he brought the women gifts—of cosmetics, perfume, and blue jeans. "They block every line in the district so my calls can get through. Whether my factory needs cement, steel, or transportation, the leaders always turn to me, since I'm the only one with all the right back doors."

However, the thought of all this success seemed only to make him unhappy. He seemed on the verge of drunken tears. "What I do is nothing compared with what people like her can do. How can someone like me compete? I can buy a hard sleeper ticket on the express train, so I'm better off than the peasants who have to take any slow train that stops in their town. It takes me no more than three days to get from Chengdu to Shenzhen. But she could go by plane if she wanted to, and get there in a few hours! She's been doing business for only a few months, and already she answers to no one. Do you think it's because she's smart? No, it's just because she's the daughter of an old Red Army man!"

His friend tried to calm him down. "Now what's there to be so upset about?" he said soothingly, twisting the duck apart and passing over a greasy thigh. "It's not as if you haven't known about people like her for a long time! Most companies are run by *gaoganzidi*. It's not just the economy, but the political reforms, too, the third echelon. Aren't most of them *gaoganzidi*?"

I was well aware of this situation. Since Deng Xiaoping had begun emphasizing younger, educated, revolutionary leaders to replace the so-called second echelon, the Soviet-oriented generation in their fifties, many of my friends had come into positions of some power. (The "first echelon" was represented by leaders of Deng's own generation.) But the really influential new leaders —the vice-premiers, ministers, governors—were mostly children of high-ranking cadres, especially children of Red Army veterans. These young people, because of their parents' impeccable credentials, satisfied the need for continuity with the revolutionary tradition and heritage. They were one way of defending the departures from orthodoxy, while retaining enough links with the past to keep the tens of thousands content who still had so much invested in the revolution. I admired Deng for moving some of the most stubborn old Red Army men out of power in a peaceful way, but I also felt worried, because the newly promoted *gaoganzidi* had grown up in an elitist atmosphere of special privileges. It was certain that they would retain some of the most feudal aspects of the old system. It seemed to me that in the course of its attempted reforms, China had ended up reviving some of its own worst cultural traditions. Foreign trade conducted through power, hierarchy, and personal relations was only an example. It would not surprise me if, in the future, a wealthy new urban commercial class was formed primarily of high-ranking cadres' children. This would truly be a Chinese-style merchant elite.

Our black-turtlenecked friend had stopped drinking, at his companion's urging. Judy peeled a banana and handed it to him. His face was still purple with drunkenness. He was sweating and had partly unzipped the big shiny zipper at his neck. If Miss Fu hadn't been due to return soon, his mutterings probably would have gone on through the siesta.

"Eat up, she'll be back soon," said the man in dungarees. "Don't forget, the most important thing is to establish the relationship. A friend like her could do a lot for us."

Reminded of this incontrovertible fact of life, the buyer seemed to pull himself together. He poured what was left of his whisky back into the bottle and put it away. He leaned back against a pillow and closed his eyes. I followed his example. The loudspeaker had been given a rest.

In the silence that fell over our small group, I reflected that in Miss Fu, this Red Army daughter, lay part of the explanation for the embarrassed confusion we had encountered in Zunyi the day before. True, the Red Army had been heroes, uneducated and oppressed peasants and social outcasts who traded their legs and arms, their health, and their lives to make a new China. At first it had probably seemed only natural that they should enjoy special treatment, for they had earned the gratitude of the people. But their children had not been heroes, yet they rarely questioned their right to use their parents' status, rarely felt ashamed or thought of it as a form of corruption. Some were even known to have raped and murdered with impunity. Now, propaganda appeals to the "Red Army spirit" seemed not only meaningless but a travesty. Those who volunteered to "eat bitterness" were often regarded not as heroes, but as fools.

It seemed to me that the disillusionment of people with revolutionary symbols like the Red Army could be understood as one aspect of the current crisis in values, of the materialistic trend and the worship of the West. Without an accepted common myth of its origins and destiny, the life of any nation will seem fragmented and purposeless. China's wealth of shared public symbols was once unparalleled. Now, however, many of them had become devoid of meaning, or poisoned with negative associations. The Red Army, the Long March, the Zunyi Conference, the song "The East Is Red," the revolutionary color red, and the image of Chairman Mao himself, his once omnipresent statues, busts, and portraits: these symbols no longer spoke to most Chinese people any longer. They had lost their power to inspire and to explain the world.

Miss Fu came back, looking a bit red in the face too. Judy and I politely yielded our seats and moved again over to the window. We understood that to the buyers, time with Miss Fu was precious. All that afternoon in the clattering, shaking train, accompanied by the ceaseless din of local opera over the loudspeaker, the two buyers expertly and patiently drew their relationship. Sometimes I fell into contemplation of the scenery; sometimes I turned to look at the arrogant athlete leaning back against the pillows in her corduroy pants suit and tall boots, and at the two men, bent over with their elbows on their knees, plying her with cigarettes, smiling at her, hauling the thermos from beneath the table to freshen her tea.

ENGINEERS OF HUMAN SOULS

I WAS IN NEW YORK during the campaign against spiritual pollution, but the fear of Chinese intellectuals was palpable even there. A number of visiting scholars telephoned me to ask for help in extending their stay abroad, for few wanted to go back to accusations that while in the West they had become steeped in decadence. I myself was convinced that another Cultural Revolution could be on the way, for tales of red-armbanded youths brandishing scissors against stylish haircuts reminded me all too well of the nightmarish search raids of my childhood, in which Father's neckties and books ended up on the bonfire. Accounts filtering out to us in the West about repression in life-style—clothing, social dancing, and pop music—were far less alarming to me than tales of writers forced to make self-criticisms. That was how the Cultural Revolution had begun.

During the autumn of 1983, younger writers, in particular, came under attack, with older ones mobilized to speak out against them. In their work, the young members of my generation had been exploring the roots and costs of the Cultural Revolution, the harm done to basic human relationships by making political values all-important, and the value of self-expression and the individual for art and society. Now they were being charged with "creating disorder in the minds of the young" and "spreading doubts about socialism and the Communist party." It seemed obvious to me that in fact, the "crisis of belief" among China's youth had developed because of their experiences during the Cultural Revolution, not because they had read some novel in which a KMT general's grandson falls in love with the grand-daughter of a Communist.

News of the campaign against spiritual pollution affected me deeply, for I knew that had I still been living in China I could have found myself in serious trouble. The campaign brought back a flood of memories about the suffering of creative people in China, about the impossibility of producing anything free from political considerations. It made me remember with particular vividness the height of my own struggles with the artistic bureaucracy, my college years. At that time, I was always waiting for the postman, hoping for a favorable response to one of my literary efforts. I was invariably disappointed.

The first time I sent out a story was in 1974, when I was still working at the lubricating oil factory. It was a harmless tale about brave workers trying to overcome the problem of waste and laziness in their plant. The editors wrote back that before they could consider my submission for publication, they needed to see a letter of introduction from my factory's Political Work Office validating my family's class background and my own "political performance"; I also needed a letter from the Propaganda Office attesting to my enthusiasm for revolutionary art and my activism in my unit's mass propoganda activities. Of course, I had always done my best to avoid the leaders of these offices; my class background, intellectual, was one of the worst, and I was hardly an eager participant in such programs as learning to sing *The Legend of the Red Lantern* or any of the other eight "model operas." In fact, at the time, most of the surviving writers who had any integrity were still in the countryside or labor camps, or had long ago been frightened into silence. To be a writer in Mao's China was simply to be an officially recognized propagandist for party policies.

That didn't discourage me from wanting to write, however,

and I was far from alone. One of my greatest enjoyments was to meet on Saturday nights with a small group of friends, during the electricity outages that were so frequent in those days, passing around manuscripts, reciting poetry, and discussing literature by the flickering light of a kerosene lamp. My own specialty was reciting Shakespeare's sonnets, as translated into Chinese before the revolution, in (as I imagined) a properly grandiose oratorical style. I remember many of the poems today, and the thought of those daring and emotionally charged evenings fills me with nostalgic affection.

After Mao's death and the fall of the Gang of Four, the emphasis on writers' class backgrounds gradually decreased, although the political content of their works was still very important. The literary sensibilities of my young friends and I developed too, from naive revolutionary aesthetics to an awareness that there were other possibilities for literature, that it might be about life itself, not merely an educational tool or propaganda for the current party campaign. When I was in college, I began to submit my stories again.

But magazine editors were invariably unhappy about the dangerous social effects of my work. Often they didn't bother to respond at all; at other times, my manuscripts would be returned with letters criticizing my "thought," "helping" me to improve my attitude. I sent out so many stories that there were fat rejected packages waiting for me several times a month in the wooden rack at the entrance to the dormitory. I was the envy of my classmates, who told me that if so many publishers were writing to me, surely there must be hope.

Once I sent a story called "Price" to a Nanjing literary magazine. It was about the suffering of a couple unable to live together for their entire married lives because of the "needs of the state," a very common situation in China at that time, and one that exists even today. The rejection note said, "The story you have told is not typical in our society. The political message is of exceedingly base quality. We hope that you will pay more attention to your political study. As an 'engineer of human souls,' a writer's first task is to raise his political consciousness . . ."

Aside from such disappointments, these efforts cost me at most a few *fen* for stamps, and many hours of hand copying (there were, of course, no Xerox machines), for which, I am ashamed to confess, I often enlisted the help of various girl friends. But my adventure in screenwriting was another matter. It cost me months of scrimping on my meager worker's salary, months of cutting down on cigarettes, of accepting the criticisms of my department leaders for my absence in class, and weeks of late night copying, for it was a very fat screenplay indeed.

Film was a passionate interest of mine for a time, and I spent every spare moment reading scripts, and books on the history of film and the technical aspects of production. The filmscript I spent so much time on was about Dr. Norman Bethune, the Canadian doctor made by Chairman Mao into a symbol of communist internationalism. Of course, a movie about his glorious life as a hero had already been made, but according to some things I had read, Bethune had many ordinary human traits as well. I thought there should be another version. When my work was at last done, it seemed too important simply to send off through the mails. Against the advice of all my friends, I resolved to go to Beijing on my hard-saved money to approach a director myself.

The guard at the gate of the Beijing Film Studio treated me as if I were not in my right mind. Not only wouldn't he notify any directors of my arrival, but he wouldn't even let me in, staring at me with suspicious eyes as I tried to persuade him, then criticizing me for not peacefully attending to my studies. Only reluctantly, to make me go away, did he allow me to leave my script with him. I am quite sure that it never made it inside.

A bit daunted, I went nevertheless to the army's August First Film Studio, also in Beijing. There, I was received better. The soldier on duty, moved by my tale of devotion to film, made a phone call and arranged for me to go inside to the screenplay office. The writers there were polite about my innocence, patiently explaining that an ordinary person had not a chance in the world of having a script accepted. Film was centrally controlled, and they themselves learned only by directive what subjects were to be treated and which of them was to write what. The head of the office accompanied me out. "There is already a state-approved film on the life of Bethune," he told me kindly. "How could there be a second one? I'm sorry, but on the strength of this alone, you have wasted your time." He saw me out of the compound with pitying finality.

Back in Changsha, my more realistic friends thought it a grand success that I had been allowed in the gate.

This painful experience put an end to my fascination with scriptwriting. My enthusiasm had been rebuffed, and it took me months to get over the humiliation. Perhaps if I had been born into another world, I would be working in film today. Ironically however, although my filmscript went into the fire, many of my unwelcome stories were published years later in overseas Chinese newspapers and magazines. Undoubtedly, if Chinese arts officials saw them, they found them full of spiritual pollution.

The campaign against spiritual pollution ended suddenly in early 1984, but I continued to worry about the fate of those writers who had been attacked, unsure whether the movement's repercussions would be so short-lived. Even if the phrase "spiritual pollution" had fallen into disfavor, that did not necessarily mean that the damage had been repaired. In returning to China, therefore, one of my priorities was to meet with writers and artists. Two of the most revealing encounters took place in Xi'an.

I knew that a young writer named Jia Pingao had been one of the most prominent victims of the campaign, singled out for criticism by the prime moving force behind it, Propaganda Chief Deng Liqun. As any Chinese knew, when you were "criticized by name" the situation was far graver than in cases where your name was not mentioned, even though everyone knew who you were. In early 1981, for example, in the aftermath of Changsha's democratic election movement, "the thought of a certain student"—me—was repudiated in loudspeaker broadcasts, but I knew that as long as my name was omitted, I was physically safe. Jia's name, on the other hand, had appeared in some of the most influential national literary magazines, along with detailed criticisms of the negativism, cynicism, and lack of heroes in his work. One story in particular, "Ghost Town," was attacked. It was a tale of violence and revenge among Cultural Revolution factions in an isolated peasant village, and of the friendship painfully established among the crippled survivors. Critics said it implied that relationships among people in modern socialist China were equally tense.

My plan was to reach Jia through a local literary magazine editor with whom I had had some correspondence. The editor said he knew Jia but did not know where he lived. He suggested that I go see a certain man named Zhao, another writer and an editor at the Shaanxi People's Publishing House. Zhao could lead me to Jia, for the two were close friends.

The publishing house dormitory proved unusually difficult to find, and when at last Judy and I located the right street, we realized that part of the problem lay in our assumption that the building would be inside a large work-unit compound with a gate. In fact, the dormitory lay at the end of a narrow alley, bordered on two sides by ordinary one-story wooden residences with laundry hanging on lines outside and a ditch running with wash water. The cement-block building was entered at one end by a wet, black corridor lit only by two small yellow light bulbs, and the common toilet stank. It reminded me of the Hunan Teachers College dorms, where I had once lived with seven classmates in a single room.

A little girl who had been rinsing a rag mop in a large

washroom sink directed us to Zhao's room, where a lovely older woman opened the door, her hair tied up in an ornate classical style and her beauty contrasting with the plainness of her surroundings. Beyond her we saw a typical urban room, with new-looking, overvarnished blond furniture and a small coal-burning stove set on the cement floor in the center, a tubular metal chimney leading out a hole in the window. Trying to hide her surprise, the woman invited us in. When we introduced ourselves, she apologized gracefully in a strong Shaanxi accent for the absence of her husband, and sat us down on padded chairs and poured us tea. From our new vantage point, we noticed on the desk a group of framed black and white photographs of her in heavy makeup and various costumes. She must be a performer? A retired singer of local Shaanxi opera, she confessed, with becoming embarrassment. She had decided not to return to the stage after she and her husband had been "sent down" to the countryside for reeducation more than fifteen years earlier, she for her performance of "reactionary" historical roles, he for his love of classical literature. She felt life was simpler and safer this way.

When we inquired after Jia Pingao, she told us that she and her husband came to know him in the countryside, when he was an "educated youth" sent to live among the peasants. Her husband had agreed to take him on as an unofficial private student, and even now he came often to see them. But she didn't know where Jia lived. She offered to fetch her husband from a hotel room that had been rented for him by the publishing house. He was finishing a historical novel there, she explained, because it was too noisy in the dormitory.

We were reluctant to disturb him but, with characteristic Chinese hospitality, his wife insisted that he would certainly wish to meet guests from so far away. We were equally firm, suggesting that we come back later in the afternoon so he would have a full day in which to write.

When we returned, Zhao, a thin, handsome older gentleman,

answered our knock. The narrow room was already thick with cigarette smoke. The actress was nowhere to be seen, but inside sat a young man—Jia Pingao—and a young woman. They all shook hands with us warmly and urged us to take the padded chairs. Zhao and Jia Pingao, an unprepossessing, wiry young man nearly buried in a heavy navy-blue down jacket, drew up low, backless bamboo stools. The woman, a fresh-faced, wholesome-looking person in short, conservative braids of a style quickly being permed out of existence, perched on a small sheet of green plastic on the edge of the wooden bed.

Zhao welcomed us with a literary language delivered in a rich, deliberate voice. It was easy to believe that he wrote historical novels, for his speech was unusually measured, full of the four-character compounds common in the traditional operas his wife had once performed. It was difficult to tell whether his formal manner was habitual or inspired by our presence: it was surely the first time foreigners had come to his home.

The younger two seemed to share little of his sense of ceremony. They besieged us with questions about the Western literary world, about the publishing system, about the relationship between writers and editors. We learned that the young woman, whose name was Li, had also been a student of Zhao's in the countryside, and later Jia's editor at the Shaanxi People's Publishing House. Now she was a party official at the Provincial Publishing Bureau, an organization that oversaw the several publishing houses of the province. She was yet another of those educated young people being promoted as part of the drive to bring in new leaders.

"Jia Pingao's stock has just gone up," Miss Li joked. "Since the campaign against spiritual pollution he's become famous!" Jia blushed modestly. He didn't look much like a writer at all. He had a peasant's short-cropped hair, dark skin, and occasionally incomprehensible local accent. He was a quiet man, a good listener, with great personal charm that emerged suddenly when he spoke and laughed. When we asked him what the campaign had been like for writers in Xi'an, he deferred to his old teacher.

Zhao said that he himself was a writer of uncontroversial war novels set in ancient times, so he had been exempt from attack, but he had been worried on Jia's behalf. "I believed Jia had done nothing wrong, and I urged him not to be afraid," he said. "Certain leaders are unused to reading about real people. They couldn't find the usual revolutionary heroes in his stories, and it disturbed them that they couldn't figure out what 'types' his characters represented." The older man glanced at Jia, who looked healthy and carefree, rocking comfortably back against a wardrobe with his boots resting on a crumbling red brick beneath the stove. "After the Cultural Revolution, the fuss about spiritual pollution seemed like nothing at all. Compared with the physical attacks, the book burnings, the public humiliations of those days, it was just a tempest in a teapot."

Jia spoke, drawing deeply on a cigarette between words. His forefingers were stained deep tobacco yellow. He smiled as if at an amusing memory. "They used to call me over to the Propaganda Department in the Municipal Party Committee just so they could give me special help with my reeducation. They would read me documents from the center issued especially about me and my work, and then I would write self-criticisms for the rest of the day." He told us that officials had to search through the whole city to find another writer willing to come up with a statement criticizing him. Everyone found an excuse. Finally, when they found somebody who couldn't get out of it, the man went secretly to Jia's house to warn him and apologize in advance.

"I was put in charge of criticizing him for the Publishing Bureau," the young woman told us, continuing the story. "I had just been given a post supervising ideological work. There we were, Jia, me, and a few others, with me in charge of criticizing the writing of one of my best friends! It was an absurd situation," she said, her smile revealing a row of straight white teeth. "I had edited a lot of those works. The two of us had invented tricks to persuade the leaders to let some of the sticky passages pass. I had always been Jia's first and most trusted reader ever since we were Teacher Zhao's students together in the countryside."

Party officials had often used this strategy, I knew: pitting friends and relatives against one another was one of the best ways of demoralizing a criticism target. But this time it didn't seem to have worked.

"If you had asked me for my personal opinion," Miss Li continued, "I would have said that Jia's work was just what we need in China: stories about ordinary people, about the suffering caused by the Cultural Revolution, about common human relationships."

"So what did you do?" asked Judy, fascinated.

"I went to his place as soon as I heard what I was supposed to do, and we talked about how to handle ourselves."

"And I told her that whatever happened, it wouldn't change our friendship," Jia said. "We both knew we had to go through the motions."

"So I criticized his negative thought, the lack of positive models in his work, his implication that socialism is not good." Miss Li spoke as if she were reciting a familiar list. "I said you couldn't see the greatness of the Communist party in his stories, that there was no 'bright socialist future' to contrast with the tense Cultural Revolution relationships he described. It was all in the literary magazines, so I knew the exact words to use: 'Jia Pingao is a talented young writer, but he should earnestly study Marxism-Leninism, and use a Marxist-Leninist standpoint and method to analyze life. Only then can he progress in his creative work . . .'"

The memory of these sessions seemed to afford Jia and his friend huge entertainment. "I acknowledged it all," said Jia with a mock-serious expression. "I said I hadn't taken seriously my glorious responsibility as a socialist writer to write constructive spiritual works. I hadn't produced literature in accordance with the requirements of our socialist times, hadn't given my readers confidence, hope, and strength. But," he continued, "I never stopped writing. I just got used to the idea that pretty much anything I wrote would be criticized. Under those circumstances, I might as well write whatever I pleased."

Times seemed to have changed. When I was ordered to "draw a clear line of distinction" between myself and my "rightist" mother, I did so, and thus cut her out of my life just when I needed her most. When I was told to write criticism reports about my "bourgeois journalist" father, I did so, and it ripped the heart out of me. During the Cultural Revolution, many were forced to criticize parents, teachers, and friends. If you couldn't bear it, the only alternative was often to kill yourself, as the Guiyang woman's daughter had done. Betrayal was an accepted part of our morality: the closer you were to the person you denounced, the more gloriously revolutionary you were. We barely resisted, whether the victimizations in which we participated, or those which we silently witnessed, not daring to interfere. But if there was anything to be said for that era, it was that the lessons learned then seemed to have made it possible for this writer and this editor to preserve their friendship despite the state's effort to destroy it. The criticizer and criticized had seen through the whole enterprise, and this turned it into an empty ritual without force.

We were told that Jia Pingao's unfortunate situation continued some months after the campaign officially ended. He was unable to publish his stories, and some people dared not appear too friendly to him. During that time, popular rumor in the literary world had it that what had lain behind the campaign was, as is so often the case, not artistic concerns but political ones. The real problem was not the content of the writers' works, but rather the opposition of some ideological hard-liners to the reformers'

Western-oriented open door policies and liberalization of the economy. Some even said that it had been a personal vendetta by Propaganda Chief Deng Liqun against General Party Secretary Hu Yaobang, who had been expanding his power by placing his old associates from the Communist Youth League in key positions.

Then in the fall of 1984, talk had turned away from the campaign against spiritual pollution to the national Writers' Conference, which was to be the first convened in China since the lively and emotional one held in 1979. It was expected that it would be far less liberal than the earlier gathering—the slates of delegates from each province had been chosen under the shadow of the campaign against spiritual pollution, and many of the more outspoken writers had not been included. Jia told us that he had not, of course, been on the Shaanxi Province list.

My writer friends from Hunan had told me that they were at first quite uninterested in participating. The October preliminary meeting presided over by the Propaganda Committee and the almost equally hard-line arts organizations under the Ministry of Culture had sounded warnings against "bourgeois liberalism." This was reminiscent of the 1981 crackdown on writers, which focused on criticism of *Bitter Love,* Bai Hua's famous screenplay about the unrequited devotion to China of an artist who is persecuted to death during the Cultural Revolution. ("This is not a typical situation," critics complained—but who among educated Chinese did not know an artist who died through violence or injustice during those days?)

Jia confirmed what I had already heard: the tight preconference atmosphere had loosened drastically when Wan Li and other reformers gave a series of "internal" speeches. The Communist party had never understood literature and art, they said, and it had no business interfering. Why, it was only just beginning to understand the first thing about economics! . . . Soon after this Jia, together with several other prominent writers whose names had been conspicuously absent from the delegates' lists, received special invitations to attend the meeting.

The big news when he arrived in Beijing was that a number of unpopular arts leaders, including Propaganda Chief Deng Liqun, hadn't even shown up, claiming illness. An absentee of a different sort was Zhou Yang, a senior arts official whose writings about alienation under socialism and about the importance of humanistic values in literature had made him one of the primary targets of the campaign. He was unable to make it because of genuine poor health, and the applause that followed his telegram of greetings went on for a full five minutes, contrasting embarrassingly with the cold silence that had greeted Deng Liqun's message. The ovation moved many delegates to tears. The meeting thus came to seem a celebration of victory over the hardliners, and for the first time artists and writers were promised full creative freedom under Communist party rule.

Like other writers with whom we had spoken in Hunan, Guangdong, Beijing, and Sichuan, Jia Pingao's feelings about the conference were mixed. Emotions were very different from those during and after the 1979 meeting, he said, when writers naively believed that extreme leftism had truly been dealt a death blow. Then, the campaign against "bourgeois liberalism" that followed not long after had come as a shock to them. This time, many writers were wiser. They were happy, of course, with the events of the conference—with the liberal keynote address, with the changes in delegate slates, and with the elections that squeezed out some of the least popular arts officials and brought in some of the most outspoken, including Jia himself, who was made a member of the Writers' Association's Board of Directors—but they were also acutely aware that the conservative leftists present were too silent, as if biding their time. Why weren't they being forced to "express an attitude," as so-called rightists had been so many times in the past?

"In China, there will always be fluctuations between looseness and tightness," said Jia Pingao. "Few people think that the current 'warm' climate will last indefinitely." But he said that since the conference he had been publishing freely again, and would continue to do so for as long as he could, at which point he would once again write what he called "drawer literature," writing that stayed in his desk until it could be taken out, just as I myself had once done.

"It's easier for young writers not to be afraid," commented the old historian to us, lighting yet another cigarette and inhaling deeply. "We older ones have suffered through too much." He then told us about Wu Zuguang, one of the speakers at the conference, a respected novelist. Wu had told the audience how his wife, whose life had been ruined because of remarks he had made in 1956 just before the Anti-Rightist movement, had read over his speech draft repeatedly, modifying it to make it safer. She even threatened to rise in the middle of the meeting and disrupt it to prevent him from continuing if he was too truthful.

A famous actress, she had been ordered by the minister of culture to divorce her "rightist" husband. When she refused, she herself was persecuted. She was too famous to be forbidden to perform, but, as soon as the applause was over, she was sent to clean outhouses. After seven years of digging air-raid shelters, she had a stroke and lost the use of one of her hands. We all agreed that it was understandable that people like her greeted promises of complete artistic freedom skeptically.

Zhao's wife had come in with a net bag of dried noodles and cabbage while we were talking about Wu Zuguang and his wife, and was quietly sweeping up the cigarette butts and peanut shells, pouring fresh hot water into our teacups, opening the window to let out all the smoke and coal gas. Now she remarked tartly, "Old man, if you wanted to go around giving speeches about artistic freedom, I wouldn't agree to it either. Only a fool forgets the pain of a wound as soon as it's healed." The conversation must have resonated with many of her own memories.

Judy wanted to know if things had changed for writers since the conference.

"It's hard to say," answered the old historian. He pointed out that many older writers had been treated as tools for propagandizing socialist values and party policies for over thirty years. Some of them struggled courageously on the borders of the acceptable and occasionally paid the price, but many more had become political weathervanes, or had chosen, as he had, to find relatively safe areas in which to work, like science fiction or history. In these genres, by very careful handling of material, oblique discussion of social problems was still possible. Some of the greatest of China's writers, like Shen Congwen, had gone almost completely silent. "So now you tell them they have artistic freedom," said Zhao, "and they don't quite know what to do with it. In some ways, it's harder than ever to be a writer. For so many years we've been chafing against the restrictions, dreaming of the great literature we could create if we were free. Well, now we have to struggle primarily within ourselves, not against political limitations. A lot of writers are finding it even more difficult. And of course, we all know that a tighter atmosphere cannot be far off."

I could understand the hesitancy of the older generation very well. Although in general Chinese literature since the death of Mao was far better than the sterile "blend of revolutionary realism and revolutionary romanticism" that had preceded it, it was the middle-aged and younger writers who were doing the more interesting work. Among writers of Zhao's age, the habit of self-censorship was deeply ingrained. They had lived through so many political movements that their spirits had been all but destroyed. The well-known writer Ding Ling, for example, had spent close to twenty years of her life in prisons and labor camps, but if anything, the experience seemed to have made her less independent of mind: she was little more than a party hack now. It was too late for her, and too late for the others who had waited so many years for acceptance into the only system they knew.

Even younger artists had trouble taking off their blinders.

The views of my friend Peng Ming, who was now running the drama division of the Hunan Television Station, had been a disappointment to me. He seemed to want to encourage dramatists to write only about heroic reformers, to stage plays that "educated, inspired, and entertained," as the official line now permitted. Even China's most open-minded apparently knew few alternatives to the principle that art should focus on life's bright side, depict individuals worthy of emulation, and represent "typical" conflicts and situations. Many artists had learned their lessons too well, and were concerned almost exclusively with the social effect of their work. To the most courageous of them, freedom seemed simply to mean freedom to criticize. They wrote primarily in order to expose abuses, and their characters were still painted in black and white.

"What kind of literature would you like to see in China?" I asked.

Jia hesitated modestly, and the young editor spoke for him. "Some of the best young writers are looking for an art less influenced by politics," she said. They emphasized self-expression, while drawing on both China's primitive folk traditions and on modern Western literary techniques. A lot of them were reading South American writers, she told us, because they shared China's third-world social concerns while creating expressive, almost mythical fictional worlds. She mentioned the names of several young Chinese writers, and among them was that of a friend of mine, a former classmate in the Chinese literature department of the Hunan Teachers College.

When I had seen this man in Changsha, he had been about to embark on a foot journey in the Miao, Tujia, and Dong ethnic minority areas of West Hunan. He hoped to collect local legends and witness folk rituals—to discover modernity in ancient themes. Without the economic reforms, taking such a trip on his own initiative would have been impossible, but now he was able to withdraw temporarily from his position as editor of a literary magazine, giving up his salary but not his position. Jia Pingao said that he too often went to the countryside north of Xi'an, to stay with the peasants in their caves and listen to their stories.

"China hasn't produced world-class literature since the 1930s," Zhao said with a sigh. "Many of us have been expecting that now great literary works will begin to emerge. But it's been almost ten years since the end of the Cultural Revolution, and still there's been little of lasting value."

"They'll be written," asserted the young editor with conviction. "It's just a matter of time now!"

Privately, I believed that in addition to political constraints, the Chinese intellectual tradition was also a factor in the lack of good writing: educated people had a deeply ingrained view of themselves as aides to implementation of official policies, as constructive critics rather than as people with their own rights and independent visions. Most of them lacked the bitter irony and confrontational defiance commonly found among writers in the Soviet Union and Eastern Europe, although they had many problems in common with them. Still, there was reason to hope: Judy and I had recently seen many changes in China, much "liberation of the mind," just as the slogan advocated. Now there was much more contact with the outside world; foreign literature in translation was widely available and its influence was already being felt. But I feared that if the door were to close again and contact with world literature cut off, an essential condition for Chinese writers to develop would disappear.

Time had passed quickly. It was already past the usual hour for dinner. Old Zhao and his wife tried to make us stay and eat with them, but we were expecting a guest that evening at our hotel.

"Who's that?" asked Jia Pingao, as he signed his name into a collection of his short stories, edited by Miss Li, for us to take away.

"Wu Tianming," I answered.

"Wu Tianming!" There was general excitement. Wu was a film director, one of the more famous names in Xi'an and indeed in China. Now they urged us to hurry, not to be late. In a warm group, Jia Pingao, Miss Li, Old Zhao, and the lovely former opera singer saw us out the long, cluttered alleyway, and waved us onto the busy evening street.

BACK AT THE HOTEL, as we stepped off the elevator on the third floor, a group of nine or ten white-jacketed floor attendants awaited us. There was an excited murmur, and then we heard disappointed voices, "He hasn't come, he hasn't come yet." I realized with dismay that my phone call to Wu, made from the service counter because there were no telephones in the rooms, had been overheard. News of the director's visit had been transmitted all over the hotel, and we had here not only the workers whose shifts rotated on this floor, but several from other floors as well.

Judy took our key and went back to the room to prepare for Wu's arrival, but I stayed by the elevator to meet our guest, as courtesy dictated. Director Wu was the pride of Xi'an, his young fans told me enthusiastically. There were only seven or eight feature film studios in China, but theirs had always been one of the worst—until, that is, Director Wu had made two wonderful films, *A River Without Buoys* and *Life*. Now the Xi'an studio was famous all over China.

The elevator opened and a man of middle height who looked to be a bit over forty got off. His hair was thick and dense, long but carefully swept back off his forehead, and he had a plump, strong face considered good-looking in Chinese men. An admiring tremor shook the waiting group.

Wu Tianming seemed accustomed to the attention. With controlled graciousness, he nodded and smiled to the eager young people, and signed an autograph for a breathless girl who held out a picture postcard of an actress in one of his films. Concerned that he would be upset with me for leaking word of his visit, I extricated him and led him down the dark, faded hallway to the cramped room, where Judy had set out tea and snacks between the heavy gray armchairs.

I spoke first, so Wu would have a chance to size us up. I dared not relate the embarrassing story of my own film ambitions, but I could tell him honestly that until I had seen *A River Without Buoys,* I had despaired of China's movie industry. I had come to hate the moralistic, flat films whose endings you could predict as soon as you knew which political line was being pushed. In college I had all but given up going to the movies, even though life was so dull that there was often almost nothing else to do at night. After I moved to the United States, however, I occasionally went to a film from the mainland, just as a way of staying in touch with the arts situation. When I saw *A River Without Buoys* in New York's Chinatown, I found it so much better than most Chinese films of recent years that I saw it three times.

The film is set during the Cultural Revolution, and tells of three men living on a river raft. One, an old bachelor, has been unfairly attacked during the early part of the revolution; the second is struggling to feed his big family; the youngest is distraught because his fiancée is being forced by a new district leader to marry another man. During the film, the fiancée escapes onto the raft, and the former district leader, who has been victimized and put to hard labor, also seeks their aid. At the end, the old bachelor loses his life in an attempt to save them.

In comparison with many Western films, *A River Without Buoys* was still heavy-handed, but in the context of Chinese film history, it was like a miracle. Before this, I had seen several emotionally stirring films of outrage at the Cultural Revolution and at the Anti-Rightist movement, but these were almost as full of political statement as those of the campaigns they were denouncing. Wu Tianming's film was instead alive with the local color of West Hunan, seeming to take as its starting point the simple tones of reality rather than an ideological lesson. And most unusual of all in Chinese film, its conclusion was ambiguous.

Wu had been only vaguely aware of the generally favorable reception of *A River Without Buoys* abroad. He had never seen the many good reviews that had appeared in the overseas Chinese press. My tales of its success were obviously sweet to his ears.

"Do you have any idea how hard it was to make that film?" he asked. He had evidently decided to trust us. He was clearly a man most comfortable on center stage, and now he became master of the conversation, as if we were the guests and he the host. He was so full of vitality that he seemed to have trouble sitting down, and he was soon pacing about our tiny hotel room as if he were an actor delivering a monologue in an enormous theater.

The script was based on a prize-winning short story by Ye Weilin, a Hunan writer whom we had met in Changsha. (In this regard, China was freer than in the old days—Ye was not a film studio employee!) Still, Wu told us, when Ye offered his screenplay to the local Hunan studio, the Xiaoxiang, the conservative leaders there hadn't even dared to mention the project to the Provincial Party Committee's Propaganda Department. He offered it next to the Beijing Film Studio. In the meanwhile, Wu Tianming had read the short story and decided he had to make the film.

Wu guessed that if Hunan hadn't dared film it, Beijing probably wouldn't either. But the review process could take half a year, and he wasn't willing to wait that long. He got on a plane and sought out Ye Weilin in his Beijing hotel room. During hours of discussion, Wu promised Ye that he would respect the story's integrity, that he feared no criticism, that if there was any trouble he would bear full responsibility. At last he persuaded Ye to retrieve his script from the Beijing studio, and together, right then and there, the two of them revised it, working feverishly for two weeks until it was done.

"That was the first difficult mountain to cross," recalled Wu.

"The second was much harder." He took the script back to Xi'an, to his studio leaders. They asked for changes. The peasants were depicted as too poor, they said, without even the cash to buy salt. "Even though the story is set during the Cultural Revolution," they reprimanded, "it still takes place in our socialist China."

Unhappily, Wu made revisions to suit them—the key thing was to get permission to start shooting. Next the script went to the Provincial Cultural Bureau and Provincial Propaganda Department. Those arts officials also had their turn to raise objections: this beggar woman should be cut; that scene in which the old man takes off his clothes to swim in the river was out of the question, it would have a very damaging social effect; the title, *A River Without Buoys,* was suspicious—didn't it imply that without the leadership of the Communist party, China could still remain afloat?

Such language was like a lingering Cultural Revolution disease, I told Wu sympathetically. People saw black-and-white political symbolism in everything. My own father's essay about the self-reliance of a sunflower had been interpreted to mean that he was advocating China without Chairman Mao. That was during the Cultural Revolution, and Mao was indeed commonly compared with the sun—such accusations were routine then. But today they seemed oddly anachronistic.

Finally, in 1982, China had a loose period and Wu got his permission to shoot. Alone with his crew in West Hunan, where nude river bathing was common and seemed utterly natural, he made the film exactly as he had first intended. He believed, he said, that the film's audience would be the true judges of whether he had been right.

Wu was a brave man. China's artists were so accustomed to having projects suddenly aborted for minor reasons that they had become routinely cautious, especially in film, which was probably the most tightly controlled medium of all. This was both because films were seen by a great many people and so had great influence, and because uneducated party arts officials found it easier to watch a movie and criticize it than to pore over the thousands of short stories and poems that were published in the hundreds of literary magazines every year. A large number of officials were, after all, only semiliterate.

Now the completed film had to go again to the provincial arts and propaganda authorities for checking, and if it passed, to the Film Bureau of the Ministry of Culture in Beijing. At the screening, said Wu, he sat sweating, more and more nervous as the controversial nude bathing scene approached. But to his amazement and utter relief, the province official who had objected so strenuously to it in the script laughed heartily at the sight of the old man's bare buttocks. He had apparently completely forgotten what he had said just a few months earlier.

Wu had won that point, but he had to make many other cuts and revisions before it passed all the official censors. Then almost as soon as the film was publicly released, the campaign against spiritual pollution began. The film was quickly withdrawn from circulation; money for tickets already purchased was refunded. Where were the party members in the film, critics demanded? Were the "good" people really good, or were they bad, with all that drinking and fighting going on? How could a socialist countryside be so poor? Wasn't this an insult to the dignity of the nation?

Fortunately, the campaign was short, and the movie was soon rereleased. In looser 1984, it was awarded the Golden Rooster prize for best feature film of 1983. After this success, Wu Tianming's courage to assert his own artistic principles greatly increased.

It had not been a smooth road, he told us. Even as a child he had been a passionate film viewer, once selling a new pair of shoes in order to see a Soviet film. He had entered the profession through an acting course given by the Xi'an Film Studio, appearing on both stage and screen. During the Cultural Revolution, he spent two years in prison for his refusal to participate in criticism sessions, but after he was released was able to devote all his time to reading about film. In 1976, after a training course at Beijing, he was at last permitted to direct.

At the time, leftism still dominated the arts. His first two films were, in his own view, propagandistic junk. One of them, *Longing for Reunion,* was a sentimental diatribe about reunification with Taiwan, set by artificially constructed "Taiwan Straits," although Wu himself had never seen the sea. "How sad," he said. "So much money and talent wasted to make such a false picture." He felt that leftist Cultural Revolution attitudes had become evil habits throughout China, that they were only recently being broken. "The Gang of Four trained audiences as well as leaders," he said. He told us that in another film he shot the first post–Cultural Revolution kiss on screen and was deluged with more negative letters than positive ones.

Wu seemed exceptionally proud of *Life,* his most recent effort. He himself was a Shaanxi native, so he wanted to make a film that evoked Shaanxi's special northern landscape, its folk customs and colors. Wu described the film as a love tragedy, but only on the most superficial level: it was primarily an exploration of the reasons for such tragedies, of the gap between city and countryside, and of the influence of corruption upon the lives of ordinary people.

The film was radical even in its premises: the "glorious socialist countryside" had been an entrenched feature of Chinese propaganda for as long as I could remember. In *Life,* the protagonist is not a smiling, heroic figure, but a thoughtful, even grim person seeking a way out of the poverty of his environment, a man with hard choices.

The film tells the story of Gao Jialin, a teacher at a village primary school. He is edged out of his position by a party secretary who wants the job for his own son, and he has to return to the fields. There an illiterate peasant girl falls in love with him.

Fearing that marriage to a peasant will tie him to the impoverished countryside forever, he hesitates. Finally, her devotion overcomes him and he prepares to marry her.

Gao then has a change in fortunes: an uncle of his becomes the boss of the party secretary, who tries to make amends to Gao by arranging a job for him at the County News Center. Back in town, a former classmate falls in love with him and offers to get him a real city job if he will marry her. This is a strong inducement, and Gao rejects his innocent peasant girl friend. Grieved, she marries a man she does not love.

Gao's dream of marriage and a move to the city is destroyed when he is accused of getting his new job "through the back door." At the end of the film, he is sent back to the fields, having lost both girl friends and all hope of escape from the countryside.

Wu told us that the film had been very controversial. According to traditional Chinese morality, Gao should never have rejected the peasant who was so good to him. However, many younger viewers sympathized with the young man's predicament: there was, after all, a huge gap in living standards and opportunities between the Chinese countryside and cities, and few country people would not move "up" if they had the chance.

Gao's problem was indeed a common one: it reminded me of a dilemma faced by many of my classmates. After they had spent some time in college, many found the old girl friends and boy friends they had met in factories and in the countryside were no longer their intellectual and social equals. Those who did their duty and got married often faced a lifelong unhappy relationship, while those who didn't faced popular disapprobation and gossip, which in China could be terrifying indeed. In one case at the Hunan Teachers College, the mother of a slighted girl friend came onto campus and put up big character posters denouncing one of my classmates for despoiling her daughter. He was eventually expelled for "immoral behavior."

Wu told us that many peasants, especially those of northern

Shaanxi, enthusiastically embraced the film as their very own. Some were unhappy with how their lives were portrayed, however. One group of wealthy peasants complained that the film did not reflect a "typical" situation in the countryside today, now that the responsibility system had created such improvements in their lives. They felt that a talented young man like Gao would surely have become a member of a wealthy "ten-thousand *yuan* household." These peasants had taken up a collection, raising the astonishing sum of 400,000 *yuan,* which they then offered to Wu so that he could film a sequel about Gao's life under the economic reforms. Wu had no interest in such a project and had repeatedly refused. But one peasant continued to make a nuisance of himself, following him about so that the director never knew where he would turn up next—the man once even met him at the airport on his return from a business trip.

I loved this story. It told of a new pride, a new awareness of the outside world on the part of these peasants. That they were concerned lest others think poorly of their lives was almost as remarkable to me as the huge sum of money they had collected to redeem their image.

I wondered if *Life* had been as difficult to make as *A River Without Buoys.*

Fortunately, Wu answered, the script had been passed and the film made during a very loose period in 1984. But there had still been some difficulties with leaders over the film. When it came time to select a Chinese film to be sent to Hawaii to be shown in an Asian film festival, where it might come to the notice of the nominators for America's Academy Awards, almost everyone wanted to send *Life;* but Propaganda Chief Deng Liqun fought for a silly film called *Bright Girl,* about the glories of socialism. He yielded only when others told him that *Bright Girl* would make China an international laughingstock. Still, he continued to object to the English subtitle for Wu's film, *A Youth's Frustrations in Contemporary China.* He was so worried that it would reflect badly on socialism that "experts" from the *People's Daily* had to be brought in to give an exact Chinese translation of the word "frustrations." Wu shook his head in anger and pronounced his judgment: "Deng Liqun's understanding of film is worth a fart!"

In Hunan, the writer Ye Weilin had told us that Wu had recently become the head of the Xi'an Film Studio, and Wu confirmed that in the autumn of 1984 there had been elections for new leaders, as part of the economic reforms. He himself had been out of town at the time. In the first round, 116 cadres were permitted to vote. Ninety-six votes went to Wu, while the previous studio head got only 4. In the second round, open to a broader group of 420 people, Wu got 395 votes.

At first, the Provincial Culture Bureau hesitated to offer him the job, for at forty-five, Wu was considered inexperienced. They tried to make him vice-head, but he refused: "I was unwilling to be 'an ear on a dragon,' " he recalled. "If I was going to give up so much of my own time to become an administrator, I wanted either a lot of power or none at all." Finally, after a third popular vote came out overwhelmingly in Wu's favor, the bureau acquiesced.

The problems awaiting Wu were enormous. The studio had been set up along lines adopted from the Soviet Union during the 1950s, with a great many layers of bureaucracy. Even the Soviet Union had long ago abandoned the system as unmanageable, but the Chinese had clung to it, calling the Soviets revisionist. The red tape had become so tangled that in Xi'an a director needed to get more than ten stamps of approval from ten different offices in order to shoot a scene or even to buy an electric wire. It took two weeks to complete work that should have been done in a day. And workers were so lazy and indifferent that in their studio of twelve hundred employees, two to three hundred were utterly superfluous.

These were problems similar to those faced by most urban enterprises, and drastic measures were needed. Listening to Wu

Tianming speak, I felt as if at last I could see some concrete solutions, after all the abstract talk we had heard about the problems of urban bureaucracy.

Wu had gotten rid of two entire layers of officials who had stood between the top studio leaders and the workshop heads. These people, I knew, would have been primarily political cadres, whose main talents lay in reading newspapers, drinking tea, and saying "no." To have abolished them was an amazing achievement. Just that afternoon, Jia Pingao's friend Miss Li had flushed in embarrassment when we asked whether there was any real use for the Publishing Bureau to which she had been promoted: she told us that there had been discussions about getting rid of it the previous year, but the seventy-odd cadres who would have lost their jobs had protested so vigorously that it had been retained after all. In a socialist country, people said, you couldn't just leave all those senior officials to fend for themselves!

Wu Tianming was handling this problem, and that of the unwanted extra workers, in a most practical and forceful manner. Each workshop had been asked to turn in a list of the workers who were really useful. Everyone not on the list, and all those cadres whose jobs had been abolished, had to report to the personnel office, or they wouldn't get their salary. The small number who didn't report, or who hadn't shown up at the factory in months, were dismissed outright.

The rest were given the opportunity to negotiate new jobs at other work units or to acquire skills that would be useful at the film studio. They could be reassigned to other workshops for a period of internship, or they could return to their old workshop on probation. If they wanted to withdraw temporarily for retraining—to attend Television University, for example—they were encouraged to do so. As for the uneducated old cadres—Wu Tianming could not hide a certain amount of glee—if they showed themselves willing, they could learn to be go-fers, production assistants. Wu liked to conduct the old cadres' oral examinations himself: for example, what would the candidate do if a truck essential to shooting a certain scene didn't arrive on time? Good answers included: go find the driver and give him a carton of cigarettes; go find the driver's leaders and give them cartons of cigarettes so they put pressure on him from above; go to another unit and give the leaders cartons of cigarettes so they approve the loan of a different truck; and so on.

The unplaced people were under great pressure to find solutions. After one month at the personnel office, they could draw only 80 percent of their salary; after six months, only 60 percent. No one innocent of a major offense was fired, but eventually the useless drew the bare minimum wage, forty *yuan* per month. It was just enough so that they were able to eat.

Another of Wu Tianming's reforms was of the salary structure. Under the old system there had been no way of rewarding good workers and punishing bad ones, and salaries rarely reflected position or ability. Wu had adopted a variant on a wage structure I had heard about in other enterprises experimenting with economic reforms. There was a basic salary of forty *yuan* for everyone. On top of that there was more, depending on the nature of the job and the length of tenure at the studio (one *yuan* for each year over five years). Then there were discretionary *hongbao,* "red packages," or bonuses, that Wu could issue at the end of the year to those who had made special contributions. Wu Tianming himself made 160 *yuan* a month, he told us. This was a modest sum, about 57 U.S. dollars.

Already Wu saw great changes in the workers' attitudes. Average salaries were now much higher than they had been before Wu became head, usually 100 *yuan* per month more than in the past. Under the new system, whereby an enterprise could keep its profits after it paid the new taxes, instead of simply turning everything over to the state, the greater the studio's income, the greater workers' own income would be. The interests of the studio were thus linked to the interests of the employees.

Wu laughed. "Even the old no-shows are at least coming in and signing their names before slipping off again!"

Workers were now on a contract system: there would be no more "eating out of one big pot." Wu himself, with a tenure of four years ("like your president!"), offered four-year agreements to actors and directors, one-year agreements to ordinary workers. Because of his reforms, he had managed to attract many talented people to provincial Xi'an, on a contract basis, even those whose residence cards were for Beijing and Shanghai. He could not help boasting: "The Xi'an Film Studio is becoming known throughout China as an oasis of artistic freedom!"

Wu told us that the script review process had now been decentralized so that individual studios had approval power, although the films themselves were still reviewed by provincial and central propaganda and culture authorities. There were still three questions Wu was required, according to document regulations, to ask of a script, but he found they were consistent with his own beliefs about his responsibilities as a filmmaker: Does it harm the interests of the country? Does it do moral damage to the people? Is it pornographic? The limits on the permissible were as broad as he could ever remember; still, like Jia Pingao, he fully expected that the climate would inevitably grow cooler again.

In general, Wu Tianming spoke guardedly about the chances of success for the reforms. The pressure on him was enormous, he said, and he had not won every battle. One of the most difficult had been getting rid of the old party leaders running the studio. Of an original thirty, Wu had managed to get rid of twenty-five, leaving only five. The first party secretary, an entrenched old ideologue, had retaliated by complaining to provincial authorities that Wu never consulted him about anything. At last Wu had managed to replace him as well, with a cooperative, intelligent young man in his early thirties.

But Wu had received unsigned threats against his life and against the life of his thirteen-year-old daughter; stones had been thrown at him in a dark alley after work. Some said he was trying to build a capitalist Hollywood in the middle of their socialist motherland. There was another kind of resistance, too, perhaps even more fundamental: when you talked of reforms, Wu said, everyone supported them, but when you actually tailored people's rewards to their performance, they got upset at the loss of their security. They were used to a slow and lazy life-style, and some found, after trying out the new ways, that they much preferred the old ones to the tension of having constantly to prove themselves on the job.

I remembered conversations with Judy's dancer friends, who in the first months of 1983, in an early experiment with economic freedom, had been given the opportunity to form their own troupes and book their own performances. Many Changsha artists in popular fields like local opera and acrobatics had done very well for themselves, but the dancers found that what they had to offer wasn't popular. They said they hated suddenly having to worry about whether there were ten people in the audience or a hundred. Several of them confessed that they preferred the old iron rice bowl. In Wu Tianming's studio, it seemed, these dancers wouldn't have lasted long.

I knew full well that the extraordinary changes Wu described were not representative of the situation in most film studios. Wu Tianming was a man of rare ability and ambition, and there were precious few like him, capable of working sixteen hours a day to reform a system and lead a studio, while continuing with his own creative work. I hoped with all my heart that one day he would get the Oscar nomination he so coveted, and all the international recognition that went with it.

And if Wu himself failed to do it, yet secured for his studio the creative freedom any artistic enterprise needs, and if the new experiments weren't crushed by the forces of reaction, there was every reason to think that another director from the Xi'an Film Studio might find a way.

IN
THE
NORTH

WHEN I WAS GROWING UP, even if I had known about them, I probably would have been indifferent to the Qin dynasty army of clay soldiers and horses unearthed near Xi'an. Ten years of the Cultural Revolution had completely cut off most of my generation from any understanding or appreciation of our cultural traditions. Now, almost four years after my move to the United States, Judy and I sat in one of the many tourist buses moving east from Xi'an to the digs, the cold sunlight glinting off the endless procession as if off a jointed toy snake. I thought it ironic indeed that I had to become a citizen of another country before learning to value the artifacts of my own heritage.

The excavated soldiers were spectacular, and outside the gates of the site, the peasants selling antique theatrical costumes and fierce-faced, anti-ghost babies' caps were almost as interesting as the frozen statues inside. Unfortunately, the bus schedule allowed only an hour at the tombs, and then a wretched four hours at the Huaqing Palace hot springs, the site of the Xi'an Incident, where in 1936 Chiang Kai-shek had jumped out the window in his pajamas to try to escape from a rebellious general.

Twenty minutes at the palace was more than enough. We walked out a side gate and past the parking lot, down the long main street of the county town in search of something more interesting. We continued into the suburbs and beyond, out to where the earth was flat and colorless, part of a famous fertile plain more than 250 miles long. Many peasants were in the fields, old couples working together spreading fertilizer, young ones driving donkey carts, children perched on top of their loads. We stopped at a settlement a little way off the road, where the houses stood in attached rows facing each other, and the doorways arched in the traditional northern cave style although there wasn't a hill for miles around. The dusty streets were virtually deserted. As we turned a corner, a young man wiping down his bicycle hailed us, smiling, asking if we had lost our way.

He was a sturdy-looking man in a blue cotton athletic shirt with white stripes up the sleeves. He hadn't shaved in several days, and he had a heavy beard for a Chinese. Since he looked like a townsman, we did not intend to stop. But when we explained that we were interested in talking with the local peasants, he insisted on bringing out two small bamboo stools and giving us some tea. Wiping his hands on a greasy rag, he introduced himself. His given name was Xinxian, "New Constitution," and by that I knew he had been born in 1955.

Why, we wondered, wasn't he out in the fields with everyone else on such a fine sunny day? Young Xinxian shrugged. "There's no future in growing vegetables," he said. He and some friends now had a photography stand catering to tourists, but only one person was needed to run it at a time. It brought in more money than farming, and you were more independent of the official bureaucracy.

Xinxian was a lively, articulate, and level-headed young man, and I began to feel glad that we had stayed to talk with him. In his words, I sensed not just a good business decision, but some measure of dissatisfaction as well. When I asked about the general situation in his town, he laughed bitterly and shook his head with a grimace.

"Reforms are fine," he said. "Who doesn't support them? But

I say if there are going to be reforms, let them be thorough. If they're going to give us the land, then let them really give it to us, not just write some meaningless piece of paper that they'll tear up as soon as the winds shift."

I had heard these sentiments expressed before. In a land where personal relations had long overridden law, it was hard to believe that a contract, even one guaranteeing the use of a piece of land for fifteen years, would protect anyone against political change.

But Xinxian had much more to say. The main problem here in Lintong County was the leaders, he said, the "earth emperors." The business-minded local bank officials, for example, had taken money intended for loans to peasants and hired two truckdrivers to go south and bring back loads of sugarcane, cornering the market. The officials pocketed a huge profit before returning the money they had taken from the bank. The state's shipment of sugarcane, which arrived much too late, now lay rotting in the warehouse.

"If they do that with sugarcane," said Xinxian enviously, "you can imagine how much chance we ordinary people have of competing in more serious business. I'd like to go into washing machines, but in China you can't drink a glass of hot water without connections."

Xinxian complained that the local Commerce Bureau officials had taken forcible ownership of the buildings around the farmers' market, rebuilt them into cement stalls, and were now charging the peasants exorbitant leasing fees of sixty *yuan* a month. They restricted all free trade to that area, so the peasants had no way out but to pay. Since the start of the economic reforms, the county leaders had built themselves new office buildings and dormitories, and purchased several new automobiles, all by drinking the sweat of the peasants.

"Aiya," sighed Xinxian. "The Nationalists were infamous for their taxes [*shui*], the Communists were infamous for their meetings [*hui*]." He seemed to be quoting a current black joke. "But if the Communists keep up like this, they'll get the same bad name for taxes as the Nationalists! After all those levies, there's hardly any profit left: hygiene tax, land-lease tax, agricultural tax ... and most important, there's 'face tax'—if you get on the good side of the tax collector, it's two *jiao;* if you don't, it's ten. No wonder everyone trembles and puts aside the best vegetables for them! That's why I don't work the land anymore." Xinxian wiped his dirty brow with the back of his sleeve and took a big gulp of tea. "All these officials call themselves 'reformers,' of course; they hold up the flag of reform with one hand and stuff their pockets with the other."

Encouraged by our interest, the young man told us about an even more infuriating situation. Some Commerce Bureau leaders were now trying to take over a parking lot that was being run by the Production Team to whom the land belonged. "Ask any of them," he said. "Beautiful Mountain Town, West Street Brigade, East Cave Production Team. It's right opposite the Huaqing Palace. As soon as something becomes profitable, the leaders want to take it over for themselves."

We decided to take Xinxian's advice and find out more about the argument from the peasants involved. We had never imagined that the very commonplace parking lot where our bus now stood with at least fifty others was the source of such conflict. So we wished our new friend good luck, leaving a pair of pretty barrettes for his little daughter, and went back through the town, stopping briefly to look at the new sixty-*yuan*-a-month stalls around the free market. We woke up the bus driver and told him not to wait for us when it came time for our group to go—we would be staying on to bathe in the hot springs.

The ticket seller at the parking lot wore a red armband. He was a dirty old peasant in a sheepskin-lined jacket, leaning against the still-warm front of a truck for the heat. "What kind of vehicle?" he asked, taking me for a driver and pulling out a sheaf of tickets.

"You're from the East Cave Production Team, aren't you?" I asked. "We heard you've been having some trouble."

Surprised, the old man looked at us suspiciously. He didn't answer. A younger peasant approached, a tall young man with longish hair and a clean white collar showing under a dirty blue jacket. I took out my business card and handed it to him. "I'm a journalist," I said. "One of the vegetable growers told us some people are trying to take away your parking lot."

The younger man immediately grew cordial, introducing himself as Liu Tianxun. He readily accepted a cigarette, handing it to the older peasant, and then took another for himself. He seemed quite unafraid to tell us everything.

Since its formation, their Production Team, which now had more than three hundred people comprising sixty families, had always grown vegetables. During the ultraleftist period, the whole team's annual income was scarcely 10,000 *yuan*. With the reforms, they decided to take advantage of their proximity to this major tourist attraction and, in 1980, beat the earth down into a parking lot. By expending a lot of "mouth water" on sweet words to officials, they finally got their business license. They also built a small inn with twenty rooms, a restaurant, and a concession stand for cigarettes, jars of fruit, and peanuts. With only ten people contracting to do all the work, the Production Team was now earning 80,000 *yuan* a year.

But this was not the end of their ambitions. They hoped to build joint-venture hotels with foreigners, suitable for tourists and people coming to take the mineral baths. They would turn their modest little Production Team into a major resort area, and Liu believed he had the ability to run it himself. "I don't care if people call me ambitious," he said, bursting with youth and capability. "I know I could be a good manager."

But Liu told us that the Lintong Commerce Bureau officials had gotten the red eye disease, envy, and begun harassing the peasants. First they said the parking lot should be administered with the help of two outside work units, the Electric Power Bureau and the Grain and Oil Company. Were they uneasy about whether the peasants would be able to succeed on their own, as they claimed, or was it that they hated to see all that wealth go unshared? The government was supposed to help them, Liu complained, answering his own question. Instead, it took advantage of them, presenting layer after layer of obstacles. He wished Shaanxi weren't so leftist and backward. It was frustrating to try to accomplish anything new here.

Now the situation had become even worse. The peasants' entire project was threatened. The Commerce Bureau claimed it needed this piece of land to build another farmers' market. They said they would build a different parking lot three *li* (a mile) away, all for the good of the state. Liu snorted scornfully. "Isn't there already a free market for them to get fat from in town?" he asked. "How can the tourists walk so far? Some of them are Westerners, and very fat. After they take their baths, they'll work up quite a sweat just getting back to their buses. Surely they won't stop to buy raw vegetables!"

I could understand why he was outraged. The peasants' land was such a logical site for a parking lot, and so truly unlikely for a free market. It looked to me as if this was one of those cases publicized recently, of petty bureaucrats "expropriating the interests of the people."

The peasants' main problem now, Liu told us, was that their Production Team leader was the county's man. All the peasants' efforts to replace him had failed. When they held elections for new representatives, county officials found fault with all their choices and refused to recognize them. That same collaborator had already betrayed their interests by leasing off twenty-three *mu* of good land to the county at a cheap price just because county officials ordered him to. For that, it was already too late. But this time, the peasants intended to fight.

The leader hadn't discussed a thing with them before coming to a very poor agreement with the county to lease them the parking lot for only 20,000 *yuan*. The peasants would thus be compensated only a fraction of what they would be losing in income. The local Commerce Bureau threatened that if they didn't get off the lot by March, their business license would be revoked.

March? Why, it was March already!

"We wouldn't compromise, so they extended the deadline until May," Liu explained. "If we're not gone by then, they say they're going to bring in a bulldozer and raze everything we've built."

"What are you going to do?" I asked.

"If they don't give up their plan," answered Liu, "we're going to sit here on this parking lot, every man, woman, and child of our village, all three hundred of us. We're going to eat here and sleep here until they admit they were wrong. And if that fails, we're going to take our hoes and turn up the land and grow vegetables again. We'd rather return to our poor old peasant lives than let them do this to us."

"Have you written to the newspapers?" I asked, knowing they were sometimes the best locus of appeal, better than the ineffective law courts, or the Discipline Inspection Committees, which were often run by appointees of the same leaders about whom people wished to complain. I thought there was a good chance the press would show interest in the case.

"Aren't you supposed to be a reporter?" asked the old man, speaking for the first time. I had almost forgotten that he was standing by, and jumped in surprise.

He was right, in a sense. But I was now also a foreigner, a bearer of a U.S. passport. It was a delicate position. I could not risk being accused of interfering in China's internal affairs. Still, I resolved to try to help these peasants, for I sincerely believed that the officials of Lintong County were "violating the spirit of the reforms."

As soon as we got back to Xi'an, I went, alone so that Judy's foreign face would not confuse the issue, to the offices of the

Xi'an Evening News. When I showed the journalists there my business card, they welcomed me graciously, and took me to the chief editor's office. I was still dirty and excited, and in a breath I told them what I had heard.

The journalists seemed interested, but not surprised. "Did you go to the Lintong Commerce Bureau and listen to their side of the story?" asked one. "Peasants often misunderstand government policies."

"Sometimes local officials misunderstand them, though," disagreed another, taking my part. "Sometimes successful collectively run enterprises are taken over by jealous local officials. It's been a problem here in Shaanxi."

"This is important because it's in front of Huaqing Palace!" I exclaimed, knowing what approach would get results. "If the peasants demonstrate in May, one of the peak tourist seasons, it will be a great loss of face for China! What kind of impression will it make on the foreigners?"

This did the trick. Thanking me for my concern about China's world image, the editors agreed that it was necessary to make an investigation as soon as possible. I left feeling that my visit had been a success.

Back in the hotel, a clerk with whom I had become friendly called out, "Just now someone telephoned to investigate you!"

Investigate? My heart sank.

"Don't worry. It was just the *Xi'an Evening News* calling to see if there really was such a person as the editor in chief of *The Chinese Intellectual* registered here." How typical, I thought, as I waited wearily for the elevator. In China, no one trusts you without the proper "introduction."

The following month, after our return to the United States, I learned what finally happened. A letter came, in answer to one of my own, from the editor in chief of the *Xi'an Evening News.* "Dear Mr. Liang," it read. "Thank you for your continued concern about our reforms. After you left, we made an investigation of the matter of the parking lot in front of the Huaqing Palace. It is already being turned into a free market, and the work is expected to be completed by May 1.

"The road in front of the palace will be moved to the north side of the county: in the future there will be no traffic at all on the south side, so the peasants' parking lot would have become useless. The reason is to ensure the safety of the tourists, and improve the hygiene situation . . . The county government has already built a new parking lot three *li* away . . . As for the transition from parking lot to market, now most of the peasants have agreed. Previously, many of them had failed to do so because the county government's propaganda and explanations were not sufficient. Some peasants were unaware of the plan. The county government admits that this was a shortcoming in their work . . ."

Oh. How to evaluate this new version of the truth? There was no way to know. However, as one who has heard all too many "official explanations," there was one thing of which I was sure: the phrase "now most of the peasants have agreed" really meant that there was still great opposition. I felt sad for the ambitious peasants, and particularly for Liu Tianxun, wishing I could believe that there would be some other way for him to use his energy and talent.

THIS ENDLESSLY INEFFECTUAL train from Xi'an to Tongchuan was taking us to "closed" areas of northern Shaanxi.

Before I met Judy, I had never had to think twice about which places in China were open to foreigners and which closed. Nevertheless, I had certainly dealt with the Chinese love of restrictions all my life, from libraries to which I could not get access, to films I was not considered sufficiently "progressive" to see. I often rebelled against the obsession with secrecy, believing it part of the feudal emphasis on hierarchy and degrees of privilege. Sometimes it reached truly absurd proportions. When dance parties were first held in the Xiang River foreigners' hotel in Changsha, I was handed a list of instructions in etiquette that concluded, after warnings about scallion breath and spitting, "Do not reveal state secrets on the dance floor."

But I had often found ways of circumventing the restrictions. Despite the difficulty for most foreigners of traveling freely in a land in which ultraleftist xenophobia had cut off contact with the West for nearly thirty years, Judy and I had gone together to countless so-called closed areas, sometimes with special permission, sometimes simply by taking the risk. Judy could never have known China had she limited herself to the open cities, and she was used to going pretty much anywhere I could. In fact, Chinese authorities who knew us were often aware that she was taking much greater liberties than foreigners were supposed to, but closed an eye to it because they considered her "China's daughter-in-law." Her small build and fluent Chinese meant that most people took her for a minority woman from the Russian border area, and even when we traveled in places without permission, we rarely had any serious trouble with the public security bureau. Now, however, I too was officially a foreigner, and here in the north we were strangers to the local bureaucrats.

Chinese trains were generally very efficient, but this one took nearly five lugubrious hours to travel the distance even a Chinese bus could have covered in three. It looked as if we would have to stay the night in Tongchuan, a large coal mining town that was not our destination at all: we were headed farther north, to the mountain areas. Our expressed intention was to travel to Yan'an, an open area because of its revolutionary significance as Chairman Mao's base, with many hotels considered suitable for foreigners. In fact, we hoped to stop in small villages along the way, turning east toward Shanxi Province well before we got to Yan'an.

The only amusing aspect of this train ride was the chance to watch the conductors carry out their own version of the economic reforms. Every few minutes, another would walk through the car hawking something—melon seeds, rolls, egg cakes, "champagne," cigarettes, and copies of *Railroad Travel News*. The resourceful crew had even contracted with one of the hotels in Tongchuan to sell bed tickets for them, and the conductor was more than happy to allow Judy and me to book a four-bed room at two *yuan* (less than a dollar) a bed. This arrangement worked perfectly for us, for when we finally arrived in Tongchuan, I simply presented our receipt at the hotel office window and was handed a room key, no questions asked.

After we had dropped off our bags, my urgent priority was to get some food into my stomach, and we went out onto the long street that ran parallel to the railroad. A dirty mining town, Tongchuan had little to recommend it; it was our luck that the Spring Festival lanterns were still up, every bit as lovely as those we had seen in other cities. There were more than two miles of handmade offerings, including some unusual ones, such as a huge injection needle made by the local hospital, and a large rat eating berries the size of golf balls.

However, street commerce was limited in comparison with that of the south, and we couldn't find a single noodle stand or collectively run restaurant. Judy was always happy to eat biscuits, but I needed something more substantial. Reluctantly, we went into one of the dirty-looking state-run eating houses. Inside, piles of rotting cabbages, onions, and potatoes lay in pools of fetid water on the cement floor. Crowds of hungry men with money and grain ration coupons in their outstretched hands pushed to reach the chit-seller in her cage, practically climbing up on top of each other. The bored young woman worked only intermittently, looking up from her movie magazine to sell a few wooden chits whenever someone from the kitchen remembered to inform her that there were five more bowls of noodles or another twelve dumplings to be had.

The greasy round tables were covered with empty beer bottles, bits of chewed-up bone and gristle, and chipped bowls of leftover dumpling water. On the floor, cigarettes had been ground out amid seed husks and gobs of spittle. But there was no alternative. Judy found a bench at a table, and I got at the back of the throng. Fifteen battered minutes later, when I emerged with my chits, I found her glaring furiously at a restaurant worker who had simply continued leaning against a wall when asked to wipe off the table. While I mopped up as best I could with my own handkerchief, Judy took my hard-won meal tickets through a side door directly to the kitchen. In this case, her foreign face might be useful.

She emerged relatively quickly, with two steaming bowls of dumplings for me. Fortunately, I had had the foresight to bring my own chopsticks. Just as I was about to take the first bite, an apparition came into the corner of my eye.

It was a huge, fat, brown face capped with a mop of matted black hair. The chin ran into the enormous body that supported it. The big eyes moved from my bowl to my face, in silent supplication, and then the mouth moved. "Good uncle, give us a little," the woman said quietly, in clear standard Chinese, and she stretched a metal bowl toward me.

I saw then that there was a child, too. He came to his mother's waist and was also covered with dust, so that it was hard to tell where the skin ended and the cloth began. He made a strange package, for he was not wearing clothes, exactly, but was rather wrapped here and there, wherever a piece of rag could be made to hold to his swollen body.

I was glad to give her most of what I had, for the sight of her had taken away my appetite, and she retreated to a corner to feed. After a futile attempt to eat what I had left for myself, I told Judy we might as well go.

Once on the street, however, Judy reminded me of what we had seen that morning near the Xi'an train station. It was a public security bureau roundup of beggars. Gray people in rags were pushed out of eating houses and hostels and forced onto a bus. Some of them were handled very roughly, and we saw a plain-clothes security man kick one viciously in the rear to make him climb the steps of the bus. A woman was being accused, it seemed, of trying to sell a little girl: as the woman got on, screaming that the child was her own daughter, the girl, who looked no more than ten, was allowed to wander away. No attempt was made to find out if she belonged anywhere. We also watched a very short, round-faced man-boy shuffle inconspicuously away—he moved so slowly that it seemed he didn't even understand that he was escaping, and I wondered if he was retarded.

When I went around and questioned the bus driver, he said that the beggars were being taken to be interrogated about where they had come from and whether they were being sought for crimes like theft, gambling, and child selling. If cleared, they would be shipped back to the countryside from where they had come. The roundups were conducted every few months, he said, because Xi'an was an open city, and foreigners didn't like to be disturbed by beggars.

I was curious to speak to some of these beggars, to learn whether it was winter poverty, a lack of relatives, or some other misfortune that had brought them here. Knowing China, I could not help feeling that some of them might end up in labor camp simply because they were poor. But it was impossible to ask any more questions at that point. Now in Tongchuan, Judy pointed out, here was our chance.

We turned and went back into the restaurant. The woman was putting the last of my dumplings into her son's mouth as we approached and spoke sympathetically to her. In excellent, literate Chinese, she told us her story. It seemed as if she had recited it countless times, but never before to willing ears.

"I never wanted to be a beggar," she said with tears of self-pity. "My husband was a worker at the Tongchuan Cement Factory, and we lived together in the work unit dormitories with our three children. I was a simple housewife. In the autumn of 1983, during the anti-crime campaign, he was arrested for gambling. They took him away for ten years of reform through labor. Now I have nothing to live on, and aside from letting us keep our room, the factory won't help me." She gestured toward her son. "They won't do anything for my child."

Judy and I realized at the same horrible moment that what we had taken for another piece of poorly wrapped gray cloth was actually the little boy's penis, horribly swollen with elephantiasis, looking like a nursing sow's udder between swaddled little legs. "They want a hundred *yuan* before the doctors will look at him," the woman wept. "How could an unfortunate like me have so much money? I have to beg just to feed him, and I have two more babies at home. The factory will do nothing. I've written letters to the courts, but had no response. No one will take responsibility, no one is in charge." Her voice shook. "Please help me."

Perhaps it was the horror of the child's disease that upset us so. Back in the street, we decided to go to the Municipal Party Committee and inquire about the situation. In China things often went better if you were able to jump a few levels of bureaucracy; perhaps the cement factory had never reported the situation, or perhaps higher officials were unaware of how badly it was being handled. Since we were foreigners, the city leaders would not refuse to see us, and we could be very diplomatic, saying, in puzzlement, how much we in the West admired China because we had heard that there was guaranteed medical care for all.

The Municipal Committee was not far, and there were two men in the gatehouse, playing Chinese chess. "We want to see the mayor," we announced, quite sure of ourselves.

The mayor and vice-mayors were not available, the surprised gatekeeper told us. They were out in the streets judging the lanterns for the prizes that were to be awarded the following day. He courteously invited us to sit down and wait, however, while he tried to locate someone in authority.

As he made a phone call, his friendly expression started to

change. When he hung up, the unpleasant questions began. "What is your work unit?" he asked. "Where are you from?" "What is your business in Tongchuan?" "Where are your letters of introduction?" Then the dreaded, "Let me see your travel permit."

In the excitement of the moment, we had utterly forgotten that we were not supposed to be in Tongchuan. We had delivered ourselves into the tiger's mouth. We stood up and said that we no longer wanted to bother the mayor with our small matter. The gatekeeper prevented us firmly from leaving, with the promise that the mayor was already on his way.

We saw no mayor, but soon the tiny room was crawling with officials and policemen. However, apparently the public security bureau official in charge of matters relating to foreigners had not yet been located. They stood around us anxiously, and the expression on their faces reminded me of nothing so much as Cultural Revolution secret police who have discovered an interloper without a residence card during the night. We could only pretend that we had no idea what was going on.

In whispered English, Judy and I quickly improvised another, innocuous purpose for our visit to the Municipal Party Committee—the unfortunate beggar woman would have to be abandoned to save our own necks. "You see," explained Judy in gracious Chinese, "we were so impressed with your beautiful lanterns, and we felt so lucky to be able to visit your lovely city at the time of this traditional festival, that we wanted to learn more about the origin of this ancient custom."

Judy's ploy diffused much of the tension. The officials seemed reassured that we were not, perhaps, dangerous, but merely tourists who had strayed from their appointed path. If that was what we wanted, the relieved old gatekeeper told us, warming up a bit, the propaganda director in charge of the lantern display was directing the evening's events from the courtyard outside. He summoned the man in, and for several minutes we held an animated and admiring exchange about paper lanterns. Apparently genuinely happy and proud, the a propaganda leader told us that this was the first year since the Cultural Revolution that the folk festival had been celebrated on this scale.

Our charade played out, we now had ammunition for our retreat. The propaganda chief had answered all of our questions, we said decisively. There was absolutely no need to disturb the busy mayor. Thank you all for your trouble. No, we told a worried-looking policeman, sorry, we couldn't remember the name of the hotel where we were staying. Good night, good night.

We disappeared into the crowd, our hearts in our mouths, sweating in the cold and looking back to see if we were being followed. It seemed we had rescued ourselves, if just barely.

But that night, long after we were asleep, a loud knock came on the door. It must have taken them that long to figure out what to do and check all the hotels. Outside were three public security officers, wearing their formal blue uniforms, red tabs on their collars and blue caps with stars. "Get dressed and bring your documents with you," ordered the leader, with none of the politeness customary in dealings with foreigners.

I followed them to the floor attendants' work room, where they examined our papers. They questioned me about what we were doing in Tongchuan, then "educated" me endlessly about our violation of regulations. Fortunately, this was not the first time for me to have a midnight brush with security police.

No matter how nasty they were, I listened dutifully and answered humbly. I readily acknowledged that we did not have the right to be in Tongchuan, abjectly explaining that we had underestimated the time it would take to get from Xi'an to the open city of Yan'an, our destination. "We were wrong," I repeated contritely, for that old Cultural Revolution slogan "Leniency to those who admit their crimes, severity to those who refuse" still applies in today's China. Then I found a way to bring in the story of how Judy and I were married with the personal approval of Deng Xiaoping, for I knew how Chinese bureaucrats fear to cross people with connections.

Just then Judy came in, blinking in the harsh light. She grasped the situation immediately. "Although we made a great mistake to come here," she said, sitting down on a wooden bed, "we were lucky to be able to see your beautiful city. It should be open to foreigners soon, so everyone can have the chance to enjoy it. Your coal resources and warm hospitality will certainly attract a great deal of foreign investment."

Chinese love to hear sweet words from foreigners. This reflects both the insecurity they feel because of China's poverty in the face of the world and their pride at having once been the most advanced civilization on earth. The older policeman, listening to Judy, could not hide a softening of his attitude. He began to bring the meeting to a close. "Of course, we are glad you have such a good impression of our city," he said, "but China is still a backward country, and here in Tongchuan we do not yet enjoy the conditions to be able to receive foreign visitors. You are not accustomed to our hard living standards." The lesson was almost over. "You have committed a serious error, but you have admitted your mistakes. Tomorrow, you will be leaving early for Yan'an."

Both sides were apologizing now, we for having been unable to catch an afternoon bus to Yan'an, they for waking us up in the middle of the night to carry out regulations. Finally, we were permitted to fill out temporary registration forms, and I knew the danger was past. We shook hands warmly all around, and then our three interrogators trooped down the stairs, allowing us to go back to sleep.

The next morning at six a.m. we stood with other travelers in the utter darkness, waiting for the bus north. In the icy cold, we decided what our next stop would be: any little mountain town that appealed to us along the way.

IT WAS A LONG DARKNESS, a darkness of icy rain and hail. When the dawn finally came, pale beneath heavy fog, our bus was twisting between deep gullies and cave villages set into the steep cliffs. Our feet were painfully cold in our thermal socks and rubber army sneakers, but the peasants traveling with us showed no sign of discomfort. They gnawed on their frozen, newspaper-wrapped corn *wowotou* as if they always ate them that way in winter.

We traveled many hours, more than half a day; if we didn't get off soon, I feared we might end up in Yan'an after all. The settlements were too small even for us—just a few black brick buildings at the county seats, and all the rest was caves. We finally stopped for the night in Chafang, a crossroads with an east-west road toward Shanxi Province on the other side of the Yellow River, staying in a private hostel where no one asked any questions.

The next morning, the roads were much worse. It had snowed during the night, and the barren mountains were covered with white. We slipped and fell on the way to the bus, which had neither snow tires nor chains. We had no hope of getting seats, since this new bus originated in Yan'an and was already full, so we stood squeezed into the doorway with the icy wind in our faces, our whole selves shivering. Less than an hour into the journey, we had good reason to regret that we had not stayed in Xi'an like obedient foreigners.

We were driving along the very summit beneath the sky, and below us, on both sides of the narrow, unsanded road, were deep ravines, gutted out of the forsaken land by erosion. Even the gentler slopes would eventually have rolled the bus down into sharp death drops. Big white slogans painted on the cliffs below warned, "No driving like a hero!" But there were no guardrails to help the driver, only primitive mounds of earth and stones lining the road to signal that he was cutting too close to the edge. What use were these, I groaned to myself, when the surface was sheer ice and the turns so sharp?

Even in that terrifying landscape among the clouds there were inhabited caves and farmland carved out to the very rim of the precipices. Endless snow-sprinkled mountains stretching into the far distance were smoothed and patterned to await spring wheat planting. The yellow scrub was a weak reminder of forests which, a fellow passenger said, an old warlord had cut down to prevent the Communists from hiding there; the many abandoned caves, now crumbling into themselves like old black mouths, were also relics of an earlier time, when refugees from famine came in the 1940s from as far away as Shandong by the sea.

We passed a wreck that had slammed into a lucky hillside. It was one of the many coal transport trucks whose rattling passing made our journey the more hazardous. In the cabin were two blue-clad figures, both motionless. Instead of stopping to help, our bus driver weaved on.

"My God," I said, "there were two men in that truck!"

A hide trader in a wool-lined hat with enormous earflaps was sharing the stairwell with us. He looked at me thoughtfully. "They were probably dead," he suggested matter-of-factly.

This disturbed me more. "Maybe they weren't. If we don't stop, who will?" I said.

The man shrugged. "Who could help, way up here?" He told us he often came here from his home in Gansu Province and had seen many accidents, once seven in a single day. There was no one in charge of maintaining the roads, he said, answering my questions. No rescue organization, no way to tow vehicles that were salvageable. The drivers relied on their connections for help, and if you were a stranger, it was best not to come this way at all.

The hide trader seemed utterly unperturbed. "Everyone has to die sooner or later," he said, laughing at my alarm. "I'll just wrap my head in my jacket and roll with the bus."

It was hard for me to be so blasé. Perhaps because I was afraid, I grew angry. I told the Gansu man that I had lived in America for four years, and doubted that such a thing could happen there —in fact, there was such regard for human life that every time a murderer was executed there was a big public debate about it. The trader and several peasants within earshot found this very funny. Then one said drily, "Here, they kill them like chickens." How right he was. Since our arrival, we had seen at least forty different announcements of the usual pre-Spring Festival executions of criminals, with red check marks to show that the sentences had been carried out. To these peasants, such things seemed only natural. In their world, friends and relatives were precious but strangers bore little responsibility for each other.

Four nightmarish hours later, we began our descent toward the Yellow River, the border between Shaanxi (pronounced with a lower-toned first syllable) and Shanxi Provinces. The road cleared of ice. Descending as if from the clouds, I felt myself infinitely small. There was no safety for us even here, however, no possibility of staying the night, for instead of the town we expected to see, there was only a military installation, with signs interdicting photographs.

Up we went again, and I prayed the rest of the way. Even Judy, who usually had little patience with my forebodings of doom, seemed very nervous. At last the ordeal was over, and the bus wove down onto Ji County, where it would pause and all the passengers spend the night. Ji was a clean, quiet town ringed by mountains, with the bright, thin air of a ski village. We immediately decided to stay until the snow melted and it was safe to go on.

REJECTING THE BUS STATION HOSTEL, we found ourselves yet another privately run inn, close to the outskirts of town and the peasant caves beyond. It was a mud-brick L that formed a courtyard with a donkey stall; a small, angry puppy barked from its chain in the corner, and pigs and chickens ran freely in and out of the rooms. Perhaps it was an omen: a dead flayed cat, its muscles red and drying, lay flung over the crook of a leafless tree. A shy young peasant showed us first a room reeking with rotted meat, then another permeated with coal gas. The bedding in the third was as gray as the others and obviously full of fleas and lice. But we decided to stay—we were eager to use the remaining daylight hours for our explorations of the countryside. Our host offered us the use of his own sheets, but we gave him ten *yuan* to buy us a new one, which settled the matter.

The village we picked to visit lay set far back from the road, among the hills. All the homes were caves, but the terracing was deep enough that some were enclosed in front with mud walls to make a courtyard. There were donkeys tied to dry trees hung with yellow corn, oval cave doors crowned with latticed paper decorated with colorful papercuts. I remembered the saying I had heard, "Southerners are particular about their food; northerners, about their housing and clothes," and reflected that it made sense, for here there were few fresh vegetables, but neither was there any mud to track through your home on your trouser cuffs.

We continued to climb and discovered that there were a great many more homes dug into this hillside than had first appeared. The caves ran along a winding road that led around the hill and seemed to continue up to the sky. I felt a bit shy, because although I knew the peasants of the rice paddies of the south like neighbors, the north was an alien land to me.

As we stood hesitantly before a likely-looking doorway, we heard a voice. "Eh, who are you looking for?" It was a small old peasant with a wispy beard and balding head, coming down the hill with a huge bundle of kindling sticks on his back. They were probably to fuel his *kang,* that heated northern bed that I had only read about in books.

"We're looking for you!" I answered bravely. "We've come

to your house for a visit! You see, we've traveled here from miles away, and we've never seen a *kang*."

Surprised, the old man took in our unusual appearance, and then smiled. "Of course, of course," he said, throwing down his heavy load. "Welcome, welcome."

We were very lucky. We had found ourselves an intelligent and friendly host. His name was Cao, and he had us come in and take off our shoes and climb up on his *kang,* a huge, raised all-purpose brick-and-wood platform warmed underneath by a fire that was stoked from outside.

I was delighted with the sight of my first cave. The curving walls, which were decorated with clean new posters for the new year, made a smooth arch, something like a slice of railroad tunnel, and were much cleaner-looking than the crumbling southern mud bricks. The back wall had been flattened so that storage chests and wardrobes could rest against it. The cave was much brighter inside than I had imagined, for a clear, soft light came in through the latticed paper above the door; the kitchen stove, which abutted the rear of the *kang,* vented outside so there were none of the fumes and black soot so common in the south.

Minutes later, Cao's wife arrived with a second load of wood, and she grew busy outside building up the fire. Soon she had spread the *kang* with cups of hot water generously sweetened with brown sugar, and little tin plates of seeds, peanuts, and dried corn cakes. I could see that the family was desperately poor, and urged them to restrain their hospitality. But Old Cao would hear none of it. "You see," he said, making a courteous little speech, "it is an unimaginable honor for us to receive foreigners. We Caos have lived in these hills since the Tang dynasty. This cave alone has over four hundred years of history. Your arrival today brings happiness not only to my family, but to my whole clan and to the spirits of many generations of ancestors."

As we sipped the sweet water, Old Cao answered our questions freely, sitting cross-legged up on the *kang* with us by the latticed paper window, so that the sun shone down onto his domed head and wrinkled face.

This area had been liberated early, he told us, because of its proximity to Yan'an. He had been among the desperately poor, and joined in the criticism of the local landlords. But later, he discovered that the new cadres who promised to "serve the people" began to change character. If they had been strangers to him, he said, it might not have bothered him so much, but these were people he had grown up with, they were his old neighbors. In 1962, by the end of the "three hard years," all the caves here were empty. Everyone had gone to beg. Only the brigade leaders ate. So, a few years later, during the Four Cleans movement to reeducate grassroots officials, Cao complained to visiting work teams. Later, during the movement to learn from Dazhai, the model agricultural brigade, he spoke out again, this time to disagree with the town's plan to tear down many of the houses so that they could rebuild them joined together in a row, collective-style. In fact, many peasants thought it absurd to destroy perfectly good buildings in order to conform to a political model, but only Old Cao was so foolish as to say what they all thought.

The leaders had their revenge during the Cultural Revolution. Although Cao had been classified as a poor peasant after Liberation, they now called him a class enemy who had betrayed his own proletarian interests. They accused him of subverting the movement to learn from Dazhai, and then of trying to form a secret organization to overthrow the local party leadership. They "exposed" a supposed plot of his to poison one of the cadres, and threatened to execute him. The charges against him were so ridiculous that he was sentenced to five years imprisonment instead. Fortunately, the Cultural Revolution had one of its sudden twists, and after only a few weeks locked up in one of the Revolutionary Committee offices he was released.

Old Cao smiled ruefully. "Since then, I've learned to keep

my mouth shut. I just listen to my radio here and watch what they do." He gestured toward a small oblong covered with an embroidered cloth. "The radio says one thing; the leaders do another. But I keep quiet. Someday they'll have to answer for it, one way or another."

We wondered what he meant; hadn't he showed off his vats of grain to us, fruit of the responsibility system, saying that these had been the best three years of his life?

"If I just want to fill my belly with grain and mind my own business, then I'm a contented man. But can you tell me why, even since the reforms, our Production Team leaders tax us for their salaries, when the radio says that they're supposed to be just like everyone else? And tell me why they got all the best land when it was divided up, and why people like me got the land farthest away from the river?" Old Cao was growing excited. "We were all glad to see what happened when the tools and farm machines were sold to us. Before, they were always broken and rusty, and now they're kept like new. Old tractors that haven't worked for years are running again. But where did the money from their sale go? I'm just an old peasant with no education, but I can't help noticing that the leaders have new tape recorders and furniture. And there's another thing I've noticed: who gets the bank loans to buy machines and build houses? They do," he said emphatically, "they and their friends and relatives. All they have to do is report that you're a bad credit risk, and you haven't a hope." Cao paused, resting his case. "I keep my mouth shut. I just listen to my radio, watch what they do, and keep my mouth shut."

We told Old Cao that we had visited a Production Team in the south where the peasants had replaced their old leaders through free elections.

"Free elections?" Old Cao echoed. "It could never happen here. Every time they're supposed to consult us, we have public hand raising. If anyone dares object, they call it 'opposing the party.' " Old Cao glanced again at his radio. "No, Deng Xiaoping lives up in the sky, and I live way down below on the earth. I can hear him, but he can't hear me."

I asked Old Cao if he listened to the Voice of America or the BBC. He looked shocked. "Anyone who does that is one of the 'cow ghosts and snake spirits,' " he said, using the Cultural Revolution phrase of denunciation. This was the first time I had heard those words in many years, and I was startled. It was as if we had stepped back in time. Everywhere else we had been, even party leaders listened to VOA and BBC, and students were encouraged to follow their English programs.

Old Cao's mother, a tiny old lady with a round back, came in and climbed up on the *kang,* resting her head against the wall. His wife was now busy making noodles. Her skill was astonishing: with a cleaver and some water, she turned a mound of flour into two varieties, one wide and flat, another long and round. Like a magician, she created fried cakes and dumplings; pickled carrots came from a jar. Her family ate meat only a few times a year, she told us apologetically; but we regarded the meal as a feast.

We had been handing out small gifts to the many children who had been wandering in and out—hair clips, postcards, a sweater that Judy no longer wanted. Perhaps the ancestors would be happy. Even recycled gifts from other parts of China, like a decorative weaving made in Hangzhou that had been a present from my sister, seemed as exotic and precious here as those that came all the way from America.

After dinner, the Cao family's warmth continued unabated: we must stay with them tonight, they urged, and share their *kang.* We could hardly imagine sharing a bed with eight others, however, and had no wish to intrude further on hospitality that had already been most generous. But when we got back to the inn, we realized that we had made a mistake: in the snow-covered courtyard lay the hides of three freshly slaughtered oxen, carefully plastered with mud to help them dry. The horns and bashed head of one lay bloody and mournful just outside the doorway to our room. Our path had crossed with that of yet another leather trader from Gansu.

THE FOLLOWING DAY, we moved to the much cleaner County Party Committee hostel in the middle of town, where a gruff old clerk checked us in no questions asked. Ji was a colorful but conservative place, its single street filled with ancient-looking men in dirty white turbans and bowlegged black cotton padded clothing. They smoked jade-mouthed pipes on bamboo stems and drove donkeys tied with bells. Almost every street merchant had the same goods on sale: peanuts, pockmarked apples, little puffed buckwheat spheres for a penny apiece. There were none of the shops selling tape recorders and television sets that we had seen almost everywhere else. Ji was still like the China of four years ago.

Finally, one morning, the sky was clear and it looked safe to go. The white-covered mountains were gradually going black, and the ice on the road was melting. But at the hour of the bus's departure, we found our assigned seats already occupied by five or six peasants, and more were climbing in the windows, shoving in the door. As Judy squeezed on, she lost two buttons. However, what made us give up and get off after two minutes was not the overcrowding but the dangerous sound of the brakes, which screeched horribly. It would be a six-hour descent to the plains, and I did not wish to lose my life this way.

Trapped again in the mountains and with a deadline to make (I had a magazine to publish in New York!), we decided there was no alternative but to go to local leaders for help. Although Ji was not open to foreigners, we were trying to leave, in any case. We didn't have much to lose: I would be happy to criticize myself if it would help us rent a jeep to get out of there.

The county offices were divided into two wings, the party and the government. Trusting to my experience that the party had more power, we turned right to the reception room of the County Party Committee. It was full of newspapers and locked cabinets, and on the wall was the pantheon, Marx, Lenin, Engels, Stalin, and Mao. A middle-aged official stood up and listened to our request, then went out to ask his superiors what to do.

Some minutes later, he reappeared, stone-faced. "There are no vehicles," he said.

We were nonplussed as we had seen quite clearly, on the way in, a garage with four jeeps and two cars.

"How can that be?" we asked.

"All broken. The drivers are resting."

We argued, begged, asked him to think of a way. Then the real reason for his lack of cooperation came out. "The higher authorities didn't notify us," he said dourly. "You haven't gone through the proper channels."

What bad luck to have encountered this attitude! "What's your name?" I demanded.

"Liu Dangsheng," he answered sullenly. (How appropriate, "Birthed by the Party" Liu!)

"We'd like to speak with your leaders."

"That's impossible," he said. "They're all having breakfast."

Having breakfast? At ten in the morning? "All right, we'll wait then," I said, trying to be pleasant.

"You can wait if you like, but it's no use. Even if the governor came, there would be no car." Mr. "Birthed by the Party" went out, leaving us alone in the office.

We waited for over an hour, reading the "rules governing secrecy" posted on the locked cabinets until we could have recited them. Then we began pacing the empty corridor outside. A young man came up the stairs, and we stopped him, asking if he knew where the party secretary was.

"The party secretary?" he repeated in surprise. "That's his office right there!" And he gestured at one of the unmarked doorways before which we had been passing.

I thanked him, outrage building in my heart. I knocked on

the door. There was silence, but I knocked again, louder. This time a voice told us to come in.

Inside, two men were sitting on comfortable sofas, cigarettes in their hands and cups of tea in front of them. They stood up hastily as we entered, putting down their newspapers. "I'm looking for the county party secretary," I said.

"I'm the county party secretary," said one of the men reluctantly, avoiding my eyes.

We pretended that nothing had happened, that we had never been treated rudely, never been lied to. Patiently and politely, we began our tale of woe all over again. We would be happy to pay whatever was required to rent a jeep, we repeated. If there had been any other solution to our problem, we would surely have adopted it.

"It's very difficult for us to resolve this matter," said the party secretary, still looking at the floor. "We've had no notification that you were coming, so we cannot receive you."

I understood his type well. The only way to reach him was to put pressure on him from above. In a friendly voice, I told him who we were. Then I began a frightening litany of the people we knew. We had been sent by this or that Chinese high government office; we were personal friends of this or that ambassador. To people like him, rank counted for more than anything—rank and connections.

"You see," I said reasonably, "if anything should happen to us while we are in your county, such as being killed in a bus accident, you would be held responsible." I smiled. "But if we get to Linfen and the railroad line safely because of your help, when we return to Beijing we will bring honor to your office."

The party secretary's face had been changing color as I spoke, and now he became frigidly polite. "I see," he said. "Under these circumstances, we'll have to do research on this question. Go back to your hotel and wait."

We knew we had won. Not fifteen minutes later, a green army jeep pulled into the hotel compound. For forty *yuan,* less than fifteen dollars, we were on our way. The pleasant young driver and the little daughter he had brought with him seemed overjoyed to have the chance to visit relatives in Linfen. On the way down the mountain, we passed two truck accidents and the passenger bus we had bought tickets on, skidding dangerously all over the road.

WHEN WE REACHED THE LEVEL PLAIN, we were as happy as if we had stepped onto dry land after a sea storm. The Linfen train represented high civilization to us, an embrace by an old friend.

But as soon as we entered the small station we sensed trouble: There were only two trains going north that stopped in Linfen, which was only a small district capital. We were not surprised to be told that all the second-class hard sleeper tickets, our usual mode of travel, were sold out—but there were no first-class soft sleeper tickets, either. Judy had picked up a bad cough and felt feverish, and I was determined that we were not going to sit upright all night after what we had been through.

We were experts, by now, in train ticket buying and knew there were always some special tickets set aside. So we went around to the back of the station, to the "Person on Duty" office. The day worker, a friendly, plump woman with a clipped northern accent, expressed admiration for our sophistication about the ticket distribution system. Unfortunately, she said, Linfen was such a minor stop that only eight hard sleeper tickets were usually available, five for open sale and three discretionary. Every single one had disappeared three days earlier. Why, she wondered helpfully, hadn't we asked the Foreign Affairs Bureau to help us book our berths through proper channels?

She was sympathetic when we told her where we had been, and she could see that Judy, coughing to the depths of her lungs, was quite ill. Still, her phone calls to stations earlier along the line were of no avail—all the tickets were gone. The only way, she suggested, was to return in the evening a few hours before the train came through and speak to Miss Liu, the night worker. She could take us onto the platform and speak with the head conductor for us. Surely something could be done.

We were hopeful, for although we had arrived at many stations without tickets, we had yet to spend the night in third class. So we checked our bags and went to pass the time in Linfen, visiting an old pagoda and watching half of an unbearable movie about the selfless courage of a women's military detachment during the Liberation war.

An hour before departure, we returned and found Miss Liu. She seemed to have been told about us, and promised that if any tickets turned up, we would be the first to get them. Then she led us into an Honored Guests' Room. Such waiting rooms were designed for those traveling in first-class soft sleepers, usually high cadres of rank thirteen and above. It was their privilege to avoid the terrible crush of the masses, who as a rule poured onto the platform like a tidal wave, breaking up against the third-class cars, scrabbling frantically over each other's shoulders into the windows. It was a habit with the Chinese: they behaved in almost the same way whether they had reserved seats or not, whether they were entering a train, a bus, or a movie theater. The single thing that impressed me the most when I first visited America was the orderly way in which people stood in line.

The Linfen Honored Guests' Room was heated and had leather armchairs lined up along the walls. We were the first to arrive, but soon three fat army generals came in, along with two tall young railroad policemen. The group looked at Judy with the suspicious surprise of those who have had almost no contact with foreigners.

The room gradually filled. There were old party leaders, one with a nurse in attendance, and big-bellied bureaucrats. Judy and I were exhausted, and we shut our eyes.

Suddenly, the sound of a satisfied voice intruded itself into my consciousness. "Thank you, Old Zheng, and thank your son here for all his help." The generals were talking about tickets, and all my nerves grew alert.

Another voice, deprecating, with a thick, arrogant accent came back: "Never mind. Any time you need tickets, I'll have them for you."

A younger voice chimed in. "We even have two more! Too bad you didn't have other friends going north!"

No wonder we couldn't get tickets, I thought. They were all controlled by these *gaoganzidi,* these high-ranking cadres' children!

Judy seemed to be asleep, but I sat up straight, eyes now wide open. The handsome young policeman was leaning back comfortably, one foot on his knee, two tickets in a hand flung out onto the back of the sofa. Just then, Miss Liu came in.

"Everyone has their tickets?" she asked officiously. "Everyone has tea? In just a few minutes, I'll be letting you onto the platform first. We'll give you plenty of time before everyone else."

She went and sat down familiarly next to the policemen, with whom she seemed very chummy. "I still have two tickets," said that young man. "What do you want me to do with them?"

"I'll get rid of them for you," answered Miss Liu.

My ears stuck up like a dog's, staring as the tickets changed hands. Surely those must be for us!

I stood up with a smile on my face but, unbelievably, the tickets disappeared into one of Miss Liu's inner pockets. I was about to protest when she turned and said to me, "Come on, you still have to buy two tickets."

Overjoyed, I followed her out of the room.

In the big, crowded waiting room, several desperate people spotted her and rushed up, money in their hands. "Any tickets?" they asked confidingly. Surely these must be Miss Liu's connections.

Without stopping, with a deliberate, subtle sign, Miss Liu indicated that one of the men should follow her. Now there were two of us in her wake. Then she pointed to a closed ticket window and told me to go stand in front of it. I obeyed, and she and the man went off in a different direction.

There was no one in line here, for this was obviously a "connections window." I waited five, ten minutes, and it still hadn't opened. Finally the wooden cover slid off, and a male voice said, "Give me the money."

Two tickets came back, but with much more change than I had expected. I was so angry that my heart almost burst. These were ordinary third-class tickets that I could have purchased at any time, even when we had first come to the station that afternoon! But the window shut before I had a chance to react, and there was nothing to be done. I took the tickets back to the Honored Guests' Room. Moments later, the man who had followed Miss Liu came in with a friend, laden with bags. They were beaming.

Controlling myself, I told Judy in a low voice what had transpired. She too had overheard the conversation with the policeman and assumed because of Miss Liu's earlier promise that the tickets were ours. Judy was even angrier than I and said she was going to go up and ask for an explanation.

The situation reminded me of a conversation we had had with the driver on the road down from the mountains. He had told us with cynical amusement how the Linfen district leaders had taken advantage of the economic looseness to exchange state-owned Linfen coal for two Toyotas, imported by Guangdong Province officials, for their own use. To avoid the registration tax on imported cars, they had bribed a plane company to airlift the cars over the checkpoints around the city of Guangzhou. Compared with shady deals on that scale, what was the underhanded exchange of a few train tickets?

With typical American directness, Judy had already approached Miss Liu. In front of all the generals and party leaders, leaving the woman with no face at all, she said in clear Chinese, "You thought I couldn't understand. You thought I didn't know you were selling those tickets through the back door. But I know exactly what happened."

The whole room fell silent, staring at the scene with amazement. They had probably never seen anything like this in their lives. The young policemen were doubtless regretting their public airing of privilege, and Miss Liu's face had gone a bright red. All her delicate skill in "the science of relationships" had been for naught.

In a sharp, nasal voice, she replied, "There's been nothing of the sort. You've misunderstood. There's no backdoorism in this station."

The train was arriving, and the interchange ended there. Miss Liu angrily unchained the platform door, and the troop of privileged marched onto the platform, their entourages in tow. Judy had only made the situation worse. Now we could expect no help from Miss Liu with the trainmaster. We would have to speak to him ourselves.

Walking up and down the platform, we spotted his triangular green armband at last. He was a youngish, strong man who spoke true local Beijing dialect. "Get on," he said pleasantly. "We'll see later if anything can be done."

We were far from the only ones begging the trainmaster for sleepers—there were at least twenty in the same predicament. We climbed up with our bags, waiting near the doorway.

But before the train pulled out, I heard that sharp nasal voice again. It was Miss Liu, speaking to the trainmaster in the blackness outside. "Be careful," she was saying. "There are two American spies on your train. They are very dangerous. They came to our city without the permission of the Foreign Affairs Bureau, and are trying to undermine the economic reforms."

I had managed to calm myself down before, but this was slander. My fury burst from me. I leaned out the door, shouting,

"It's you who are undermining the reforms! You who are going through the back door!"

Miss Liu whirled around, screaming up at me. "Who went through the back door? You come down here and say that!"

"You did," I shouted, losing all control. "I saw what you did, I heard what you said! It was just you!"

Her police friends were standing by. "Your mother," one cursed me. "Are you Chinese or a foreigner? If you are Chinese, you must obey us. If you are a foreigner, you must respect the regulations of our country." Then, to my disbelief, he grabbed onto my sleeve and started to pull me off the train. I grasped the iron handrail and held tight.

"Don't fight, don't fight," came the trainmaster's northern voice. "It's not right to treat a foreign guest like that. It's not right to pull people." At his sharp words, the policeman let go of my sleeve. "Now let's forget it," my rescuer said. "We have a train to move."

He helped me back up and pulled the metal stairway in, sliding the door shut. Thank heavens for a Beijing train, I thought. Thank heavens for a Beijing trainmaster.

As we pulled away from Linfen, I began to calm down. How could I have been so stupid as to fight with them? I had made the worst possible mistake in China, losing my temper. I had seen similar things for years, had taken them for granted for so long. But it seemed I had lost the ability to swallow my anger and put up with them anymore.

The train's speed picked up, and Judy and I stood patiently with the others waiting for beds. All they could do was smile and hope, trying to look important. Then the trainmaster made a general announcement: the best he could do was let us all buy dining car seats for the night, which would be far more peaceful than the crowded third-class compartments.

Philosophical now, I prepared to stand in line with the rest, but the trainmaster patted me on the shoulder. "Not you," he said. "Wait a minute." When everyone was gone, he led us to his "on duty" compartment and invited us to sit down and have tea. He closed the metal door, chatting sympathetically to us about what had happened, saying that of course I had been right, the railroad was like that everywhere. All the decent tickets were controlled by connections. He seemed tireless, but all Judy and I could think about was where we were to sleep.

Then he changed the subject abruptly. "You are foreigners, so you must have Foreign Exchange Certificates?"

We understood now the price of his help for two beds. With FECs, he would be able to shop in special stores for foreigners and buy imported goods, from 555 cigarettes to inexpensive color televisions. What could we say? No matter how we hated the practice of connections, mutual favors were the very substance of most Chinese relationships. You had to abide by those rules or you could not survive. Satisfying our new friend by changing 300 *yuan* for him, we were at last allowed to pay the supplement for two second-class beds.

IN
AGRICULTURE,
DON'T LEARN
FROM DAZHAI

DAZHAI'S SILENCE WAS EERIE, but rustic tranquillity was the model brigade's natural state. This out-of-the-way country village of only 124 families should always have been this quiet.

That was the opinion of Chang Wenzhi, a grizzled actor from Taiyuan, the provincial capital. He looked like the robust and rather ugly peasant which he specialized in playing. He had come for a television role as an old Dazhai labor hero who gradually sees the merits of the agricultural responsibility system. The film crew and the handful of journalists there to cover the project were the only guests besides ourselves in a cavernous if rather basic hotel with beds for hundreds. Where Dazhai had once been a revolutionary mecca for thousands of political pilgrims a day, Judy and I had found no public transportation scheduled to go there, and had to get off at a crossroads and walk in.

In some ways, the film crew was in Dazhai for the same reason we were: they too had come to see what the Mao-era symbol of the leftist agricultural line was like under today's policies.

Taking advantage of the cold afternoon sun, Judy and I left the dusty and deserted hotel and walked out to try to find some answers. The brigade itself, like some sort of a living museum, had as its entrance a gateway adorned with the name Dazhai in two huge red characters. Inside the town, the gray brick cave-form dwellings appeared as I had seen them so many times in films and photographs, attached in rows like barracks for the collective life. Small yellow mountains of bright dry corn dotted the stone streets, but all the doors were closed and there wasn't even an animal to be seen. Finally, attracted by the sound of a machine, we discovered a middle-aged couple shucking ears of corn.

"Hello," I said, smiling, and using the opening line that usually brought such a friendly response. "We've come from the United States to see how your lives are today. How are things going for you now?"

"Very well, very well," they answered, nodding automatically.

Although the man wore the black cotton padded clothing and the woman the dark wool kerchief we had come to associate with hospitable northern peasants, behind their smiles and obligatory responses to our questions we saw no hint of welcome, no move to turn off the deafening machine or stop grinding the yellow ears against its sharp teeth. Discouraged, we said good-bye and continued to walk through the village.

Dazhai's fame had begun with a natural disaster, when a 1963 flood wiped out the villagers' homes and possessions. Their struggle to rebuild caught Chairman Mao's attention: their land had been pitted with deep gorges, but basket by basket they had filled them up with earth, and out of nothing created level farmland. In 1964, with a single sentence, Chairman Mao hoisted them to glory: "In agriculture, learn from Dazhai."

Dazhai became Mao's showcase. When a new wind blew, the people of Dazhai performed. They taught us how to judge the value of a day's work in terms of a person's political ideas and class background, how to emphasize class struggle through criticism/self-criticism sessions. We learned how it was bourgeois to leave the fields to visit relatives or friends, how agricultural sidelines were capitalist. The people of Dazhai went to work together at dawn, ate their meals side by side in the fields, and returned after dark to hold struggle meetings and study the works of Chairman Mao. Hardship was regarded as collective happiness and glory, an opportunity to temper themselves. When one of their members died, they held revolutionary commemorations, and no husband or wife was so individualistic as to weep for long.

At the height of its fame, Dazhai was a model for a new social and cultural order. It was studied and admired not only in China but all over the Third World and even by leftists in some capitalist countries. Red Guards camped in the fields, sometimes tens of thousands a day, and foreign visitors came in droves.

There were few Central Committee leaders who had not visited at least once: Mao's wife, Jiang Qing, the most notorious member of the Gang of Four, was said to have loved to ride through the hills on a favorite horse she brought with her for the purpose. Deng Xiaoping had been there twice, and had fallen from power for the second time after a row with Jiang Qing at a meeting in the county seat only twenty minutes away. As late as 1977, Mao's immediate successor, Hua Guofeng, said that all China should try to realize Dazhai-style counties by the end of the century.

But after Deng Xiaoping came back to power that same year, one of the first things he did was to negate the Maoist model. By 1980 the newspapers were attacking notions of class struggle and the value of collective life as impediments to China's development. Dazhai was derided as a lie foisted upon the Chinese people to make them believe phenomenal success was possible only through phenomenal self-sacrifice. In the space of a few months Dazhai fell from the height of revolutionary glory to the depths of political humiliation.

For me, the visit to Dazhai was far more than an intellectual exercise, for Dazhai had played a large role in my own personal odyssey. As a twelve-year-old Red Guard exhilarated by Maoist ideals, it had once been my great sorrow never to have seen Dazhai with my own eyes. In my politics textbooks and geography classes, on film screens, in the words of songs and in news photos, Dazhai and its people were utterly familiar to me, as they carried dirt and broke stones to remold the very face of the earth.

The Dazhai slogan had been everywhere in China, in huge white characters on the sides of peasant homes, in little red ones on tin cups, handtowels, canvas bags, and even on tubes of toothpaste. I felt as if I knew Brigade Party Secretary Chen Yonggui, frequently pictured shaking hands with delegations of foreign visitors, always retaining his white peasant turban despite the glory China eventually accorded him by making him deputy premier. I imitated the spirit of Dazhai and "put politics in command," "let thought take the lead," "struggled bitterly," "was self-reliant," and "loved the nation, loved the communist spirit of the collective." I burned to help China achieve true communism and to witness how our high political consciousness and collective life-style would lead us as a nation to perform superhuman feats.

But later, as I followed my "capitalist journalist" father to the countryside to be reeducated, I understood the suffering caused by the Dazhai ideals. I witnessed the senseless slaughter of privately owned ducks and chickens and saw a peasant woman weep over a dead pig blown up by commandos out to "cut off the tail of capitalism." I shared the home of people without the means to buy oil or salt because no marketing was permitted, and was driven by my empty belly out into the fields by night to steal raw sweet potatoes. My father's health deteriorated as he dutifully stood in the paddy fields declaiming the quotations of Chairman Mao to illiterate and uncomprehending peasants; we both endured the endless political meetings and rituals of political worship that had nothing to do with alleviating poverty and exhausted everyone.

Like most Chinese, I was glad when the Dazhai model was at last dropped, its successes exposed as fabrications and its leaders' names dragged in the mud with those of the Gang of Four. Yet on seeing the silent ghost town Dazhai was today, I felt less sure of myself. Who were these people who had welcomed Maoism into their bosoms with such enthusiasm? Would they be willing to speak to someone who remembered their hour of glory with such antipathy? What would they, in their shame, now have to say about their past? Dazhai might well prove an unfriendly bastion of leftism, I thought, and wondered if we ought to have come at all. For the first time in our travels, I hesitated to knock on those silent doors.

As we stood wavering on the dirt road, a great truck suddenly rushed by, stirring up dust such as is possible only in northern China and obscuring everything from view.

WE HAD ALWAYS GONE to the grassroots with as little official help as possible, even going out of our way to avoid it. However, here it looked as if a formal entrée would be essential. We dropped by the brigade (now *xiang*) offices, where a young cadre was busily separating the day's newspapers into piles for different departments. After looking at our travel documents (we had gotten permission to be there), he recovered from his surprise and promised, with genuine warmth, that a government official would be in our hotel room within two hours.

He was true to his word. The cadre who arrived seemed delighted that two foreigners had remembered to visit Dazhai, and on the following morning we were treated to an escorted official visit, just like hundreds of thousands of our predecessors in another time.

County Foreign Affairs Director Kun led the way, his blue

cadre's suit buttoned up so tight it seemed the only explanation for why his head sometimes shuddered spasmodically. The sky was so blue and the sun so bright that the dry yellow hills seemed full of promise after all.

"I've walked this road almost twenty years," Director Kun said. He had worked in Dazhai since 1965, having been transferred away only recently to the county seat. "Four or five kilometers. But at the busiest I used to walk it seven or eight times a day." He sighed. "All kinds of people. Red Guards, foreigners, Jiang Qing, Premier Zhou. The only one who never came was the man who said people should learn from Dazhai."

I hadn't known that Chairman Mao had never been here, but it recalled to me immediately the absurdity of so many Cultural Revolution policies. Mao had his ideals, but how often he had lacked an understanding of realities! Perhaps he did not care to know whether the Dazhai model really worked. To him it mattered only that a symbol exist to embody the values he thought would create a new human being, and that he had something concrete to point to when other leaders called for different methods.

Following Director Kun in a large sweep around the brigade, we passed neat fields that climbed like broad steps into the hills where Jiang Qing had gone riding, saw the tops of the gorges that had once cut deep into the earth. The brigade's coal mine, opened only in 1984 after the end of the state coal monopoly, was one big change in Dazhai. This and the similarly contracted-out apple orchard, chicken farm, and deer antler project were now providing 70 percent of the brigade's income. The chicken farm, run by a "specialized household," showed that in Dazhai, too, profound changes were taking place: amid a sea of talkative hens, the farmer could hardly hear our shouts.

But most interesting to me was the woman in mourning we encountered on our descent into the town. Dressed entirely in spotless white and followed by two daughters in white headdresses, she sang and wailed her sorrow for all the mountains to hear. After nearly twenty years in that rarefied leftist air, the old practices had been remembered. That, to me, was a surprising testimonial to the depth of traditional culture.

BEFORE VISITING SOME HOMES, we stopped for an interview with the new party secretary, Zhao Shuheng. A fifty-six-year-old Dazhai native, he had been an accountant in the early seventies before becoming a "worker-peasant-soldier student" of water conservancy, chosen for his political performance, at Beijing's prestigious Qinghua University. He was a large, slow-speaking northerner, a nose picker and inspector of results, but a seemingly honest man who was frank about the difficulties of being a local official.

He told us that the Dazhai peasants had been uncomfortable with the new policies, and that land had been divided late there, not until early 1983. However, it had been obvious that a change was necessary. Under the old system, more and more people had become adept at political sloganeering, and fewer and fewer were actually doing any work. After an initial unsuccessful period during which the brigade was split into smaller units, the land was finally contracted out to the families themselves.

Since the land division, grain yields had increased dramatically. In 1979 a *mu* had produced about 800 *jin,* mostly of corn; in 1983 it produced 1,200. Annual cash income, which during the Cultural Revolution had been only about 70 or 80 *yuan* per family, now averaged 600, with some families earning 1,000 and none less than 200. In early 1984, stored grain stood at a million *jin,* and even after a 1984 drought, remained at 600,000. The brigade had made an arrangement with Hebei Province to exchange Dazhai's corn for its wheat, and now the peasants were eating more fine grain than they ever had before. The main problem now, especially since the central government was planning to purchase less grain, was to help peasants find their own markets for the surplus and encourage them to develop sidelines and other uses for the land.

These statistics were similar to those we had heard all over China. In Dazhai, we were more interested to hear how this new secretary, who had known the village through most of its history as a model, now saw its political past. We asked first for his opinions about how leftism had been manifested there.

Secretary Zhao seemed eager to talk about this. "For political reasons, our ordinary village became famous. Falsification of production figures was inevitable under all that pressure. Where other brigades measured dry grain, we measured wet, so for their eighty *jin* we got one hundred. And the distortions became even worse at the county level, after Qiyang County was renamed Dazhai County and there was even more political pressure to succeed. Distortions reached tens of millions of *jin*." Zhao paused, inhaling his hand-rolled cigarette deeply. "In the past, people thought that if the big river was full, the little streams would never run dry. But now we know that it's the little streams that feed the big river."

We asked why, if so many visitors came to Dazhai every day, the fabrications had never been discovered. Before replying, Zhao blew his nose into his fingers and wiped his hand on the bottom of his shoe, a common country habit that I was finding difficult to get used to again.

"Our peasants never knew what the figures were. Only the leaders knew. And the visitors never questioned the peasants directly, they just toured under the direction of a guide, like Director Kun here. But even if the peasants had known the numbers were false, how could they have dared to tell anyone?"

Zhao's words reminded me how often people had been executed for speaking the truth. Hadn't my mother spent two years in labor camp for criticizing her leaders? Party Secretary Zhao was right, the peasants, even the leaders, had little choice. Now, however, I heard Zhao telling us that when his superiors urged him to bring the peasants' income up to an average of 1,000 *yuan* a year, he told them it was impossible. "It isn't that easy," he explained. "Not this year, not until we can develop trade with the outside."

IN THE SUNLIT CAVES, we dutifully admired comfortable and clean *kangs,* nice furniture, dust-free plastic flowers, porcelain cats for dispensing soy sauce, and apple-shaped knickknack boxes. Some rooms were filled nearly completely with grain in huge brown earthenware vats. We were told proudly that Dazhai had been a "television village" ever since the brigade had contributed fifty *yuan* a head toward the purchase of sets in order to overcome peasant nervousness about the obvious manifestations of prosperity.

The peasants were old hands at receiving foreign guests on official visits, and I noticed a Japanese doll and a small bottle of French wine in one home, presumably gifts from earlier visitors. They seemed to answer our questions honestly, but without freshness. As elsewhere, we were told how they now felt free to work and free to stay home, and that they now had much more fine grain and were using the coarse grain to feed the pigs.

Still, one smiling and hearty-looking woman confessed that she found the new life lonely. "Before, we used to sing together as we worked. Now it's me alone or just me and my old man. The mood isn't the same anymore." She gestured outside to the narrow street defined by long rows of cave dwellings built for the collective life. "And our homes just aren't set up to care for donkeys and oxen. We have no courtyards, no sheds. If we tie them to our doors, the streets become filthy and it's hard to get through."

Although we had come to Dazhai expecting that here, if anywhere, there would be some unhappiness with decollectivization, the nostalgia in her voice was startling. After traveling to so many places and finding such enthusiasm for the new ways, those words had an almost illegitimate thrill to them.

I experienced another sort of thrill a little later when we were taken to meet Jia Jincai, an elderly, short man whose trousers were so thick and stiff that they looked as if they were empty, balanced on his two huge feet. His face was open and weatherbeaten, and he greeted us warmly. When Director Kun said his name, I realized why something about him seemed familiar.

Jia Jincai, the indefatigable breaker of Dazhai rocks, had once been a national hero. He had been portrayed on film and television; a commemorative postage stamp had been imprinted with his face. Here was the ultimate model laborer from the model brigade! I couldn't help feeling excited, for Jia was a person of history.

When he spoke, his voice was soft, but it was a cry of pain from the heart. Seemingly indifferent to the presence of Director Kun, he told us an ordinary tale of sorrows that could have been those of any older peasant family without labor power. But how very sad and peculiar it sounded coming from this man who had once been received by dignitaries all the way up to Chairman Mao!

Because his children were in the army, he and his wife had to till their plots alone, and even the few *mu* they had were proving too much for them to handle. "A man grows older year by year, and life grows worse year by year. The lively days are behind now, and no one pays attention to us." He coughed and drank from his tea. "I am seventy-six now, and it hurts me even to walk."

Jia Jincai had once paid for the attention of the world with superhuman dedication to hard labor, and now, surely, his joints must ache more than most. I could not help feeling that in his old age he should be repaid for the use propagandists had made of him. But today there would be no glory for the citizens of

Dazhai, only an obscure sunset as they tried to recover their sense of what life might have been had politics left them alone.

I WAS AN OUTSIDER, visiting in Dazhai for the first time. There were others who felt more deeply than I did and understood much better. That evening, as we went to have a look at the cave-style hotel room Jiang Qing was said to have preferred, we ran into Chang, the television peasant actor, and invited him to come with us.

In the dimming light, Jiang Qing's cave was nothing special, just an old and dusty place, part of a row that was shut up and empty. Where once China's highest leaders had stayed, there were now only a few small black pigs foraging about. I commented on the silence and told the actor some of my thoughts of the afternoon.

He sighed deeply and shook his head, clapping my shoulder heavily with his strong peasant-like hand. "Young man," he said. "You have no idea how right you are. You never saw what it was like. I know Dazhai almost as well as the peasants who live here. Remembering the past and seeing today, my heart is nearly broken."

Apparently Chang had a great deal to say. We brought him to our room and poured him a cup of strong green Zhu Ye Qing liquor. When we told him how we had met Jia Jincai, Chang's eyes grew wet. "Please forgive me," he said. "I cannot control myself. I myself have just been to see my old friend Jia, and I am too sad. In fact, I have been thinking about these same questions ever since I arrived three days ago, but I could not bring myself to go see him until now."

In a deep, resonant, and slow voice, his expressive, ugly actor's face full of feeling, his trained performer's hands giving his words the right emphasis, Chang told us how he had known Jia Jincai since the 1960s, when, as a much younger actor, he had been sent to Dazhai to learn to portray the turbaned brigade secretary, Chen Yonggui. He had slept together with the peasants on their *kangs,* worked the fields and broken stones with them, sat in on all their political meetings.

Now once again he was to play the part of a Dazhai labor hero, this time modeled after Jia Jincai. But after he had accepted the assignment, he had learned that the script portrayed Jia as a stubborn old man fallen behind the times, one who is eventually convinced by disco-dancing young people to get with the reforms. Saddened by this inaccurate and superficial picture, Chang worried that the drama would hurt the local peasants deeply. But this afternoon, when he had gone to confess his role in the project to Jia Jincai, the old man had seemed to care only that his old friend had returned, treating him like a long-lost brother.

"You should know," said Chang, "that nearly all the rocks that built this hotel, nearly all the rocks that built this village, were struck from the mountains by Jia Jincai." Chang's forehead was creased with deep emotion. "I saw with my own eyes how, every morning at four, he would prepare a pot of corn gruel and a little pickled vegetable, his food for the entire day, and carry it with an enormous iron hammer set on a thick willow branch up into the hills to break rocks. When it came time to eat, the gruel was often frozen solid. That red flag of 'learning from Dazhai' is dyed with the blood of Jia Jincai."

Chang's tears were flowing quietly, and his anger showed as well. "Do you think the people of Dazhai liked to suffer? Do you think they were made of something special? No, they were just honest, innocent, obedient, very ordinary Chinese peasants. Peasants!" He slapped his knee and gestured to the air. "What do they know of politics? Yet politics forced them to it. A big crowd of journalists and propagandists would arrive to see how they carried out class struggle. Do you think they had any way out? People would come to watch how they worked day and night without sleep. Under those circumstances, how could they rest?

Jia Jincai always liked it when I came to visit him, because then he could wrap dumplings, bring out a bottle of wine. I tell you, he didn't want to eat gruel and pickles all day. How he enjoyed his food! Peanuts, dumplings, liquor—he loved them all."

Ordinary people were to be pitied the most, I thought. Their lives and self-respect had to float with the political wind. "The red flag of Dazhai has been thrown to the dirt," Chang continued. "As a model it was a disaster for China. But that was not the fault of the Dazhai people!"

Then Chang talked about the script, complaining that as now written it could be about any village in China. "Dazhai's reputation was false to begin with. Now, once again, they are distorting the true situation for political purposes. How could there be disco dancing in Dazhai, when these people are still afraid to buy themselves a new undershirt? The tragedy of the Chinese people is that they do not speak the truth, preferring to imagine impossible utopias and perfect human beings. It is because of this that the so-called Dazhai experience was invented."

"Do you think that any film should be made about Dazhai?" we asked.

"Of course!" Chang exclaimed. "But it should be made as a tragedy, the tragedy of how politics poisoned the lives of ordinary peasants. But the greatest tragedy"—Chang lowered his voice—"is that people like Jia Jincai even today do not realize that they were used. They feel confused and abandoned, but they cannot understand what happened well enough to feel angry about it."

That night I thought about Chang's words for a long time. The next morning, the winter sun still hidden in the mist, we left Dazhai. The hundreds of victims of the Cultural Revolution I had known—the suicides and prisoners, the counterrevolutionaries, capitalists, intellectuals and rightists, the victims of factional warfare and the people sent to the countryside—all these paraded through my mind. Yet here I had met another breed of victim, a totally unexpected one: the reddest and most revolutionary, those of most advanced thought and highest political consciousness, those who enjoyed the Chairman's greatest love and protection. In one way or another, almost all of us had been sacrificed on the altar of Mao's revolution.

AFTER THE NIGHTMARE

*I*T WAS AN EARLY SPRING Beijing evening, and the air was dry and windy. Bicycles flowed home from work through the walled streets like rivers through conduits, carrying anonymous figures with their heads swathed in gauzy scarves against the dust. The only pedestrians were gathered in dark clusters at the bus stops. Compared with the exposed street life of southern cities, the broad boulevards of the capital seemed oddly empty.

Judy and I walked along Changan Avenue, then turned up a side street into a tangled nest of *hutongs,* those maze-like, distinctively northern alleyways so evocative of old China. In the falling darkness, it was difficult to make out the square blue street numbers. We were looking for the home of a retired middle-school teacher named Jiang, for we had one last obligation to fulfill before our departure from China the following day.

Hundreds of years from now, it seemed to me, Chinese would still be asking each other to "help carry things" to their friends and relations, as if the postal service did not exist. Sometimes the little favors were so numerous as to daunt anyone contemplating a trip. Of course, there were good reasons why this was common practice in China: fear of the red-eye disease, the need to avoid tariffs, the difficulty of packaging hard-to-obtain delicacies such as fruit—but even my father's sister, who lived in comparatively modern Taiwan, used this ancient method. In New York, I often received phone calls from strangers bearing gifts from her, once from a pilot who said I had to meet him at the airport within the half hour, before he took off again.

This time, we were the messengers. Jiang was the younger brother of a historian who had left China before 1949 to study abroad and hadn't been back since. The professor had written me that my memoir of the Cultural Revolution had helped him understand what lay behind his brother's careful letters: I wrote a courtesy note back, mentioning that Judy and I would soon be returning to China for a visit. Another letter from the professor arrived, saying he was sending some medicine for us to take to his ailing brother. The mission was hard to refuse.

We finally found the address, in a narrow *hutong* lined with smooth, mud-plastered walls. It was an old-style, single-story dwelling of the type soon to be seen no more: Two old stone lions with chipped faces guarded the doorway, and inside there was a courtyard. Before the Cultural Revolution, this would probably have belonged to a single family; now, since the political upheavals and the population explosion (Chairman Mao encouraged us to reproduce, so that by sheer weight of numbers only we Chinese would survive a nuclear war), there would be many households living here. Jiang's doorway was in a corner, behind a scraggly attempt at horticulture in a large broken pot.

A man of about thirty-five with a broad, bony face and bristling haircut answered the door, and we assumed this must be Old Jiang's son. He seemed immediately to know who we were. His uncle must have written that we were coming.

Inside, seated at a square table beneath a single dim light bulb, was an emaciated, stoop-shouldered gentleman dressed in a black padded jacket and woolen scarf. The deep, burnished wooden surface was set with a simple supper of meat buns and red bean porridge. Old Jiang made as if to stand to greet us, but he was obviously very weak, and the younger man urged him back into his chair, a standard institutional one of the borrowed type, with

Such-and-Such Middle School painted on the back. Representing Old Jiang as host, the younger man began hastily to clear the food away, to our embarrassment, and to search in a cupboard for snacks with which to receive us. Only when we protested vehemently did he return to the table to take up his bowl and chopsticks to finish his meal.

We didn't intend to stay long, so we immediately took out the medications sent by the American professor: a box of packets of high blood pressure medicine; a large assortment of vitamin pills; penicillin; powdered ginseng as an old age tonic . . . it looked as if Old Jiang could use every bit of it.

He wasn't able to speak much, for he was prone to fits of coughing, during which his son would pat his back gently to help him spit. After a fit like this, he would breathe easier again for a few moments, only to begin coughing again if he tried to talk. His hands were pasty and trembling, and he had difficulty feeding himself, so as we spoke, the son tore the steamed buns into pieces with his chopsticks, and lifted them to the father's mouth, one small morsel at a time.

The room was damp and dark, serving as bedroom, kitchen, and sitting room all at once. The young man seemed concerned that we not make a troubling report to the professor about Old Jiang's living conditions, explaining there was some chance that the old man would be given one of the new apartments at the school, with central heating. Then he asked the inevitable hospitable questions about what cities we had visited, about how Judy had learned her Chinese, about the weather in Beijing as compared with where we lived. Old Jiang whispered a question of his own only once, and his son bent his head down to listen closer. "Oh," he said, with apparent reluctance. "His brother said in his letter that you've written a book about the Cultural Revolution?"

We told them that we wrote it because we believed that the tragedy should be recorded and discussed, not sloughed off like a bad dream.

The old man whispered, in a voice so faint that I could barely hear it, "We will always remember in our hearts."

Old Jiang's son seemed oddly uncomfortable about the turn the conversation was taking, and now began busily to pour warm water from a tin kettle into a metal basin, plunging a handtowel into it and wringing it out. "He mustn't get overtired," he explained apologetically, washing his father's face with practiced gentleness. "It's time for you to rest now," he said firmly into the old man's ear.

We stood up to leave, but the young man stopped us, saying, "I'll just put him to bed and go with you. It's easy to get lost in these *hutongs*." The custom of seeing people out was an unvarying one, and we feared he would feel he had been discourteous if we did not allow him this ritual. We sat down again to wait, watching him prepare his father for bed.

He unfolded the heavy cotton comforter, filled a heavy glass bottle from a hot water thermos, wiping it dry with a towel and placing it beneath the quilt to take off the chill. A medicine vial came from a wardrobe, from which he poured a dark liquid into a spoon for the old man to take obediently in his shrunken mouth. Supporting him by the elbow, he helped him sit on the bed, then gently removed his outermost jacket, pulling first at one thick black sleeve, then the other. He pulled off the shoes, old wool ones, and raised the limp legs onto the bed, unfastening the cotton pants and working them carefully off over the gray knit wool ones in which the old man slept. Then he smoothed the quilt over him, gently tucking it around his feet and neck. I envied the old man for this good son, regretting that my time to care for my own father had been so short.

The young man picked up a heavy coat. "Ready now," he said to us, and to his father, "Sleep well." As we stepped into the courtyard, he pulled the cord to turn out the light.

We walked a while in silence. The young man had pulled his hood up and didn't seem to want to talk. When we reached the first wide street, we told him it was unnecessary to see us out any further.

"It doesn't matter," he answered. "I'm going home anyway."

I was confused—I had thought he might live with his wife and children in another room off the same courtyard. It was unusual that a son let a man so feeble live alone. But perhaps he had no choice but to live at his work unit.

He was a bit of a queer fish, I decided, sometimes friendly and conversational, then suddenly almost sullen. I didn't want to press him. The three of us walked briskly, the young man buried in his thick hood, Judy with her scarf twisted around her head and neck. At last we came out onto Changan Avenue.

"You can find a taxi at that duck restaurant," said the young man pointing across the way to a neon sign in front of which were parked several imported tourist buses for foreigners.

We told him we planned to walk, since the night air was so fresh. Now the broad thoroughfare was very quiet, the dull lamps shining bright on pavement still wet from a passing night sweeper.

"I'll go with you a bit longer, then," he said. "I live over by Chaoyangmen."

"That's quite a distance you have to go to see your father," said Judy. "Do you have supper with him every night?"

The young man hesitated. This ordinary question seemed oddly tough to answer. Several bicycles, bells ringing, came from behind and saved him the necessity of reply. We walked a few more minutes in silence, until we could see Tiananmen Square in the distance. Suddenly he said, "Teacher Jiang isn't really my father, you know. I just call him that. My name is Hu Bo, and I used to be his student." He seemed relieved to have spoken it out at last. "In fact," he said to me, "although you and I are from different cities, we have a lot in common."

He seemed quite natural again. He told us that just now, when the subject of the Cultural Revolution came up, he had been very interested, but feared that the topic might cause Old Jiang to become overexcited. Even more important, he confessed, he lacked the face to discuss the events of the past in his teacher's presence. "You and I share the same past," he said. "But now you don't live in China anymore, and you don't have to deal with the people who lived through it with you. It's easy for you to say it should be remembered. But as for me, I usually want to bury it forever."

When the Cultural Revolution began, he told us, he was just graduating from upper middle school, and was preparing to take the examinations for Beijing University's Chinese literature department. He was from a workers' family—his father was at a steel plant, his mother manufactured textiles. If he was accepted, he would be the first in the history of his family to attend college.

He was interested in literature and had read a great many historical novels, poems, and traditional legends. When his special aptitude was discovered by his Chinese teacher, Old Jiang, he received special encouragement. Teacher Jiang was a devoted instructor. He often urged his students to become professors, engineers, scholars, and writers. "He used to say, 'The more famous you are, the prouder I will be.' " As Hu recalled this, his voice grew quiet and came close to breaking.

Although dedicated to all of his students, Teacher Jiang corrected Hu Bo's compositions particularly carefully, and once nominated him for an essay-writing contest open to Beijing's middle-school students. Young Hu won, and his parents brought a bottle of good liquor to Teacher Jiang's house to express their thanks. When Hu was reviewing for the examinations, Teacher Jiang invited him to his home after dinner for private coaching.

The teacher's daughter, also preparing for the exams, used to study together with him. The three of them spent hours in that room we had just visited, sitting around that same small square table. Young Hu found himself observing the girl secretly, her intelligent demeanor and pretty face, smelling her clean scent as they sat across from each other, learning the grammar of ancient times and looking quickly away when they accidentally met each other's eyes.

Then the Cultural Revolution broke out, and the hopes of Hu Bo's parents, of Teacher Jiang, of the daughter, and of Hu himself were dashed. The ambition to become a scholar became not only an impossibility but a crime. The universities were filled with cries of revolution; it would be a full ten years before students were once again enrolled in universities on the basis of ability.

But Hu Bo had another, even more glorious route open to him, because of his "good" working class background. His parents' lack of education was no longer a handicap to him but a source of pride. The battle lines were clear, with students of "bad" background and teachers on one side, the scions of the revolution on the other. Workers' and revolutionary cadres' children became masters of the middle school.

Considered the most dangerous "reactionary scholarly authority" of all was Teacher Jiang. His crimes were innumerable: he had encouraged students to become famous, so he was deliberately poisoning the revolutionary new generation with elitist ideas; he was from a landlord background, so his bourgeois capitalist attitudes were deeply ingrained; he had a younger brother in America, so he was an imperialist spy. Fully one-fourth of all the big character posters that covered the school walls denounced him; he was locked in a classroom between struggle sessions, only rarely permitted to see his family.

Hu Bo's hesitations were swept away by the mass revolutionary fervor and his desire to protect Chairman Mao. There was no middle ground. He had to become an activist or risk being accused of lagging behind, and his feeling for Mao quickly overcame his respect for Jiang. His parents had been saved by Mao from poverty, and their great, unquestioning reverence for Mao's authority had been instilled in him from childhood.

When the first Red Guard groups were organized in his school, he became a minor leader. By this time he was convinced that Teacher Jiang's encouragement of his studies had truly been intended to infect him with dangerous notions. It seemed quite natural, even glorious, to stand up in criticism sessions to repudiate Old Jiang, and to tell stories of the pernicious private tutoring sessions.

As Hu came to this part of his story, we arrived in Tiananmen Square, with its great, desolate expanse of concrete and stone. It was deserted, except for a few pairs of lovers, slowly pushing their bicycles as they walked side by side. The Martyrs' Monument looked large, lonely, and obscene. By unspoken agreement, we strolled toward it, memories linking me to Hu.

After several months, Hu recalled, Chairman Mao issued a new slogan, "If you don't attack what is reactionary, it will not fall down." Each day, the students promenaded their teachers in humiliation, making them clean bathrooms and sweep garbage, beating them publicly. One hot afternoon during a mass criticism session, an elderly physics instructor fainted from the heat. Teacher Jiang met the eyes of his old student, who was supervising the rally, and asked humbly that they be allowed to move into the shade. "I shall never forgive myself," said Hu Bo heavily. "I beat him. I took off my leather belt and beat him until my arm hurt."

Hu Bo sat down at the base of the Martyrs' Monument, the angles of his face illuminated hollowly from below by the surrounding ring of night lights. Judy and I joined him silently. We could feel how this sorrow weighed on his heart.

The relationship between Old Jiang and Hu Bo today was extraordinary, I thought. Most Chinese had little choice but to work sleeve by sleeve with the same people with whom they had lived through the Cultural Revolution, for China's work-unit system determined that people often spent their entire lives with the same few co-workers. At my old college, middle-aged teachers, who had once been on opposite sides in factional warfare, today prepared their lessons in the same small teaching groups;

they attended assemblies in the same rooms that had once been used for criticism sessions. One woman I knew lived across the hall from the man responsible for the suicide of her father: she couldn't move away, so she had to suppress her anger and memories, chatting with her neighbor when they happened out on their balconies at the same time to hang their laundry, fetch a coal briquette, or water their plants.

At the *Hunan Daily,* when I was negotiating my father's return, I had been astonished to see how many people I recognized, childhood friends, "aunties" and "uncles," even an old teacher or two. My father attended a "tea and talk" party for retired cadres a few days after he moved in, and among the officials in charge of distributing candies and cigarettes to the old editors I noticed one of the very same radicals who had locked them up and stood guard at their humiliations. Now, the old victims had little choice but to accept his sweets, shake his hand, smile, and ask after his family. They all had to live together. But in their hearts, who knew what emotions raged? Surely few were capable of the kind of friendship that existed between Teacher Jiang and Hu Bo.

Hu Bo continued his story. In late 1968, he said, when the intellectuals were sent away from the cities to the countryside, the only teachers allowed to remain at the school were possible candidates for incarceration, people whose "questions" were not yet "made clear." Old Jiang was among them.

Then one day, Hu Bo escorted a group of teachers to the train station to make sure they departed as scheduled. By sheer chance, amid the huge crowd he spotted Jiang's wife and daughter. He found the girl as beautiful as ever, although her long braided hair had been chopped off into a short bowl. They were under the supervision of another group of Red Guards, probably from the wife's work unit. Apparently they too were being sent away.

All his secret feelings for the girl came back to him in a rush. But he couldn't bear to face her now. After the way he had treated her father she must surely despise him. He tried to hide himself in the crowd, to avoid those pretty brown eyes and intelligent gaze.

But the girl noticed him, and her face brightened as if at the sight of an old friend. She stood up and waved to summon him over. Then her mother nudged her and she sat down and looked the other way—they were being watched. In confusion, Hu Bo stood fast by his own group, and a few minutes later the platform entrance doors opened. As the girl passed through the gate, she turned and looked at him one more time, her eyes full of tears.

Later, Hu realized that her father must never have told his family about what was happening to him at school.

Old Jiang went to prison; Hu Bo became an increasingly influential political leader. Then he himself was sent to the countryside, as an "educated youth," to a rubber-producing area in faraway southwestern Yunnan. From the headiness of revolution, he was cast into a life of bitter loneliness and poverty. For the first time, he had a chance to think seriously about Old Jiang and his daughter, and what he had done to them. Many of the other ex–Red Guards sent to the border area with him tried to escape through the hills to Burma and thence to Thailand. Hu Bo had opportunities, but he was set on returning to Beijing.

When his father died in the mid-seventies, Hu Bo was given the chance to take a city job in his place, according to the policy of the time. After six long years of hard rural life, he was assigned a job as a ticket seller on an electrified tram line. Dull as it was, he threw himself into the work, trying to make something of his life again. He tried to forget, to repress his angry thoughts about the education he had lost that came flooding forth whenever the tram passed the universities in the northwest part of the city. At home, he cared for his aging mother as best he could.

Some months later, he learned from a classmate that Old Jiang's daughter had been sent to Heilongjiang, China's coldest province; there she had become desperately ill and died in an epidemic—she had been unable to get adequate medical treatment. Her mother died soon after. The classmate also told him that Teacher Jiang was now living alone in his old home and had been in failing health since his release from prison in 1971, during the slight liberalization following the Lin Biao Incident. "As soon as I heard, I wanted to go," said Hu Bo. "But I felt guilty. If I couldn't explain my actions to myself, how could I have faced him?"

Then one day, by sheer chance, Hu Bo had an errand to do in Old Jiang's district, and he ran into him on the street. His teacher looked so different, so much older and thinner, limping with a cane, that Hu was a few feet away before he realized who he was. He turned his head down and tried to pass without speaking, but it was too late: Old Jiang had recognized him. He called out to him, and Hu Bo had to stop. "To my great shame, he greeted me warmly," said Hu Bo with emotion. "He made me come with him to his room and gave me tea. When I tried to apologize for the past, he didn't even want to hear me: he said I had been only a child then, and could hardly be blamed for what had happened.

"From then on, my course became clear. I treated him like my own father." Hu Bo paused, and said simply, "You see, he has no one else."

I had never met anyone before who had chosen such a direct route for atoning for his crimes; few were prepared to confront their roles in the tragedy. Everywhere, you could meet victims, but few confessed that they had been victimizers as well. Still, I understood why Hu Bo could not speak of the past with Teacher Jiang. The scars were too deep to heal.

We had been sitting on the cold stone for so long that I had begun to shiver. We seemed to have attracted the attention of one of the green-coated military sentries on duty, and he walked by to take a curious look at us, staying at an unobtrusive distance. Hu Bo must have felt the time too, for he raised his hand to look at his watch, and exclaimed, "I have to hurry. My last bus leaves in a few minutes."

We walked him to his stop, past the Mao Mausoleum to Qianmen. Hu Bo grew reticent again, as if embarrassed to have spoken so much to strangers; at the same time, he seemed sorry to say goodbye. I was reluctant to let him go, too, for his story had evoked a flood of thoughts, and now there was no time to express them—the headlights of his bus were already flashing in the distance. "I'm glad to have met you," Hu Bo told us with sudden warmth, shaking hands before he boarded. "I hope we'll have other opportunities." Then he added, as if he had just remembered the occasion of our visit, "Tell Teacher Jiang's brother not to worry, he's being taken care of." He climbed in, the bus nearly empty at this late hour, and found a seat by the window. We stood and watched as his white hand, waving farewell, moved out of sight.

Perhaps because I hadn't shared my own memories, my mood was heavy. Judy and I walked slowly back through the square. Again we passed the Mao Mausoleum, the white marble edifice seeming unusually large and empty in the deserted concrete plain, like a vanity. Perhaps it appeared that way because it was still inhabited by a single man. I had no desire to linger nearby: Hu Bo's story was connected with Him too directly.

It was a sad and difficult paradox, I thought: our survival as a nation depended in many ways on whether the lessons of the Cultural Revolution could be transmitted to future generations. At the same time, Hu Bo and his teacher's relationship proved that it was essential that people do their best to forget, to put the anger behind them. Tragedies like that of Hu Bo and his teacher were common in many Chinese families, to different degrees. Why they had occurred was a question that Chinese of our century had to face.

To my mind, there was a long list of complex contributing factors: thousands of years of feudal tradition of obedience to authority; the Communist party's tight control of us; the many years of emphasis on political movements, which made us well-practiced machines for criticism/self-criticism; the special privileges and abuses of power by the new party elite, which elicited our envy and thirst for revenge; the lack of routes for expressing discontent and appealing injustices, which made us feel so bottled up inside; Mao's taste for categorizing people as members of ranked classes, exacerbating tensions . . . of course, the struggles within the party leadership over which road to socialism China should follow contributed to Mao's own paranoiac and desperate acts. But no matter which of these factors were most important, it seemed clear to me that as they flowed together tragedy was inevitable.

Even in my short lifetime, China had seen changes as extreme as those in any country I could think of. Looking toward the feeble light on the gate tower, I reflected that many of the actors in these changes had played their roles right here in Tiananmen Square, the very symbol of China's heart and soul.

In 1966 I had come here with thousands of others to stand in front of the portrait of Chairman Mao and swear my undying fealty. Here, I had joined a sea of Red Guards struggling for a glimpse of our Great Helmsman—perhaps Hu Bo too had been in the crowd. Here Mao had set the country on fire and forced nearly everyone into one of two roles: victim or victimizer.

Ten years later in 1976, also here in Tiananmen, tens of thousands of people who like me had lived through violence, struggle, family upheaval, hunger, and the insanity of leftist policies gathered in an illegal protest against the Cultural Revolution and the dictatorship of Mao. They all focused their attention on the speakers at the Martyrs' Monument where we three had just been sitting. The occasion was April 5, the traditional day of mourning for the dead, but the Gang of Four had decreed that there would be no ceremonies commemorating the recent death of Premier Zhou Enlai, who was known throughout China for his moderate views and protection of intellectuals and cultural relics. It is said that it took three days to wash away the blood spilled that day, but the sacrifice was well made: few doubt that it prepared the way for the events of that autumn, after Mao's death, when Tiananmen celebrated the fall of the Gang of Four.

Now, nearly twenty years since the beginning of the Cultural Revolution, and ten since the death of Mao, a new revolution was under way, a modernization revolution. Not long ago, in yet another parade, a high-tech robot had been trundled through this great square as if to symbolize still more radical changes. As Judy and I had learned in recent months, the effects of these changes were being felt among all Chinese, from the poorest Hunan peasant to the dissident recently out of prison; from the most ordinary neighborhood noodle seller to the most thoughtful artist or intellectual.

Now the nightmare was over, Mao was truly dead, lying waxed and slowly shrinking not one hundred yards away. Most of the huge white statues and portraits of him were long gone, and his body would soon be joined in that hideous white mausoleum by other corpses whose lives had been less sinister in their effects. But in the excitement of earning money, modernizing, and enlivening the economy, I wondered how many people were like Hu Bo? After the long nightmare, how many were looking seriously at themselves, beginning with the basic question of their behavior toward other human beings? I knew that in China the clouds of the past would not dissipate, not for the next fifty years at least, for too many of us had been shaped during that terrible era, and our relationships with each other and our attitudes to the world around us had been affected too deeply.

Of course, anyone could see that the reforms, within the limitations of socialism, were putting China on a better course. But if you looked deeper, even in this golden time of growth and relaxation of controls, you would still discover just below the surface many of the familiar failings, habits, and distortions of reality that had brought the nightmare upon us in the first place. It was easy to fear that the seeds of new disasters lay amid the optimism, and that China's way into the modern world was still bound to be a troubled one.

A NOTE FROM THE AUTHORS

Our collaboration is unusually complex and interdependent.
Although we have chosen to write in the voice of Liang Heng,
responsibility for this work is shared by both of us.
Liang Heng and Judith Shapiro

ABOUT THE AUTHORS

Liang Heng and Judith Shapiro collaborated in writing Son of the Revolution, *a memoir of Liang's life during the Cultural Revolution and after. They were married in his home town of Changsha, in 1980 (after receiving permission from Deng Xiaoping himself), and now live in New York City. Liang, who became an American citizen in 1984, is founder and editor of* The Chinese Intellectual, *a quarterly magazine; Shapiro writes for a number of publications.*